A Modern Relation of Theology and Science Assisted by Emergence and *Kenosis*

A Modern Relation of Theology and Science Assisted by Emergence and *Kenosis*

Bradford McCall

WIPF & STOCK · Eugene, Oregon

A MODERN RELATION OF THEOLOGY AND SCIENCE
ASSISTED BY EMERGENCE AND KENOSIS

Copyright © 2018 Bradford McCall. All rights reserved. Except for brief quotations in critical publications or reviews, no part of this book may be reproduced in any manner without prior written permission from the publisher. Write: Permissions, Wipf and Stock Publishers, 199 W. 8th Ave., Suite 3, Eugene, OR 97401.

Wipf & Stock
An Imprint of Wipf and Stock Publishers
199 W. 8th Ave., Suite 3
Eugene, OR 97401

www.wipfandstock.com

PAPERBACK ISBN: 978-1-5326-4212-8
HARDCOVER ISBN: 978-1-5326-4213-5
EBOOK ISBN: 978-1-5326-4214-2

Manufactured in the U.S.A.

I dedicate this book to my two theological mentors, one largely in retrospect and one mostly in prospect. Amos Yong: you have modeled theological scholarship for me through your voluminous writing over the last decade, and I hope to have a measure of your output, in terms of both quantity and quality. Philip Clayton: you have inspired and formed me for over a decade with the advocation of emergence theory and panentheism, and I look forward to actually studying under you, though I feel as if I already have . . .

Contents

Preface | ix
Introduction | xi

Part 1: Delineation of Theology & Science Models
    Chapter 1   A Delineation of Models on the Relationship Between Theology & Science. | 3

Part 2: *Kenosis* & Emergence
    Chapter 2   Making Sense of Emergence: A Critical Engagement with Leidenhag, Leidenhag, and Yong. | 15
    Chapter 3   *Kenosis* and Emergence: A Wesleyan-Relational Perspective. | 36
    Chapter 4   The *Kenosis* of the Spirit into Creation. | 59
    Chapter 5   Thomistic Personalism in Dialogue with Modern Depictions of *Kenosis*. | 71

Part 3: Teleology & Theology
    Chapter 6   Divine Action in an Evolutionary World: Toward a Teleological Model of Causality in the Theology & Science Dialogue. | 85
    Chapter 7   Aquinas, Teleology, and the Modern Evolutionary Synthesis. | 104
    Chapter 8   Charles Sanders Peirce's Evolutionary Developmental Teleology. | 118
    Chapter 9   Evolution, Emergence, and Final Causality: A Proposed Pneumatico-Theological Synthesis. | 132

Contents

Part 4: Pneumatology, Philosophy, & Science
    Chapter 10   A Modern Depiction of Natural Theology in Dialogue with Aquinas, Darwin, and Whitehead. | 145
    Chapter 11   A Critical Analysis and Response to Hume from a Pneumatological Perspective. | 156
    Chapter 12   Causation, Vitalism, and Hume. | 176
    Chapter 13   Triangulating Peirce, Gould, and Conway Morris into a Thematic Understanding of the Theology and Science Relationship. | 185
    Chapter 14   Conclusion | 202

Bibliography | 207

Preface

AT THE BEGINNING OF the ninth month of 1995, my life forever changed. I was involved in a head-on collision, which resulted in me being in a coma for several months. When I emerged from the coma months later, I became enamored with the notion of a "loving God." This enamored state lasted for a couple of months, but when I realized the enormity of my injuries and the lack of my memory, I found myself angry. Extremely angry. I took out my anger on everyone, but mostly on my parents. What I have done *to* them will scar me for the remainder of my life. What they have done *for* me will also.

I earlier said that I took out most of my anger on my parents, and while that is largely true with respect to other humans, the bold and bare truth is that I took out more anger on God, the one whom I thought was responsible for my predicament. My anger only intensified as I re-learned how to walk, talk, read and write, and so forth. Anger might not be the right term. Nay, pissed is more like it. Soon thereafter I found alcohol, and I began to be a recluse.

This reclusion in retrospect was perhaps beneficial, for I learned the power of self-discipline with respect to my studies, and being exposed to eighteen years of learning in a compact period of time needed such. But I took it too far. In focusing on my biology studies to the exclusion of people, I began to lose part of myself, which was only fueled by my concurrent alcoholism. Then I met God in a cotton field on Highway 27 in Vienna, Georgia, on 7/24/2000. This meeting radically reoriented my life, and led to a change of my name and destination. To the degree that I formerly hated God and cursed his name, to that same degree I began to adore him. Totally bipolar, in a sense.

I started attending church again, and even became a preacher a few years after my conversion. As is common in mid to late life conversions,

Preface

I at first clung to an overly fundamentalist understanding of God and all things Christian. Became a Pharisee, really. In due time, however, I encountered the thought of John Wesley, and that was the beginning of my metamorphosis. After graduating from Asbury Theological Seminary, I began searching for post-graduate degree programs. I found one in Virginia Beach, Virginia, at Regent University School of Divinity.

When I enrolled in Regent's PhD in Renewal Studies program in 2006, I truly matured in in a theological sense, both in mind and spirit. Amos Yong, one of my professors there, inspired me to return to where I began my secondary education: the undergraduate biology degree. Little did I know that he was pushing me not only confront the demons of my past, but he was also preparing me to become what it was that I previously despised. Indeed, through his leadership, I faced what I had earlier thought to be the damnable devils of Process theology and liberal Christianity. I remember him telling me that I had to come to terms with my aversion to Process Theism. Little did he know at that time that I would eventually become an adherent of that philosophical system! Nevertheless, he continued to stretch me mentally, and I began to grow toward an advocation of Process Theism.

It was during my time of grappling with my biological past that Amos told me that I could make significant contributions to the theology and science discussion. He began to coach me toward emergence theory, and thereafter I fell in love with the writings of my doktorvater to-be (Philip Clayton). While I did not successfully complete my PhD with Amos, and this failure is one of my most regretful occurrences, I profited immensely from knowing him and the other friends I gained while at Regent. Iron sharpens iron. His pushing me to reclaim my biological heritage forms the basis of this current volume. These essays were written and published over the span of a decade while I grappled with the interaction of theology and science. They all were composed with the intention of me reconciling the faith that I profess with the scientific views, particularly the biological ones, that I also propound. These essays are almost biographical in that one can see me struggling with matters of faith and revelation through them. I hope they can inform scholars within this community in the same way that they did me upon their writing. Beginning in 2018, I get to try my hand at working on another PhD, and the conversation that this book models will be continued. I honestly feel so fortunate to count as my predominate influences Amos Yong, David Bradnick, and Philip Clayton . . .

Introduction

IMPRESSED BY WILLIAM PALEY's logic and eye for detail, the young Charles Darwin accepted the conventional observation that organisms were adapted exquisitely to their environments. This remarkable fact, Darwin agreed at the time, could only be explained by reference to the existence of an intelligent and benign creator.[1] Having overcome the initial objections of his father, Charles accepted Capitan Fitzroy's offer to be his gentlemanly companion on an exploration of various unknown lands, setting sail in 1831 on what would turn out to be an endlessly fascinating five-year voyage around the globe on the Beagle. It was a journey that would give surprising new direction to Darwin's own life and also provide information about nature that has agitated the religious sensibilities of many Christians ever since.

After returning home, Darwin's earlier belief in the special creation of each distinct species transmutated into a strong suspicion that the origin of different living species had occurred gradually, in a purely natural way. Among the many questions that Darwin and other naturalists who thereafter studied the specimens he collected on the voyage began to ask was, Why do small but distinct variations appear among geographically distributed species of birds and other animals? Specific differences in species, Darwin began to suppose, could be accounted for without divine special creation if there had been minute, cumulative changes in living organisms over an immensely long time. In fact, following his return from the voyage of the Beagle, Darwin writes of his own views, "The old argument from design in nature, as given by Paley, which formerly seemed to me so conclusive, fails, now that the law of natural selection has been discovered. There seems to

---

1. Haught, *Making Sense of Evolution*, 6.

Introduction

be no more design in the variability of organic beings and in the action of natural selection, than in the course which the wind blows."[2]

In offering the mechanism of natural selection, Darwin gave a new kind of answer to what had previously been viewed as a strictly theological question. After he published his theory in 1859, Darwin effectively made natural science the new kind of ultimate explanation by making science itself able to provide a new answer to a very old theological question. Indeed, in the wake of the *Origin of Species*, religion underwent a significant reformulation. God, who had been seen as the primary artist of nature in former years, began to be viewed as a more distant deity—even more so than the developments of Newton had relegated him. Responses to the theory of evolution by religious communities proceeded along several lines, from outright rejection by the fundamentalists, to cautioned acceptance by the religious moderates, to unquestioned acceptance by theological liberals. Fundamentalists viewed Darwinism as an attack on the tenets of Christianity, and therefore rejected the insights gleaned from the science of evolution. Scientifically, there were also mixed reactions to the advent of Darwinism, ranging from outright rejection, to qualified acceptance, to full embrace.

Following his famous teacher Georges Cuvier, Louis Agassiz asserted that the major groups of animals do *not* represent ancestral branches of a hypothetical evolutionary tree but, instead, document a great plan that was used by the Creator to design the many different species in existence today. Asa Gray, however, was a Presbyterian Christian scientist who heartily accepted Darwinism. Gray spent much of his life arguing on both a popular and a scientific level for the compatibility of evolutionary theory and religion by contending that natural selection was not inconsistent with a deity superintending the process of evolution. Another response to Darwinism comes from the likes of Thomas Henry Huxley, who represented a ferocious attack on the tenets of Christianity, veiled in the guise of his newly coined terminology of "agnosticism." After all, if natural science can account for something as complex as living organisms, including things as simple as the fish's eye and eventually as complex as even the human brain, had not science then taken over theology's place in the task of making life's designs fully intelligible? If natural selection is the ultimate cause of apparent design, do classic theological explanations matter at all? What good is

---

2. Charles Darwin, *Autobiography*, http://darwin-online.org.uk/content/frameset?itemID=F1497&viewtype=text&pageseq=1.

INTRODUCTION

theology if science can provide a satisfying answer to one of humanity's most burning questions? These questions are still quite alive today—over one hundred and fifty years later.

People throughout the ages have attempted to understand the universe and their place within it. In attempting to develop a worldview that explicates their position in the world, religions have typically played a very important role, but since the scientific revolution, and particularly since the biological revolution onset by Darwin, science has also played a crucial role. How should we attempt to understand the relationship between religion/theology and science? In this book, I will attempt to answer this overarching question by examining several attempts in the past to classify the theology and science relationship. I will also develop my personal view of the relation between theology and science, and thereafter discuss some contributions to this project of understanding theology in an evolving world from extant literature. I then argue that emergence and kenosis can add to the discussion of understanding the theology and science relationship, particularly when viewed through panentheistic Wesleyan-Relational lenses.

Whenever one collects various essays for (re-)publication, especially when their composition spans over a decade, the methods and manner of their presentation inevitably arise. Where and in what order are they best presented, one queries. While I concede that another presentation of these disparate essays is possible, I have chosen the present format intentionally, and this introduction will attempt to make this placement apparent. Part one of this book is comprised of a single programmatical chapter that constitutes an introductory essay toward a modern relation of theology and science. Indeed, in "A Delineation of Models Regarding the Relationship Between Theology and Science," I review some contributions from other scholars that directly impacts and/or illustrates my advocation of a monistic Process-based view of the overlapping relationship between theology and science. In light of the current worldview, marked by the scientific notion of evolution, new models of divine action are necessary. I contend that Process philosophy is an apt mediator between theology and science. Process philosophy is based on the conviction that the central task of philosophy is to construct a cosmology in which all intuitions grounded in human experience can be reconciled. In the broadest sense, the term "Process philosophy" refers to all worldviews holding that process or becoming is more fundamental than unchanging—or static—being. The task of reconciling theology and science involves the replacement of the materialistic worldview with "panexperientialism," which allows religious experience to be taken seriously.

Part two of this title is constituted by four chapters. It explores emergence and kenosis in view of a modern relation of theology and science. In the second chapter, "Making Sense of Emergence: A Critical Engagement with Leidenhag, Leidenhag, and Yong," David Bradnick and I argue that Amos Yong's teleological understanding of emergence, largely, goes untouched by a recent critique of the same. In fact, we argue that Yong employs emergence as a framework to discuss special divine action as well as causation initiated by other spiritual realities, such as angels and demons, which bears directly on how one may view the relation of theology and science in the (post-)modern world. Mikael and Joanna Leidenhag, however, have issued some reservations about the use of emergence in the theology and science dialogue. In this chapter, Dr. Bradnick and I provide a summary of emergence and address each of the criticisms set forth by Leidenhag and Leidenhag.

Chapter 3 is comprised of an essay entitled, "Kenosis and Emergence: A Wesleyan-Relational Perspective." This essay is the fulcrum upon which the entire book depends. As fundamentally relational, God both affects and is affected by those with whom he relates. This is essential to the notion of a loving God, which I repeatedly, following Thomas Jay Oord, refer to as characterizable by "uncontrolling love." In this chapter, after reviewing and interacting with Philip Clayton, I suggest that he contributes four things, principally, to a Wesleyan-relational perspective on emergence: first, emergence is in direct opposition to reductionism. Second, any position on creation in an evolving world must take seriously both evolutionary continuity and the increase in organizational complexity marked by organisms within the natural environ. Third, strong emergentism focuses more so upon the whole than upon the parts, yet is inherently monistic. And fourth, emergence theory represents an explanatory ladder of nature that eventually leads outside the natural sciences, opening up new avenues to possibly speak of a deity.

In chapter 4, I note that recently a collection of essays by theologians and scientists explored creation as *The Work of Love,* pointing to divine action as kenosis. The resurgence of kenotic theology has been helpful in reformulating divine action in an evolutionary world. The kenotic theology that I advocate in this fourth chapter, "Kenosis of the Spirit into Creation," maintains that the Spirit of God, who *is* uncontrolling love, completely shares and imparts himself *into* creation. Indeed, the Spirit "poured himself out" into creation, thereby causing it to leap forth from chaos and become a structured and orderly system of life-bearing entities. Affirmed in this chapter is the notion that creation is a kenotic act of *self-offering* insomuch as the creation of matter and the world has its ontological origin in and through the agency of the Spirit.

Chapter 5 is constituted by an essay that delineates what Thomistic Personalism, especially drawing upon Karol Wojtyla's *Love and Responsibility*, may contribute to a modern relation of theology and science. In that particular work, Wojtyla characterized love as the inherent affirmation of the value of the person. Yet, there is a form of love that is pre-eminent, which he refers to as betrothed love, the defining characteristic of which is self-donation. I build on Wojtyla's characterization of betrothed love as self-donation, noting that the bible gives good grounds for illustrating the Spirit as the active agent of God in the world, particularly regarding the Spirit as *life-giver* and *animator* of all creation through self-donation (or self-giving). In this chapter, I note that the Spirit is the effectual arm of the Trinity that was active as the Son spoke each word in the primal creating moments. The Spirit, I postulate, is ultimately responsible for both the conditions for life, as well as life itself.

Part three is again constituted by four chapters. This section covers teleology and theology broadly considered, and how teleology relates to a modern relation of theology and science. This section begins an exploration of theology and science in largely chronological terms, which will also extend through the fourth part of this book. In chapter 6, "Divine Action in an Evolutionary World: Toward a Teleological Model of Causality in the Theology & Science Dialogue," I investigate whether contemporary models of divine action are coherent and kosher. If they are, that is well, and my book is not needed. If they are not, I suggest herein that a turn to teleological explanations is more than warranted and fruitful for further research. This development of a teleological perspective on divine action will be the foundation of my research for the foreseeable future.

In chapter 7, I explore "Aquinas, Teleology, and the Modern Evolutionary Synthesis." Because the modern evolutionary synthesis is still the paradigm in evolutionary biology, the question of whether Thomistic teleology is inconsistent with the modern synthetic theory of evolution is an important one. In conducting this investigation, Aristotelian philosophy is employed, since Aristotle is the father of teleology and his philosophical system relies on the concept of function. In this chapter, I explore whether Aquinas's teleology—which includes an intentional agent—is compatible with the modern synthetic theory of evolution. I contend that no modification of Aquinas's system of theology is necessary to render it compatible with Neo-Darwinian orthodoxy.

In "Charles Sanders Peirce's Evolutionary Developmental Teleology," which constitutes chapter 8, I constructively dialogue with Peirce in order to derive from him a novel conception of teleological causation. In fact, this chapter reaps insights from Peirce that are critical to a modern relation of theology and science. Peirce was a novel thinker in terms of both originality and in application. One area of his originality was his evolutionary developmental teleology. Another area of originality is his novel conceptioning of evolutionary causation, which is founded upon his foundational and fundamental three categories of Firstness, Secondness, and Thirdness. Herein, I argue the notion of a "developmental teleology" is applicable to Peirce's idea of teleology in general. Seen as such, final causes evolve, and they are not static. This contention means that teleology emerged out of the increasing complexification of life on earth, and continues to be general, not specific in its derivation. Moreover, in Peirce's agapasm, as explicated in part two of this chapter, God gives himself away in acts of uncontrolling love without any conditions as to the potential responses to that love, as well as to what responses may fulfill that love. Rather, it is completely reckless and overflowing. Seen as such, the many and varied manifestations of complexity that macroevolution has given rise to are to be seen as a fulfillment of the teleological goals of God.

The ninth chapter is entitled, "Evolution, Emergence, and Final Causality: A Proposed Pneumatico-Theological Synthesis," and it argues that an unprecedented challenge and opportunity for philosophy today is to mediate the emerging dialogue between science and religion. It has been said that creation and evolution, between them, exhaust the possible explanations for the origin of living things. However, this chapter offers another option—a pneumatological (re-)interpretation of emergence, one that "reads" the philosophical concept of emergence through theological lens, which is beneficial because it opens up the possibility of teleology (or final causality). This chapter makes a key presentation of the metaphysical basis of emergence theory.

Introduction

In the fourth section of this title, which is similarly comprised by four chapters, I interact with pneumatology, philosophy, and science, lifting principles from each of them in working toward a modern relation of theology and science. In fact, chapter 10 discusses a revised form of natural theology in dialogue with Thomism, Darwin, and Whitehead. It argues that in order to be kosher and pertinent, a modern relation of theology and science informed by natural theology must "read" nature as giving reasons that are promotive of belief in a God, not proof that there is a God. I glean insights regarding how the enterprise of natural theology has, if anything, been given a new lease of life through the rise of evolutionary thought. The traditional approach to natural theology is merely one option among many; the rise of evolutionary thought supplemented an existing and vigorous theological critique of this approach. Natural theology needs to emerge from the shadows of this traditional approach and rediscover, retrieve, and renew alternative approaches. Natural theology cannot be understood to concern *proving* God from nature.

Chapter 11 is the first of two chapters that react to David Hume's contributions to a modern relation of theology and science. In this chapter, I discuss how a pneumatologically informed position can effectively circumvent the criticisms levelled by Hume toward Christianity. Indeed, in the course of the history of Christianity, one of the most advocated and denigrated concepts is the verity of the miraculous. One finds that the opponents of Christianity have perpetually attempted to belie the status of the miraculous in order to overturn the entire worldview of the Christian. On the other hand, one also finds that at various times Christians have overemphasized the importance of the miraculous to their worldview in general. The situation in which the Scottish philosopher Hume lived (1711–1776) was riper for the apparent refutation of the miraculous than any time in the history of the movement. After a lengthy critical analysis of Hume, it will be argued in this chapter that he did not successfully negate either the *possibility* or the *plausibility* of the miraculous.

In chapter 12, we again dialogue with Hume, noting especially how causation has troubled philosophers at least since the time of Aristotle. The main reason for the quest to clarify causation concerns its implications for other philosophical issues, as clarity regarding causation is intrinsically vital for clarity in the areas of metaphysics, epistemology, the philosophy of science, the philosophy of language, as well as the philosophy of logic. To believe in causation is simply to believe that there is something fundamental about nature in virtue of which the world is regular in its behavior and that something is *what* causation is, or is at least is an essential *component* of what causation involves. In the seventeenth century, there was much debate regarding the notion of vitalism, and this debate heavily influenced the discussion regarding causation. During this early modern period, many philosophers questioned the intelligibility of causal interactions and the notion of causation itself. As a consequence of this debate, causes were no longer seen as the active initiators of a change, but as inactive nodes in a law-like implication chain instead.

In the thirteenth chapter, "Triangulating Peirce, Gould, and Conway Morris," I attempt to construct an introductory (of sorts) relation between Charles Sanders Peirce, Stephen Jay Gould, and Simon Conway Morris in order to derive a from them a thematic evolutionary developmental philosophy of the theology and science relationship. I note that two themes regarding the nature of evolutionary thought—that of it being pictured as descent with modification and as it being marked by an over-reliance on genetics and a high emphasis upon contingency—mark the historical development of Darwinism broadly construed. As I develop it in this chapter, I would like to hope that we, in the twenty-first century, can move beyond these two models, and enter into a Darwinism as being marked by an evolutionary developmental philosophy assisted by Peirce, which would result in a proposed period of stability between the competing extremes of an overemphasis on contingency on one side and strict predictability on the other.

Part One

Delineation of Theology
&
Science Models

1

A Delineation of Models Regarding the Relationship Between Theology and Science[1]

IN THIS CHAPTER OF the book, I delineate several aspects of previous models of the relationship between religion/theology and science. John Hedley Brooke and Geoffrey Cantor, for example, argue that neither religion nor science is reducible to some sort of timeless essence; rather, both must be understood in their historical particularities—they are inextricable from the times in which they arise.[2] Within the academy of higher education today, there are four general ways of responding to the main question of this chapter. On the one hand, we have those who think they there are no real limits to the competence of science, what it can do, and what it can explain. Richard Dawkins, for example, writes that since we have modern biology, we have "no longer . . . to resort to superstition when faced with the deep problems: Is there a meaning to life? What are we for? What is man?"[3] According to Dawkins, science can address and answer all of these questions. Mikael Stenmark calls people like Dawkins "scientific expansionists."[4] What they have in common is that they think science can and should be

---

1. A significantly revised form of this essay appeared in *Wesleyan Theological Journal* 51 2 (2016) 156–73.

2. Brooke and Cantor, *Reconstructing Nature*.

3. Dawkins, *The Selfish Gene*, 1.

4. Stenmark, *How to Relate Science and Religion*, xi. Note that Stenmark gets the terminology of "scientific expansionists" from Graham, who notes that expansionists write in such a way that the boundaries of science "include, at least by implication, value questions" (Graham, *Between Science and Values*, 6).

expanded in such a way that the only kind of knowledge that we can have is of a scientific variety.

On the other hand, there are people that contend science should be heavily informed by or shaped by religion. These thinkers aver that the boundaries of religion—not those of science—can and should be expanded in such a way that religion dictates science. Stenmark calls these individuals "religious expansionists."[5] For instance, in this camp one will find such thinkers as Alvin Plantinga, who, while noting that it is naive to expect contemporary science to be religiously or theologically neutral, advises us that it would be wise that, "a Christian academic and scientific community ought to pursue science in its own way, starting from and taking for granted what they know as Christians."[6] I contend that we must take religious expansionists as serious as we take scientific expansionists.

There is yet another group of views on the theology and science relationship, one that contends science cannot be ideologically neutral. Steven Rose, Richard Lewontin, and Leon J. Kamin, for example, are representatives of this view; they write that they "share a commitment to the prospect of the creation of a more socially just—a socialist—society. And we recognize that a critical science is an integral part of the struggle to create that society."[7] Stenmark calls these thinkers "ideological expansionists."[8]

In contradistinction to the three above mentioned models, there is a fourth group of thinkers that defend the idea that science and theology or ideology ought to be restricted to their own separate areas of inquiry; Stenmark calls these people "scientific and religious restrictionists."[9] An example of this type of thinking can be found in the writings of Stephen Jay Gould, who argues that science and religion should exhibit a respectful non-interference, and are in fact autonomous, non-overlapping "magesteria."[10] The magisterium of science regards the empirical realm, whereas religion regards questions of ultimate meaning and moral value.[11]

It should be noted that both science and religion have social dimensions, and as such, they are social practices, meaning that they are "Socially

---

5. Stenmark, *How to Relate Science and Religion*, xii.
6. Plantinga, "Science: Augustinian or Duhemian?," 377.
7. Lewontin, et al., *Not in Our Genes*, ix–x.
8. Stenmark, *How to Relate Science and Religion*, xiii.
9. Ibid., xiv.
10. Gould, *Rock of Ages*, 5.
11. Ibid., 6.

established cooperative human activities through which their practitioners . . . try to achieve certain goals by means of particular strategies."[12] I agree with Stenmark here. I contend that science and theology have social practices that *overlap*. It is often claimed that science is the paradigm of dispassionate inquiry, where positions of truth are critically examined, and nothing is believed on the basis of authority; instead, the scientific community disinterestedly applies the scientific method. I question this claim, and contend instead, with Thomas Kuhn,[13] that all scientific truths are socially constrained. Moreover, since the practice of science is a learned activity, it, like religion, employs the usage of authority. Philip Kitcher agrees, writing, "individual scientists identify certain people within the community as authoritative in issues that are not agreed on throughout the community."[14]

Personal Model of the Science and Theology Relationship: Overlap

Early in my postgraduate education, I encountered Process philosophy, and my life has been forever changed as a result. This section of the book will briefly recount the results of this encounter with Process philosophy, its continuing relevance for me, and how my advocacy of a monistic Process-based view of the overlapping relationship between science and theology looks like fleshed out in practice. In my studies over the last fifteen years, I have interacted heavily with Process philosophy, and have invariably inculcated much of what I have been exposed to since my entrance into a postgraduate degree program. In these postgraduate studies, I have consistently sought to *integrate* my new learning with my undergraduate degree in biology. So then, in the chapters that follow, one may find an explication of how I have come to view the science and theology relationship as one that should be characterized by a *monistic* understanding of the two domains that is based on a Process worldview (i.e., ideologically based), and is discernable by an *overlapping* of the two fields of inquiry.

While I here use the term "integrate," this should not be taken to mean that I indiscriminately agree with Ian Barbour's characterization of what he calls the "Integration" position of the theology and science relationship.[15]

12. Stenmark, *How to Relate Science and Religion*, xvi.
13. Kuhn, *The Structure of Scientific Revolutions*.
14. Kitcher, *The Advancement of Science*, 84 n.36.
15. cf. Barbour, *Religion in an Age of Science*, 77.

PART ONE: DELINEATION OF THEOLOGY & SCIENCE MODELS

Due to this highly read book, most of the discussion post 1990 has classified the science and religion relationship as being one of conflict, independence, dialogue, or integration. Because I view the notion of there being a "conflict" between science and religion as a specious concept, based more so on John William Draper's polemic against the Catholic Church, as expressed in his *History of the Conflict between Religion and Science*, as well as my contention that the putative relation known as "dialogue" is nebulous (regardless of which view one might hold, they should be committed to "dialogue" with opposing views), I would—if I had to use Barbour's delineations—be an integrationist. But overall I agree with Brooke and Cantor[16] and van Huyssteen[17] who argue that Barbour's classification scheme is too a-historical, universal, and static to fruitfully map the way science and religion have interacted.

Process philosophy is based on the conviction that the central task of philosophy is to construct a cosmology in which all intuitions grounded in human experience can be reconciled. Whereas cosmologies were traditionally based on religious, ethical, and aesthetic as well as scientific experiences, cosmology in the modern period has increasingly been based on science alone. In the broadest sense, the term "Process philosophy" refers to all worldviews holding that process—or becoming—is more fundamental than unchanging—or static—being.[18] The term has widely come to refer in particular, however, to the movement onset by Alfred North Whitehead and extended by Charles Hartshorne.

So what does my monistic advocacy of a Process-based view of the overlapping relationship between theology and science actually look like? On one side, this task of reconciling theology and science involves the replacement of the thoroughly materialistic worldview, with which science has been associated primarily since the nineteenth century, with "panexperientialism," which allows religious experience to be properly considered. The term panexperientialism was coined in 1977 by American theologian-philosopher David Ray Griffin, and is a combination of the terms "pan," meaning all, and "experience." The theory of panexperientialism is summarized in Griffin's book *Unsnarling the World-Knot: Consciousness,*

---

16. Brooke and Cantor, *Reconstructing Nature*, 275.

17. van Huyssteen, *Duet or Duel?*, 3.

18. One can find advocation of these views in an anthology entitled *Philosophers of Process*, which includes selections from Samuel Alexander, Henri Bergson, John Dewey, William James, Conway Lloyd Morgan, Charles Sanders Peirce, and Alfred North Whitehead, with an introduction by Charles Hartshorne (Browning, *Philosophers of Process*).

Freedom, and the Mind-Body Problem,[19] in which he argues that in panexperientialism, Whitehead advocates a monistic metaphysic; thus, the traditional problems of mind-body interaction are not present in Process metaphysics because reality, at its base, is not bifurcated into purely mental or physical categories. This Process metaphysical doctrine states that all individual actual entities—from electrons to human persons—are essentially self-determining and possess a capacity for "feeling" or a degree of subjective interiority. The self-determining nature of all entities is consistent with an uncontrolling love of God perspective as advocated by Thomas Jay Oord in manifold books over the last decade. Although all actual entities possess experience, it is not necessarily conscious experience; Whitehead argues that consciousness presupposes experience, but not vice versa. Panexperientialism is a significant departure from the dominant metaphysical theories of idealism (all is mind), dualism (mind and matter are equally fundamental), and materialism (all is matter).

The other side of the task of reconciling theology and science involves overcoming exaggerations from the theological field that conflict with necessary assumptions of science, the main exaggeration of which involves the idea of divine power. Whitehead and Hartshorne believe that a metaphysical description of reality points to the necessity of a supreme agent to which the name "God" can meaningfully be applied. But they—and I—strongly reject the traditional view of divine power, according to which God, having created the world *ex nihilo*, interrupts its causal processes at his whim—a doctrine that not only creates the problem of evil, but also conflicts with the assumption of methodological naturalism that no such interruptions can occur. Their alternative proposal is that the power of God is persuasive, not coercive, with power intermediate between the omnipotent God of classical theism and the absentee God of deism (see, e.g., Whitehead 1929,[20] 1933;[21] Hartshorne 1984).[22] Brooke and Cantor's position finds support from Thomas Jay Oord's uncontrolling love of God concept. This book will often refer to this posit, for I contend that this is a better portrayal of God, especially in view of the long and winding road of biological evolution through the processes of natural selection. Indeed, with Barbour, I contend

---

19. Griffin, *Unsnarling the World-Knot*, 11.
20. Whitehead, *Process and Reality*.
21. Whitehead, *Adventures of Ideas*.
22. Hartshorne, *Creativity in American Philosophy*.

that process metaphysics is the most promising mediator between theology and science in today's academic environment.[23]

Catholic Contributions to my Personal View

My advocation of a monistic Process-based view of the overlapping relationship between theology and science is aided by the interaction with the sciences modeled by the history of philosophical inquiry in the Catholic tradition, which gives me a method to emulate in its re-articulation of Aristotelian positions by Thomas Aquinas, for example. I see much value in employing science as a "handmaiden" to theology, a role first envisioned by Philo Judaeus in the first century, later expressed in medieval theology by Augustine in the fourth century, and fully embraced in the early twelfth century by Hugh of Saint-Victor. Our current Pope, Francis, in the Apostolic Exhortation *Evangelii Gaudium*, offers something akin to this position, writing that, "The Church is herself a missionary disciple; she needs to grow in her interpretation of the revealed word and in her understanding of truth. It is the task of exegetes and theologians to help 'the judgment of the Church to mature'.[24] The other sciences also help to accomplish this, each in its own way."[25] I suggest that this means that the other sciences, biology for example, can critique, hone, and refine theology, thereby making it more robust. The Pope goes onward to state, "For those who long for a monolithic body of doctrine guarded by all and leaving no room for nuance, this might appear as undesirable and leading to confusion. But in fact such variety serves to bring out and develop different facets of the inexhaustible riches of the Gospel."[26]

The Catholic philosopher and theologian John Haught takes pains to let science be science, and to simultaneously let theology be theology. The scientific method, Haught insists, should have nothing to say about purpose, values, or even God's existence. Rather, it should stick to dealing with physical causes and avoid attempting to give ultimate explanations. To understand how theology may in some sense be explanatory of life's apparent designs without posing as an alternative to evolutionary accounts,

---

23. Barbour, *When Science Meets Religion*, 34.
24. Second Vatican Ecumenical Council, *Dei Verbum*, 12.
25. Pope Francis, *Evangelii Gaudium*, 34.
26. Ibid., 35.

one must develop what Haught calls a "layered explanation."[27] By layered explanation, he simply means that everything in our experience can be explained at multiple levels of understanding, in distinct and noncompeting ways. The idea that there can be a plurality of compatible explanations for a single event or phenomenon is an ancient one, endorsed by great thinkers such as Socrates, Plato, Aristotle, Augustine, Aquinas, and Kant, and Haught argues that it is a valid methodology—even in this age of science.

In other words, ultra-Darwinists like Dawkins and Dennett need not insist that natural selection rather than divine creativity accounts for living design. In a layered understanding, different levels of explanation are simultaneously operative. Just because natural selection can account for the design of a fish's eye at one level of understanding, for example, this does not necessarily exclude divine creativity as an explanation at a deeper level. Since theology operates on a different explanatory level—alongside of, and not in conflict with—from scientific accounts of phenomenon, evolutionary biologists should not expect to see divine influence intervening directly in the life-process at the level where natural selection is operative. Nor should they conclude that they have ruled out divine creativity as a valid theological idea just because they see no "evidence" of direct divine manipulation in the formation of biological complexity.[28]

Moreover, thinkers from Plato to Whitehead have acknowledged that things cannot be actualized without being patterned (or ordered) by some "formative" principle(s). In contemporary scientific usage, information is identified—at various levels—as the set of principles that organize subordinate elements into hierarchically distinct domains. Haught avers one dimension that gets lost in modernity's simplistic reductionism is the dimension of "information," which means, he says, that more is going on in evolution than merely molecular or atomic activity. Indeed, complex organizational principles inform the more elemental levels, and he loosely assigns the name "information" to these principles, noting that information is not reducible to its constituent matter and energy.[29]

When faced with information, Haught contends, contemporary science has alighted against something distinct from the material causes that had lent credence to reductionist views of life (and by extension, to mind). Analytically basal, the DNA molecule appears to be composed of

---

27. Haught, *Making Sense of Evolution*, 23.
28. Ibid., 25.
29. Ibid., 50.

simple "chemical components," but at a deeper level of understanding, the informational arrangement of genetic codons—A, T, C, and G—is the most significant feature of the cell. The specific sequence of genetic codons of entities is, after all, what determines what the entity is phenomenologically. Chemically speaking, if you look at DNA, one will not notice the informational content that the constituent atoms and molecules are carrying. However, at a deeper "reading level," the informational arrangement of the codons is all-important. My existence as a member of *Homo sapiens* has to do not only with my evolutionary ancestry, but also with the specific sequence of nucleotides in my DNA.

Haught states that even if I descended continuously from a common living ancestor, and even if my genetic makeup differs quantitatively from that of chimpanzees and bonobos by only a minute amount, the "informational" difference is great enough to produce both biological and ontological distinctiveness. In the arena of information, then, I am discontinuous with the rest of life. Even though I remain continuous with all animals at the level of my evolutionary, atomic, molecular, and metabolic constitution, the specific informational content embedded within my genes is what counts the most. It must be stressed that this informational aspect is naturally derived, with Haught stipulating that the information content is not an instance of "intelligent design."[30] What Haught proposes, however, is that an awareness of the informational content "silently at work in the universe"[31] offers at least one way to understand how different levels of both being and value can descend from earlier instantiations of the evolutionary advance without being completely reducible to them (i.e., they are emergent—I am using the distinctively philosophical sense of the term as it will be developed later in this book).

We are also aided in our endeavor to understand theology in an evolutionary world by Thomas Aquinas's characterization of God working through secondary causes. Catholic priest and philosopher Denis Edwards stipulates that Aquinas perceived God to act in and through creatures, or natural causes, enabling them to be truly causal in their own right, by enabling them to be, to act, and to become.[32] Aquinas notes that God acts through intermediaries, imparting to them the dignity of having causal powers. In respecting their dignity and integrity, God grants secondary

---

30. Ibid., 50–51.
31. Ibid., 51.
32. Edwards, *How God Acts*, 80–81.

causes their proper autonomy. Edwards points out that for Aquinas, God is "always and everywhere at work" through secondary causes.[33] I resonate with Aquinas's attempt to salvage the particularity of divine action in our scientifically driven world.[34] In contrast to Aquinas, however, I view God to work not only primarily through secondary causality, but also *exclusively* through it, through the perhaps unknown laws of nature, much alike to Denis Edwards.[35]

Preliminary Conclusions

In this chapter, I have attempted to explicate how one should understand the relationship between theology and science. In so doing, I have noted that the scientific expansionist, religious expansionist, and scientific and religious restrictionist positions all fall short of an adequate explanation of the relationship between theology and science. Additionally, I have developed my personal view of the relation between theology and science, which is demonstrable as a monistic Process-based view marked by an overlapping of the two domains. In so doing, I have highlighted the panexperientialist aspect of my personal view, which implies that not just humans but even subatomic particles have a capacity for some level of subjective interiority. Also, I noted that the other side my personal view of the relationship between theology and science involves overcoming the exaggeration of divine power, with this chapter opting to view God's power as one of persuasion rather than coercion.

My advocation of a monistic Process-based view of the overlapping relationship between theology and science is aided by the interaction with the sciences modeled by the history of philosophical inquiry in the Catholic tradition, which gives me a method to emulate in its re-articulation of Aristotelian positions. In particular, I highlighted Haught's advocation of a layered explanation, by which he means that everything in our experience can be explained at multiple levels of understanding, in distinct and noncompeting ways. Moreover, in this chapter I examined how Haught advances the notion that information is identified in contemporary scientific usage as the set of principles that organize subordinate elements into

---

33. Edwards, *How God Acts*, 81.
34. Ibid., 83; cf. Aquinas, *Summa Theologiae* 1a.105.7ad1.
35. Edwards, *How God Acts*, 83.

Part One: Delineation of Theology & Science Models

hierarchically distinct domains, a concept that points to realities beyond what the principles of physics alone can explain.

Following this, I argued that in light of the current worldview, marked by the scientific notion of evolution, new models of divine action are necessary. In sum, I view a monistic Process-based view of the overlapping relationship between theology and science as the most constructive and tenable response to Darwinism in today's society.

Part Two

Kenosis
&
Emergence

2

Making Sense of Emergence

A Critical Engagement with Leidenhag, Leidenhag, and Yong[1]

BY DAVID BRADNICK[2] AND BRADFORD MCCALL

A NUMBER OF THEOLOGIANS engaged in the theology and science dialogue—particularly Pentecostal theologian Amos Yong—employ emergence as a framework to discuss special divine action as well as causation initiated by other spiritual realities, such as angels and demons. Mikael and Joanna Leidenhag, however, have issued some reservations about the use of emergence in the theology and science dialogue. In an article entitled "Science and Spirit: A Critical Examination of Amos Yong's Pneumatological Theology of Emergence," they argue that Yong uses supernaturalistic Pentecostal themes—including divine interventionism—that renders the concept of emergence obsolete.[3] Further, they claim that Yong's employment of emergence theory is inconsistent because he highlights the ontological independence of various spirits in the world concurrently with his advocation of supervenience theory. In view of these concerns, Leidenhag and Leidenhag urge Yong to depart from his aim of harmonizing

---

1. A previous version of this essay appeared in *Zygon: Journal of Religion and Science* 53 1 (2018): 140–57.

2. David Bradnick is a professor of philosophy, Stevenson University; e-mail dbradnick@stevenson.edu.

3. Leidenhag and Leidenhag, "Science and Spirit," 425-35.

the spirit-filled imagination of Pentecostalism with the scientific culture of the twenty-first century, at least via the use of emergence theory.

In what follows, we plan to provide a summary of emergence and address each of these criticisms set forth by Leidenhag and Leidenhag, since emergence has been an important interlocutor for both Yong and the authors of this current chapter. While we are aware of two other articles in this area, one by Mikael Leidenhag (2013)[4] and one by Joanna Leidenhag (2016),[5] we tend to focus upon the metaphysical consistency of an emergence theology herein, but the latter part of this essay begins to address some of Leidenhag's (2016) theological concerns. Notably, in her article, Joanna Leidenhag argues that emergence faces several theological problems, particularly in the area of Christology and Pneumatology. Space does not permit us, however, to address all of these concerns. We will now move on to a general overview of emergence theory.

An Overview of Emergence Theory

Emergence is the "theory that cosmic evolution repeatedly includes unpredictable, irreducible, and novel appearances."[6] These novel occurrences, which are naturally produced, include—but are not limited to—structures, organs, and organisms. In brief, emergence claims that it is possible to get "something more from nothing but."[7] As such, emergentists argue that reductionary tendencies within natural science are not tenable. No longer can one seek to explain all things as being thoroughly reducible to their physical entities or microphysical causes (i.e., physicalism). Whereas substance dualism was the dominant metaphysical view in Western history from Plato to Kant, numerous scholars contend that adherence to a bipartite construction of physical components and spiritual components is no longer reasonable. The revolution in metaphysics first wrought by Kant has undercut physicalism and dualism. The earth, in the emergentist view, is an active and empowering environmentment that brings forth life by various interdependent processes.

Philip Clayton is a leading theorist of emergence inasmuch as he offers a third way of understanding the world and human relationships.

4. Leidenhag, "The Relevance of Emergence Theory."
5. Leidenhag, "A Critique of Emergent Theologies."
6. Clayton, *Mind & Emergence*, 39.
7. Goodenough and Deacon, "From Biology to Consciousness to Morality," 802.

He presents emergence as a viable option and a fruitful paradigm for evolutionary progress, in contrast to the waning explanatory power of its competitors, physicalism and dualism.[8] In fact, "actualizing the dream of a final reduction 'downwards', it now appears, has proven fundamentally impossible."[9] In view of this implausible task, Clayton has sought to resurrect and re-appropriate the positions of early twentieth century emergentists. He contends that three general claims undergird emergence theory in the philosophy of science. First, empirical reality divides naturally into multiple levels, which means that new emergent levels evolve over the course of evolutionary history. Second, emergent "wholes" are more than the sum of their parts and require new types of explanation adequate to each new level of phenomena. Third, such emergent wholes manifest new manners of causal interaction, so biological processes, for example, are not merely reducible to physics, but require genuine biological explanations instead.[10]

Within *Mind & Emergence* Clayton modifies the four features of emergence as advocated by Charbel Nino el-Hani and Antonio Marcos Pereira (EP), who were late twentieth century emergentists.[11] Specifically, he converts EP's construct of ontological physicalism into a more realistic paradigm of ontological monism, arguing that all matter (i.e., reality) is composed of one basic type of "stuff" and that mere physics (i.e., physicalism) is not sufficient to account for the various manners in which this "stuff" is expressed in the world. Clayton essentially adopts EP's construct of property emergence, which entails the notion that genuinely novel properties emerge from complex systems when material particles attain an appropriate threshold of organizational complexity. EP's notion regarding the irreducibility of emergence is modified by adding that there are forms of causality that are irreducible to physical causes, and that causality should guide our ontology.[12] Finally, EP's conception of downward causation in reference to emergent systems is virtually adopted, with Clayton defining

---

8. Clayton, *Mind & Emergence*, 3.

9. Clayton, *Mind & Emergence*, 70.

10. Clayton, "Emergence of Spirit: From Complexity to Anthropology to Theology," 294.

11. el-Hani and Pereira, "Higher-Level Descriptions," 118–42.

12. Clayton, *Mind & Emergence*, 5.

the concept as the "process whereby some whole has an active non-additive causal influence on its parts."[13]

Before offering his definition of emergence, Clayton draws from Bedau the classification of *strong* and *weak* emergence theories in the twentieth century.[14] Strong emergentists postulate that evolution produces ontologically distinct levels of organs/isms that are characterized by their own distinct regularities and causal forces. In other words, new, or emergent, ontological realities supervene upon their constituent substrates but cannot be reduced to them. Strong emergence also involves "downward causation" from the whole to the parts. In contrast, weak emergentists maintain that, as new patterns emerge, the causal processes remain those that are fundamental to physics.[15] A property of an organ/ism is weakly emergent if it is reducible to its intrinsic qualities, so that weakly emergent properties are "novel" only at the level of description; this is in contrast with strongly emergent organs/isms in which the cause is neither reducible to any intrinsic causal capacity of the parts nor to any relation between the component parts. The largest difference, however, between strong and weak emergence is that strong emergence rejects the reduction of biology to micro-physics.[16]

Clayton asserts that weak emergence leaves us with the old dichotomy of physicalism and dualism.[17] He writes that emergence is "that which is produced by a combination of causes, but cannot be regarded as the sum of their individual effects."[18] Particularly, in offering his view regarding emergence theory, Clayton emphasizes the immanence of God. Within biology, for instance, one can see multiple instances of where that which emerges becomes a causal agent in its own right.[19] He maintains that whereas "biological processes in general are the result of systems that create and maintain order (stasis) through massive energy input from their environmentment," there comes a point of sufficient complexity after which a phase transition suddenly becomes almost inevitable.[20]

---

13. Ibid., 49.
14. Bedau, "Weak Emergence," 375–99.
15. Clayton, *Mind & Emergence*, 9.
16. Ibid., 58.
17. Ibid., 10.
18. Ibid., 38.
19. Ibid., 65.
20. Ibid., 78.

Within *Mind & Emergence*, Clayton promotes eight different characteristics of emergentism.[21] First, with respect to the world, he advocates *monism*, which he describes as the contention that there is one "stuff" of which it is made; then, Clayton argues for *hierarchical complexity* whereby "more complex units are formed out of more simple parts." Third, Clayton contends that *temporal or emergent monism* means that, "hierarchical structuring takes place over time;" as a fourth characteristic, Clayton points out that there is no *monolithic law of emergence*, and thus the emergence of higher-level properties cannot be accounted for by one single law. Fifth, there are *patterns across levels of emergence*, insomuch as emergent properties share a familial resemblance of ontological dependency, irreducibility, and unpredictability. Additionally, there is *downward causation*, which means that a high-level property can causally affect its physical constituents. Thus, given the first six characteristics, we have a clear case of *emergentist pluralism*, which refers to the idea that there is a plurality of distinct properties and levels within the natural world. Understanding all of the preceding characteristics of emergence, Clayton defends the *emergence of mind* so that human agency becomes a naturalistic, yet non-reductionist, entity. He advocates a "theological dualism" whereby reality is composed of that which is God and that which is not God. Clayton denies that God is an emergent reality (à la Samuel Alexander); instead, he views emergence as an analogical approach to understanding divine action.

Amos Yong's Pneumatological Emergence Theory

For full disclosure, both authors of the present chapter are former PhD students of Pentecostal theologian Amos Yong, and we have been greatly influenced by him. In fact, we have adopted and appropriated many of his seminal thoughts. In what follows, we shall provide a cursory explication of his views, which will both setup and provide a transition for Leidenhag and Leidenhag's critique of him.

Yong suggests that the philosophical position of emergence may provide an advantageous framework in which to bring theology into dialogue with science. He writes, "does pentecostal theology have anything to *say* in, much less *contribute* to, the ongoing dialogue between theology and science"?[22] In response to this question, Yong states that Pentecostalism,

21. Ibid., 60–62.
22. Yong, *The Spirit of Creation*, 2.

given its "embodied epistemology and nonreductionistic worldview," aids in eroding the false dichotomies created by modernism—namely "materialism versus spiritualism, rationalism versus empiricism, intellectualism versus emotionalism . . . naturalism versus supernaturalism."[23] He goes on, noting that the Spirit-nature opposition is, and has always been, a false one. Therefore, any separation of the Pentecostal experience of the Spirit from scientific explorations is, necessarily, to the detriment of both fields of inquiry. The second reason that Pentecostalism can make a unique contribution to the theology and science dialogue is that the category of "spirit," which is a central defining concept in Pentecostal theology, is present in both theological and scientific discourse. In fact, Yong's article "Discerning the Spirit(s) in the Natural World" describes sixteen different uses of the category of "spirit" in the theology and science dialogue. Therein, Yong moves from the cosmological sciences and field theory to the use of "spirit" in the biological sciences and "the emergent complexity of human life in terms of 'spirit.'"[24]

Yong sees Clayton's emergence theory as attractive because it provides a framework for non-dualistic "interactivity and co-creativity between the divine and the creation" in a manner similar to how it allows Clayton to remove the dichotomy between mind and matter.[25] This gives him the ability to employ emergence theory as a bridge between a Pentecostal reading of Scripture and the empirical sciences. Importantly, Yong does not adopt Clayton's emergent theory wholesale. He criticizes Clayton for trading in mind-body dualism for "theological dualism." He thinks the latter position is deficient and fails to account for the work of the Spirit within natural and biological processes.[26] Yong proffers that his pneumatological "theology of creation can supplement and in that sense fill out the theological content of Clayton's emergence metaphysics."[27]

Leidenhag & Leidenhag's Critique of Yong's Theology

Leidenhag and Leidenhag express two major concerns about Yong's application of emergence:

23. Ibid., 11.
24. Yong, "Emergence from Physics to Theology," 321.
25. Yong, *The Spirit of Creation*, 158.
26. Ibid., 185–87.
27. Ibid., 163.

1. Yong's Pentecostal supernaturalism "renders the concept of emergence obsolete;" and

2. His argument for emergent spiritual realities, such as angels and demons, "betrays his commitment to supervenience theory."[28]

Leidenhag and Leidenhag write further, "Given [our criticisms] can we still say that the emergence theory is compatible with the Pentecostal worldview? By changing the meaning of emergence so radically, Yong has not yet been able to answer this question positively."[29] In this section, we address each of these concerns in order. We maintain that our reading of Yong, which is a plausible alternative to the one presented by Leidenhag and Leidenhag, challenges their criticisms. Our reading preserves Yong's pneumatological emergentism, by and large, and his Pentecostal worldview that adheres to both non-reductionism and a spirit-filled cosmology, which includes angelic and demonic realities.

The first criticism raised by Leidenhag and Leidenhag against Yong is that his Pentecostal supernaturalism "renders the concept of emergence obsolete." The primary origin of this criticism stems from Yong's interpretation of the creation story, namely the advent of *ha adam*. By employing Gen 1, Yong argues that human beings emerged from the Spirit of God, who breathed life into the dust of the ground. According to Leidenhag and Leidenhag, Yong's pneumatological reading of this passage creates a "tension" with emergentist monism. They add, "Monism here, one of Clayton's eight theses of emergence theory, means that there is one world made up of one type of 'stuff.' Thus, no extra-natural forces can be causally responsible for the emergence of higher-levels according to the monist thesis . . . Thus, the tension on Yong's view becomes apparent as enspiritedness of ha'adam is not physically realised but is realised by the Spirit of God, the ruach."[30] They add, "Although Yong employs the biblical notion of 'dust' in an emergent fashion, the sole cause of ha'adam's existence remains divine, thus distinguished from (and outside of) the natural order."[31] On this point, we take issue with their depiction of Yong's theology.

Leidenhag and Leidenhag are correct in asserting that the Spirit of God, according to Yong, is involved in the creation of human kind; however,

---

28. Leidenhag and Leidenhag, "Science and Spirit," 428.
29. Ibid., 434.
30. Ibid., 429.
31. Ibid., 429.

one does not have to read his proposal through the lens of supernaturalism. Rather, we can understand Yong in such a way that the Spirit works through natural processes. In fact, Yong does not refer to his position as "supernatural," but this is an assessment imposed by Leidenhag and Leidenhag instead. Moreover, he explicitly resists supernaturalism in other writings.[32] In our reading of Yong, the advent of the human spirit is not an immediate event, but the result of slow evolutionary processes over the course of billions of years. The human spirit could not emerge until complex biological systems evolved, including the brain; it is not a creation *ex nihilo*, as Leidenhag and Leidenhag claim. Veritably, Yong writes, "A supervenience theory of mind provides an account of consciousness that is emergent from, intimately connected with, and dependent on, but finally irreducible to the material workings of the brain, even while providing a viable model for understanding the phenomenon of mental causation."[33] Thus, one is not required to understand the advent of the human spirit as a supernatural occurrence since it comes about through divine action *within* natural processes. In fact, in the article entitled "Ruach, the Primordial Chaos, and the Breath of Life," Yong argues that God, at times, allows creation to evolve and organize independently; here God is passive and creation becomes a co-creator.[34] Hence, we do not understand Yong's account concerning the emergence of *ha adam* in terms of supernaturalism since emergence recognizes that novel ontological properties emerge through the interaction of systems, including non-physical realities. We will say more will about this below.

Leidenhag and Leidenhag continue their characterization of Yong as a supernaturalist in referring to him as a dualist interactionist. They write:

> Yong's reading of Genesis still sees God creating two types of things, material "dust" which can continue to develop through the emergence of higher-levels and increasing complexity, and "breath" which is directly bestowed by God into ha'adam and which does not continue to develop or generate the emergence of new levels. The Spirit of ha'adam does not seem to emerge from matter, but only interact with matter after having been directly created by God.[35]

---

32. e.g., Yong, *The Spirit Poured Out on All Flesh*, 294–96; see also Yong, "A Review Symposium."

33. Yong, *The Cosmic Breath*, 87.

34. Yong, "Ruach, the Primordial Chaos, and the Breath of Life," 196–97.

35. Leidenhag and Leidenhag, "Science and Spirit," 429.

However, Yong uses a literary-theological reading of Gen 1 to argue against traditional dualist interpretations of humans as "embodied souls" and to argue for an ontologically holistic view of humans as emergent creatures.[36] As we noted above, the emergence of the human spirit is not the result of single act of God and also not the infusion of a different substance; instead, the human spirit arises from within nature and through the work of God. This includes countless series of biological processes that are, in turn, dependent upon various chemical properties. The emergence of the human spirit is the culmination, and perhaps the realization—or instantiation—of God's purposes within the created order. Accordingly, God does not insert new "stuff" into the cosmos but God works, instead, to bring about new levels of realities from primordial matter. Yong insists upon "the dependence and interconnectedness between the human spirit and its material substrate."[37]

It appears that Leidenhag and Leidenhag have imposed a more literal understanding of Gen 1 upon Yong's interpretation of the text. After all, Yong explicitly resists dualistic renderings of humans in many texts. The literary structure of the biblical text allows us to emphasize this culmination from a theological standpoint, but we are not bound by its literal interpretation. Reading Yong through a lens that is sympathetic to evolutionary processes, therefore, challenges Leidenhag and Leidenhag's claims that he is a dualist interactionist. For instance, in writing about the standard evolutionary accounts, Yong notes that he does not "think it plausible for us to enjoy the benefits of contemporary technology, medicine, and other applications of modern science and then summarily dismiss their overarching explanatory framework."[38] Thus, Yong appears to invite this type of evolutionary reading.[39]

Furthermore, in their characterization of Yong as a supernaturalist, Leidenhag and Leidenhag argue that Yong is inconsistent in his application of emergence and misappropriates many of its key components. Yet, we contend that Yong's pneumatological account is compatible with emergence. Leidenhag and Leidenhag are correct in asserting the emergentists' commitment to monism, but their charge that, "no extra-natural forces can be causally responsible for the emergence of higher-levels" mischaracterizes

---

36. Yong, "Ruach, the Primordial Chaos, and the Breath of Life," 200.
37. Yong, *The Spirit of Creation*, 159.
38. Ibid., 137.
39. cf. Ibid., 135–44.

PART TWO: *Kenosis & Emergence*

Yong's position as well as Philip Clayton's emergentist principles.[40] It is important to point out that most emergentists, such as Clayton, are not physicalists. While the world is composed of a single sort of "stuff," this stuff takes on many different forms and structures and can display a multitude of properties.[41] Moreover, Clayton identifies himself as an emergent panentheist and maintains that God is active within the world.[42] Thus Clayton himself argues for the influence of "extra-natural" forces within the cosmos, if what is meant by this is divine action. In fact, Clayton's entire project is an attempt to give an account of divine action that is philosophically and scientifically cogent. Furthermore, he acknowledges that certain explanations do not contradict, and some may align with, emergentist principles. He writes, "There is no obstacle to belief in an initial creative act by God . . . it becomes plausible that God could have initiated this natural process with the intention of bringing about intelligent life."[43] Additionally, while Clayton does not embrace divine action on the quantum level, he concedes that it is a possible explanation.[44] Therefore, the concept of extra-natural is not equivalent to supernatural as long as the former, in this case God, operates within the laws of nature.

Mikael Leidenhag resists Clayton's panentheistic emergentism because it "collapses into dualism."[45] He remarks, "But given that there are particular instances of divine influence on the world according to their view, that we seem to have causes that are non-natural, it seems that Clayton's and Peacock's [sic] panentheistic model is not antidualistic at all . . . the distinction between panentheism and classical theism becomes blurred."[46] Here Leidenhag fails to recognize that emergence accepts the existence of heterogeneous properties and realities that may interact and have causative effects upon one another. The problem with classical dualism is its adherence to distinct substances and its inability to account for causation between them, yet we contend below that a relational worldview moves beyond the deficit of substance dualism. As we argue here, though, what is promising about emergence is its ability to overcome this problem

---

40. Leidenhag and Leidenhag, "Science and Spirit," 429.
41. Clayton, *Mind & Emergence*, 4.
42. Clayton, *In Whom We Live and Move and Have Our Being*, 87.
43. Clayton, *Mind & Emergence*, 200.
44. Ibid., 187-91, 201.
45. Leidenhag, "The Relevance of Emergence Theory," 977.
46. Ibid., 978.

of causation for there is a plurality of distinct properties and realities that are not necessarily incompatible in terms of causative effects. Thus, Mikael Leidenhag's concern is questionable.

Given Clayton's understanding of emergence, God can work through both top-down and bottom-up means, and Yong's theological position can be located within such a framework. Yong accepts that the cosmos operates in accordance with regulatory laws, but he also embraces the notion that the universe is somewhat indeterminate and open to chance. Even miracles, according to Yong, can "be seen as basic divine actions that work within a regulatory system established by God rather than as violations of a strictly mechanistic created order."[47] Yong claims that we can understand pneumatology as working *within* the framework of natural laws, so his theology is consistent with Clayton's emergentism. Leidenhag and Leidenhag have not demonstrated sufficiently that Yong deviates from emergentism, and this renders their first critique tenuous, if not invalid.

The second criticism brought by Leidenhag and Leidenhag against Yong is that the use of supervenience throughout his arguments—specifically the ones concerning the emergence of human spirit and the emergence of spiritual realities, such as angels and demons—is inconsistent and problematic, and this "betrays his commitment to supervenience theory."[48] Here we argue that some of their concerns are legitimate, yet others are questionable. Nevertheless, a move toward a less robust form of emergence should leave Yong's pneumatological proposal largely intact.

Leidenhag and Leidenhag note that in *The Cosmic Breath* Yong writes, "a supervenience theory of mind is transformed into a relational and systems theory of minds and bodies in interdependence with each other and with nature's processes."[49] They argue that his application of the term *interdependency* "raises serious questions" because within emergence higher ontological levels—in this case human minds—are dependent upon lower-level substrates, but these lower levels are not dependent upon the higher ones. For example, human consciousness cannot exist without a body, but bodies—including other animals—can exist without consciousness. Alternatively, Leidenhag and Leidenhag suggest that, "cooperation" is a viable

---

47. Yong, *The Spirit of Creation*, 127.

48. Leidenhag and Leidenhag, "Science and Spirit," 428.

49. Yong, *The Cosmic Breath*, 87. Leidenhag and Leidenhag attribute this quote to Yong's text *Science and the Spirit* (2010), but in actuality it comes from *The Cosmic Breath* (2012), which we have correctly noted here.

term. We agree that the term "interdependence" is not an accurate depiction of emergence and warrants their criticism; however, in *The Spirit of Creation*, Yong writes that the mind and brain exist in "a relationship of supervenience."[50] He never uses the term interdependence and subsequently claims, "Human beings are minimally constituted by their bodies in an existing environmentmental web. Apart from this embodiment ... mind is non-existent and incapable of appearing."[51] So, in this case, we see either an error in Yong's earlier writing, which seems to be inconsistent with the trajectory of his principal ideas, or we have an instance where his thought develops. Consequently, one would be disingenuous to evaluate the overall value of Yong's proposal on this one (potentially dubious) instance. Removing the idea of interdependency from Yong's theology, or modifying it to an understanding of "cooperation," would do little to disrupt his overarching project—which is what we propose due to our acceptance of supervenience.

Next, Leidenhag and Leidenhag question Yong's use of supervenience concerning the Spirit of God. In *The Spirit of Creation*, Yong claims, "The charismatic activity of the Spirit also proceeds from the 'top down,' and is somehow ... supervenient upon the activity of free human agents."[52] Leidenhag and Leidenhag maintain that this should not be understood as supervenience; rather it is nothing more than "co-operation" between two agents—the human and the Holy Spirit. They add that these are "two ontologically distinct agents, neither of which emerged from the other, whose activity together brings about a common goal."[53] In our opinion, Yong does not claim that the Spirit emerges from human agents. Note that Yong refers to the Spirit's charismatic activity, which may include an act like speaking in tongues or manifestations of divine love. He is not proposing the supervenience of an agent. Furthermore, for Yong, the manifestation of these actions can only occur within and through intelligent, substantial agents. The interaction of the Spirit with humanity generates these charismatic properties, which is consistent with emergence. Emergence, as we explain above, proffers that new properties arise out of the interaction of systems, and Yong expresses an instance of these interactions. So, on one hand, Leidenhag and Leidenhag, are correct—Yong understands the charismatic work of the Spirit as a cooperative event—but his pneumatology does not violate

50. Yong, *The Spirit of Creation*, 61.
51. Ibid., 64.
52. Ibid., 95.
53. Leidenhag and Leidenhag, "Science and Spirit," 431.

supervenience, nor does he collapse the ontological distinction between humans and the Spirit, as they claim.

Leidenhag and Leidenhag also issue concerns over Yong's proposal that ontological realities—such as demonic, angelic, and ancestral entities—may arise, yet exist independently of the lower-level substrates from which they emerge. It should be noted, however, that elsewhere Joanna Leidenhag writes, "Although it seems acceptable to claim that created spirits (human souls, angelic, demonic, or ancestral spirits) are emergent phenomena, as Amos Yong suggests, it does not seem acceptable to place the Divine Spirit as a created result of the emergent process."[54] In consideration of this quote, Joanna Leidenhag's position, at least, on emergence and emergent realities is unclear. Nevertheless, their concerns here arise when Yong writes, "Once emergent the powers potentially attain a life of their own, capable of influencing and interacting with concrete historical structures, institutions, organizations, nations, and even persons and church movements."[55] Leidenhag and Leidenhag identify this as a case of strong emergence, and this appears to be a fair assessment. We agree with them that such a robust form of strong emergence is problematic, but in two other works, Yong seems to reject strong emergence. In *Beyond the Impasse*, he advocates that the demonic must be embodied. He pens, "Real evil ultimately cannot be understood as being ontologically separate from its determinate and particular incarnations."[56] He then adds, "These concrete actualities should be sufficient to convince us that the demonic does not refer to Casper-like spirits floating about in mid-heaven."[57] Elsewhere, Yong makes similar claims, describing the demonic as parasitic: "The demonic has no ontological reality of its own . . . it does not possess its own being."[58] So Yong's position is not entirely clear. He considers a radical form of strong emergence in *The Spirit of Creation*, but several of his other works reject such a position.

We contend that Yong's pneumatological assist does not fall apart if one retains a less robust form of emergence, as advocated in his earlier proposals. That is to say, spiritual realities can emerge in connection with material substrates but cannot exist independently of them. The advancement of a scaled-back emergence requires that one discard the existence

54. Leidenhag, "A Critique of Emergent Theologies," 785.
55. Yong, *The Spirit of Creation*, 205.
56. Yong, *Beyond the Impasse*, 138.
57. Ibid., 155.
58. Yong, *In the Days of Caesar*, 162.

of ancestral realities, but it does not require us to reject the existence of angelic and demonic realities. One of the authors of this chapter, David Bradnick, argues for the reality of emergent spiritual entities, namely angelic and demonic ones, without advocating their independence from their component—or constituent—base, which may include social, political, and economic, systems.[59] We recommend thamt Yong adopt this approach with reference to a weak form of emergence.

Leidenhag and Leidenhag anticipate a possible move by Yong to a "stricter" application of emergence and propose that, "his pneumatology would suffer considerably." Leidenhag and Leidenhag further elucidate this claim concerning Yong's pneumatology in stating:

> According to emergence theory, there can be no higher-level or supernatural causation from above without first a corresponding lower-level or natural event. Thus, for the Spirit to be an active part of the emergence theory, the Spirit (and its causal powers) would have to emerge. This would be much like how emergent theories describe the mind, and not like how Pentecostal theology describes the transcendence of God.[60]

But, as we argued above and will fill out below, this is a non-issue since God, who includes the Spirit, can act within the world through non-supernatural means. Thus, by restricting Yong's pneumatology to a less robust view of emergence, his overarching thesis remains cogent and plausible.

A Proposal of Kenotic-Relational Theology

We would now like to return to our earlier concerns, and argue that the Spirit can act within the world through non-supernatural means. Using an expanded view of kenosis that includes the pouring of the Spirit *into* creation offers a "pneumatological assist" to Yong's writings. In this view, the Spirit necessarily in-fills all of matter from its very origin, and as such, there is no distinction between matter and Spirited-entities. This chapter affirms the notion that creation was a result of the kenotic act of the Spirit *into* creation. Thus, this chapter also contends that the creation of matter and world has its ontological origin *in and through* the agency of the Spirit of God.

---

59. Bradnick, *Evil, Spirits, and Possession*.
60. Leidenhag and Leidenhag, "Science and Spirit," 432–33.

The Greek verb *kenoó* (κενόω) can mean either "to empty," or "to pour out." In the literal sense, its Hebrew equivalent is used, for example, in Isaiah 32:15: "Until the spirit be *poured upon* us from on high." The verb, which appears fourteen times in biblical Hebrew, refers to a cause of movement leading to a mass being poured out of a container in its original sense.[61] Thus, the word also means "to pour out" in reference to Rebekah's *pouring out* the water from her pitcher *into* the trough (Gen 24:20, the verb in the LXX is *exekenōsen*). In the original Hebrew of Gen 24:20, the term employed is a primitive root, meaning to *be* (i.e., causatively to *make*). Hence, it is appropriate to translate the term as either to *empty*, or to *pour out*. Note here that the pitcher was *emptied*, whereas the trough was made *full* by the emptying of the pitcher (which is *addition*, in a sense).[62] It is, therefore, concluded that a fruitful approach to understanding this difficult phrase is to realize that the verb *kenoó* means *to pour out* as well as *to pour into*.

Provided this understanding of kenosis, both creation and the incarnation are kenotic acts of *self-offering* since God makes space for creation and pours himself into it. Consequently, one may accurately posit that creation—in a *qualified* sense—possesses the Spirit of God from the beginning, though one needs to be wary of falling into pantheism. This kenosis of the Spirit into creation eliminates a strict sense of theological dualism between God and nature, which means that nature is indeed enspirited from its very origin.

We argue, along with Yong and Mikael Stenmark, for a multi-dimensional model of theology and science whereby these two domains overlap.[63] In other words, while these domains retain unique methodological approaches, there is room for mutual interaction. This interaction is possible because, if God is involved in the evolutionary development of the world—and we think God is involved panentheistically—then science models that very world in which God acts. Thus, we deny that theology and science are non-overlapping magisteria, as advocated by Stephen Jay Gould.

In speaking further of kenosis, it is important to note that many advocates of emergence theory highlight the basis of such a view in the panentheistic relation of God and the world.[64] Regarding Clayton's usage

---

61. Swanson, *Dictionary of Biblical Languages*.

62. cf. Wood, *New Bible Dictionary*, 643.

63. Stenmark, *How to Relate Science and Religion*, 261–68.

64. Inbody, "Reconceptions of Divine Power in John Wesley," 180–91; cf. Clayton and Simpson, *Adventures in the Spirit*; also see Saunders, *Divine Action and Modern Science*.

of it, one could say that emergence and panentheism are two sides of the same proverbial coin regarding his metaphysics and cosmology. Indeed, in an earlier essay, Clayton defines panentheism as the view that the world is within God, though God is at the same time more than the world.[65] Panentheism seeks to stress that the infinite God is as ontologically close to finite things as can possibly be thought without dissolving altogether the distinction between creator and created. Panentheism does not change biblical statements about God; it changes the philosophical framework that has too long dominated Christian attempts to conceive the relationship of God and world. Like many relational theologians today, Clayton breaks fundamentally with the Aristotelian notion of God as unmoved mover, which he finds to be sub-biblical.[66] Panentheism attributes all the functional regularity within the natural world to conscious divine intention, providing a thoroughly theological reading of physical regularities, one that is fully consistent with natural law.[67]

The fact of panentheism, if you will, is rather well documented in current scientific, philosophical, and theological literature.[68] Interestingly, John Wesley perhaps anticipated the concept of panentheism.[69] He writes, "There is no point of space, whether within or without the bounds of creation, where God is not."[70] He then adds, "Perhaps it cannot be proved that all space is filled with matter. But the heathen [Virgil] himself will bear us witness . . . 'All things are full of God.' Yea, and whatever space exists beyond the bounds of creation . . . even that space cannot exclude him who fills the heaven and earth."[71] Going further, Wesley notes the intimate presence of God within creation, saying "Nay, and we cannot believe the omnipotence of God unless we believe his omnipresence. For seeing . . . [that] nothing can act where it is not, if there were any space where God was not present he would not be able to do anything there . . . [but] God acts everywhere, and therefore is everywhere."[72]

---

65. Clayton, "The Panentheistic Turn in Theology," 289.

66. Ibid.

67. Clayton, *In Whom We Live and Move and Have Our Being*, 84–85.

68. See Cooper, *Panentheism*.

69. Inbody notes this, but he does not elaborate upon it. See Inbody, "Reconceptions of Divine Power," 176.

70. Wesley, Sermon 111, "On the Omnipresence of God," 42.

71. Ibid., 44.

72. Ibid.

The metaphor that God is the body of the world, a common claim in modern depictions of panentheism, also finds consonance with Wesley, who writes "Perhaps what the ancient philosopher speaks of the soul, in regard to its residence in the body, that it is *tota in toto, et, tota in qualibet parte*, might, in some sense, be spoken of the omnipresent Spirit, in regard to the universe: That he is not only "All in the whole," but "All in every part."[73] Similarly, Wesley elsewhere notes that, "God is in all things, and . . . we are to see the Creator in the glass of every creature; that we should use and look upon nothing as separate from God . . . who by his intimate presence holds them all in being, who pervades and actuates the whole created frame, and is in a true sense the soul of the universe."[74] One does not have to buy into Wesley's antiquated language of "soul" in order to glean from his comments that God is panentheistically—in modern terms—related to the universe.

We would like to complement the insights of Wesley noted above with those found in Sigurd Bergmann's book, *Creation Set Free: The Spirit as Liberator of Nature*, wherein grounds are given to assert that it is the Spirit who is the source of life, who is in all things, and that all things are therefore in God, insomuch as "God's Spirit is the principle of evolution."[75] One of the most valuable insights found within Bergmann's book is that the Spirit vivifies (foundationally), permeates (ontologically), indwells (incarnationally), and consummates (liberationally) creation.[76] Life, then, is a manifestation of the all-encompassing Spirit, who, in a characteristically Wesleyan-relational manner (though not noted as such by Bergmann), comes alongside the creation and relationally and uncontrollingly influences it toward greater complexity.[77]

The appeal of panentheism is that the energies at work at the physical level are already divine energies, and physical regularities are already expressions of the fundamental constancy of the divine character. Thus, panentheism claims that if the world remains within and is permeated by the divine, then it is possible to speak of divine purposes and goals being expressed, even at the stage when there are no conscious agents. The

---

73. Wesley, Sermon 67, "On Divine Providence," 538.

74. Wesley, Sermon 23, "Upon our Lord's Sermon on the Mount," 516–17.

75. Bergmann, *Creation Set Free*, 223.

76. Ibid., 170.

77. As Tyrone Inbody notes, relationships are constitutive of all reality, even divine reality (Inbody, "Reconceptions of Divine Power," 182).

lawful behavior of the natural world is an expression of divine intentionality.[78] In the concluding paragraphs of this essay, Clayton turns in a more speculative direction and attempts a constructive theological account of the evolutionary process of emergence. Scientifically, panentheism arises out of emergence theory; theologically, it arises out of the dialectic between the transcendence and immanence of God. A relationship of difference-in-sameness characterizes God's relation to the world, which is neither construed as external to God nor as identical with God.[79] Jürgen Moltmann makes a rather compelling case that a loving God could only be related to a free world of enduring significance if God contains that world and its inhabitants are within Godself rather than standing outside of it and them. His central theme, then, is panentheism.[80]

Ted Peters and Martinez Hewlett respond directly to the challenge of natural selection, arguing that although we do not directly see God's oversight in nature, we can know it by revelation to be there; God is hidden and revealed, present at the heart of nature but always transcendent, working through natural mechanisms.[81] There is, thus, no point in looking for the interface of the divine and the natural.[82] As interrelatedness epitomizes the life of the Godhead, so also does unlimited interrelatedness characterize the relation of God and creation. God can be "other" and simultaneously participate in the creation in a way analogous to the distinction and co-inherence of the persons in the Trinity. Moltmann understands creation as consisting of community and intimacy with the Creator at increasing levels of complexity.[83] In a collection of essays edited by Philip Clayton and Arthur Peacocke entitled *In Whom We Live and Move and Have Our Being: Panentheistic Reflections on God's Presence in a Scientific World*, Peacocke argues that the turn to panentheism offers great promise as a doctrinal resource for contemporary theology and its understanding of God's relation to the world.[84]

---

78. Clayton "Emergence of Spirit and Four Responses," 17.
79. Ibid., 18; cf. Cooper, *Panentheism*.
80. Moltmann, *Science and Wisdom*.
81. Peters and Hewlett, *Evolution from Creation to New Creation*, 167.
82. Creegan, "A Christian Theology of Evolution," 504.
83. Moltmann, *The Trinity and the Kingdom of God*, 19.
84. Peacocke, "Introduction," xix.

More pointedly, Peacocke notes that the Spirit makes things able to make themselves, which affirms a panentheistic perspective.[85] The immanent creator Spirit is continuously creating and continuously breathing life into the creation. Interestingly, Terence E. Fretheim writes, "God's creating in Genesis 1 . . . includes ordering that which already exists . . . God works creatively with already existing reality to bring about newness."[86] In agreement, Manual G. Doncel asserts that theologians today are correct to contemplate this long process as God's continued creation, mediated by the interplay of laws and chance.[87] The Spirit is present "in, with, and under" the processes of biological evolution within the created world.[88] The notion of emergence, it should be noted, is compatible with the working of the Spirit in empowering creation from within.

Like Clayton, Steven Crain adopts a panentheistic perspective, one in which God is in but not totally constituted by all things natural, but in a way that Crain argues is consistent with classical philosophical theism and Christian discourse about divine transcendence. Crain avers that the standard panentheistic metaphor that the world is the body of God should be complemented by the metaphor that God is the body of the world. This panentheistic grammar implies that God is radically immanent within the world in virtue of continuously giving it the gift of being. Crain contends that, "both the divine presence in the world and divine action in the world are nonintrusive, noninvasive, and noninterventive."[89] Contemporary theology should strive to understand how "God empowers the world from within, especially in bringing human free agents among God's creations" and how God is "continuously sustaining and energizing [the world's] story . . . from within."[90]

In consistently arguing for a panentheistic relationship of God and the world, Hans Küng forms the basis of his conclusions regarding evolutionary progress. According to such a view, God works in and through the regular structures of the world, being present to the world dialectically in that he is transcendent in his immanence, all the while immanent in his transcendence. Accordingly, God makes possible, permeates, and perfects

---

85. Peacocke, "The Cost of New Life," 21.
86. Fretheim, *God and World in the Old Testament*, 5.
87. Doncel, "The Kenosis of the Creator," 798.
88. Peacocke, "The Cost of New Life," 32.
89. Crain, "God Embodied In," 670.
90. Ibid., 672; cf. Clayton, "Emergence from Physics to Theology," 685.

creation, as he is in, with, and among its causal operations (being the origin, center, and goal of the process). Concerning the personhood of God, Küng asserts that God is personal, but more than a person, affirming the Augustinian conception of God as being more inward than the innermost part of our body, yet also affirming simultaneously Bultmann's conception of God as "wholly other."[91]

At the close of the ninth chapter in *Breath of Life: A Theology of the Creator Spirit*, Denis Edwards avers that a proper view of panentheism is fully Trinitarian: it does not place all of the creating activity on one member of the Godhead, nor does it contend that the creation is currently related to the Godhead by only one member of it. Further, a proper view of panentheism understands God as "wholly other" than creation, but also radically interior to everything therein due to the interpenetrating Spirit that permeates it. This view understands the universe as evolving within the life of God, with the creating Spirit enabling evolving entities to have their own autonomy and integrity. As a result, creation is a two-way relationship between God and created things; both can affect and be affected by the other.[92]

Whereas instances of emergence are well attested in the literature, and theories of emergence also abound, the uniting principle amongst these concepts is lacking. In all these cases, what is lacking appears to be the metaphysical basis of emergence theory, which is a lacuna that a kenosis-based perspective could perhaps adequately fill. Indeed, perhaps the development of a kenotic-relational metaphysical basis for emergence in the natural world will succeed in linking panentheism, emergent possibilities, and God. Here we are building on Clayton, who notes that, "emergence propels one to metaphysics, and metaphysical reflection in turn suggests a theological postulate above and beyond the logic of emergence."[93] James W. Haag, for example, notes that many scholars use the term emergence to explain *what* it is and *why* the term is employed, but too few scholars note *how* it works.[94] We suggest that one such avenue that could be further fleshed-out is the notion of *kenosis* being depicted as a "pouring into" versus merely a "self-emptying," both of which have biblical foundation. In this projection, creation would be seen as the result of the kenotic "pouring" of

---

91. Küng, "The Beginning of All Things," 109.
92. Edwards, "Breath of Life," 136.
93. Clayton, *In Whom We Live and Move and Have Our Being*, 91.
94. Haag, *Emergent Freedom*, 37.

the Spirit *into* the primal, chaotic matter that was present in the beginning (Gen 1:2). By being poured into the primal creation, God the Spirit would be present to it in its evolutionary path toward increasing complexity, relationally guiding, luring, and wooing it to his goal of communion with an "other."

Preliminary Conclusions

So what does all of this mean? We contend that a picture of the world as being contained within God, construed as such by modern theology and philosophy, offers a pneumatological model by which God can interact with the world through non-interventive ways. While we applaud Yong's overarching theological project, we think it could be enhanced by moving in a kenotic-panentheistic direction. Particularly, because a kenotic approach avoids supernaturalism—a primary critique made by Leidenhag and Leidenhag of Yong—it clarifies the modality of the Spirit's operation within the physical world. Moreover, many of those who dialogue with theology and science understand the perfecting of God's creation in relational and processive terms insomuch as the Spirit lures created things through a myriad of possibilities open to them. Seen in this light, God presents a vast array of possibilities to created things, which offers a multitude of different ways by which their complexity may be increased. This conceptioning of *kenosis* would provide also a basis for the relationality of God to the world, the result of which is the advancement of the evolutionary paradigm, of which humans are (presently) the pinnacle. This view enhances Yong's pneumatological proposal and is consistent with a viable form of weak emergence.

3

Kenosis and Emergence

A *Wesleyan-Relational Perspective*[1]

MY FIRST INTERACTION WITH Larry Wood at Asbury Theological Seminary was during the summer semester of 2004, in a course entitled "Method and Praxis in Theology." Dr. Wood's course sought to critically analyze contemporary theological methods and identify the influence of postmodern science upon contemporary doctrine. I remember Dr. Wood telling us that Wesley once said to a preacher that the study of logic was the single most important thing to study next to the Bible if they were going to understand the Bible properly and thereafter preach it effectively. The foundation that Dr. Wood gave me through that course in connecting theological method with Christian doctrine, especially the doctrine of divine revelation, has served me well in the subsequent years of my studies. This chapter is an attempt to demonstrate that methodology concerning emergence in recent philosophical reflections. It is my hope that it will serve as appropriate example of a Wesleyan-influenced theology of creation in the postmodern world. Note that I herein intend to contribute, at least minimally, to the development of a systematic theology of creation. I agree wholeheartedly with Joel B. Green who notes that a proposed synthesis of theology and the bible should proceed by clearly identifying where and how to locate the disciplinary interface, where and how to locate the structures of accountability

---

1. A previous version of this essay appeared in *The Future of Wesleyan Theology: Essays in Honor of Laurence Wood*, 155–70.

to ensure respect given to both fields, and where and how to locate the means for validating constructive work.[2]

This chapter reviews select literature regarding emergence theory, in particular its relation to theology, highlighting its basis in panentheism, and noting an implication that is emergent (pun intended) from the literature: the resultant possibilities for God. This implication creates space for a Wesleyan-relational perspective on the process of emergence, a perspective that is not only warranted, but also fruitful for further research. Several books and articles from leading voices in the field will be reviewed in an attempt to survey this ongoing debate. While understanding that this is not an exhaustive review, the reader nevertheless will have better comprehension of the current state of discussion concerning emergence theory in religion and science, especially regarding its consonance with Wesleyan-relational theology.[3]

In *Creation and Reality*, Michael Welker offers "initial steps toward correcting both the classic theistic caricature of God the Creator and a corresponding religious understanding of reality."[4] New approaches to creation are a "burning theological interest," for modern religious depictions are "boring, vapid, and banal."[5] Even when and where the bible is granted authority in faith and practice, patrons seem to no longer read it attentively and imaginatively.[6] In this chapter, then, I seek to offer a new approach to creation, building upon the notions of emergence and kenosis. I argue that the existence and viability of emergence theory depends upon the primal kenotic act of God the Spirit *pouring* himself *into* creation.

---

2. Green, "Scripture and Theology," 42.

3. The distinctive Wesleyan doctrine of prevenient grace offers a similar concept of love as entailing divine call and creaturely response. Prevenient grace might very well be best described as the omnipresent, omni-relational God acting in each moment to empower creatures to respond freely and then luring them to choose responses that increase overall complexity. See Maddox, *Responsible Grace*; and Wynkoop, *A Theology of Love*. For a Wesleyan reading of divine omnipresence, see Lodahl, *God of Nature and of Grace*, chapters 4 and 6.

4. Welker, *Creation and Reality*, 2.

5. Ibid., 4. Part of the reason why theology today is often boring, vapid, and banal is that it has "misconstrued the role of texts and the role of interpreters" (Green, "Scripture and Theology," 30).

6. Davis and Hays, *The Art of Reading Scripture*, xv.

PART TWO: *KENOSIS* & EMERGENCE

Wesleyan Theology and Emergence Theory

Wesleyan theology conceptualizes God's sovereignty and power in a manner that allows for the creativity of that which is created to be exercised within limits.[7] Moreover, Wesleyan theology in general is keen to highlight the relational nature of God's uncontrolling love,[8] a love that insists on embracing and working with creatures,[9] versus over and against them, which connotes a process marked by not only time, but also perhaps by diversions (the term "diversions" being preferable to "errors," note).[10] "Diversions" instead of "errors" also makes this process consonant with God's uncontrolling love. John B. Cobb stipulates that the Godhead constantly readjusts his aims in response to the partial successes and partial failures of the past so that some possibility of achievement lies ahead for creatures and created things. Elsewhere, Cobb notes that if the creatures or created things responded fully to God's lure in the past, that entity would be given wider possibilities in the present, but if it has resisted the lure, then less is possible in the present.[11] As the subtitle of his book indicates, "*A Relational Theology of Creation*," Fretheim argues for a "relational model of creation," one that avoids pitting divine sovereignty against human freedom, or espousing a static view of creation in which everything was created perfectly within the first seven days. Fretheim states that, "both God and creatures have an important role in the creative enterprise, and their spheres of activity are interrelated in terms of function and effect."[12] Divine sovereignty under such a model is one that, "gives power over to the created for the sake of a relationship of integrity."[13] As relational, God is affected by those with whom God relates. Mildred Bangs Wynkoop deserves the credit for highlighting the relational character of Wesley's theology in *A Theology of Love*.[14] In their book, *Relational Holiness*, Thomas Jay Oord and Michael Lodahl argue that the core distinctive of Wesleyan theology is relational love. The tehomic theology that Catherine Keller proposes is relational at

---

7. See Wesley, "Thoughts upon God's Sovereignty," 10:362–63.
8. See, e.g. Callen, *God as Loving Grace*; cf. Pinnock, et al., *The Openness of God*.
9. Lodahl, *God of Nature and of Grace*, 27.
10. See Cobb, *A Christian Natural Theology*, 251.
11. Cobb, "Human Responsibility," 106.
12. Fretheim, *God and World in the Old Testament*, 27.
13. Ibid., 272.
14. Wynkoop, *A Theology of Love*.

its core, as its relational God "remains enmeshed in the vulnerabilities and potentialities of an indeterminate creativity."[15]

Wesleyan-Relational theologians reject the idea that God is a distant monarch uninfluenced by creation. Because God *is love*, he uncontrollingly takes risks with his creation,[16] working with it over a long period of time through the processes of Darwinian evolution, rather than creating by divine fiat.[17] In fact, Wesleyan theologian Oord asserts that, "[uncontrolling] Love requires relations with others. Love cannot be expressed in absolute isolation; love is inherently relational. Loving actions require sympathetic responses to others with whom the lover possesses relations. And love involves the promotion of well-being to those with whom the lover relates."[18] He goes on, "Giving gifts to others—including the power for self-determination—is by definition part of what it means to be a loving and relational God. And a gift-giver whose essence is love cannot do other than give gifts of love."[19] This power for self-determination is principally due to the uncontrolling nature of God's love, a love that is not capable of controlling other entities. Rather, there is autonomy which God respects, even furthers. That might sound a little odd, but it is his nature to be others'-empowering. One may accurately assert that the defining theme in relational theology is that God fundamentally exists in relationship, which means that both God and creatures are affected by others in give-and-take relationships, and all that God does is for the purpose of relationship.[20]

15. Keller, *The Face of the Deep*, 226.

16. As Wesley notes, "It is not written, 'God is justice', or 'God is truth' (although he is just and true in all his ways). But it is written, 'God is love', love in the abstract, without bounds; and there is no end of his goodness." (Wesley, "Predestination Calmly Considered," 10.227).

17. cf. Lodahl, *God of Nature and of Grace*, 64–67. God accepts these risks, says Murphy and Ellis, "in order to achieve a higher goal: the free and intelligent cooperation of the creature in divine activity" (Murphy and Ellis, *On the Moral Nature of the Universe*, 246). The process of evolution, Murphy and Ellis go on to say, reflects God's "noncoercive, persuasive, painstaking love all the way from the beginning to the end, from the least of God's creatures to the most splendid" (Ibid.).

18. Oord, "Essential Kenosis," 8.

19. Ibid., 11–12.

20. Inbody notes that Wesley's understanding of God's power construes it as dynamic, relational, and persuasive (Inbody, "Reconceptions of Divine Power," 169–92). In the same volume, Lodahl argues that Wesley reconceived God's power as relational and over-abundant in its self-giving (Lodahl, "Creation Out of Nothing?," 222). For further reading on Wesleyan-relational theology and how relationality informs Wesley's theology, see Cobb Jr., *Grace and Responsibility*; Sanders, *The God Who Risks*; and the work of

Moreover, if God is uncontrolling love that is poured out for others (1 Jn 4:8), then according to Trinitarian doctrine, God has never been anything else. In other words, if the operations of God as attested to by the testimony of the scriptures lead us to confess that God is love and thus loves the *other*, then it makes theological sense that God is eternally communicating with, and communing with, a world of some sort. Thus, uncontrolling love theology views the reality of the universe and God as thoroughly interdependent. Schubert M. Ogden asserts that, "it is not meaningful to talk [about God's love] at all unless the structure of God in itself involves real, internal relatedness to others . . . to accept others as love is to be really, internally related to them."[21] However, this is not to imply that the world has always existed *necessarily*. Rather, as Michael Lodahl argues, if the world has in fact always existed, it is only because of God's overflowing love.[22] I am drawn to Lodahl's posit that Gen 1 does not make the explicit claim of *creatio ex nihilo*, but neither does it abrogate it.[23] He goes on,

> the Wesleyan tradition in the main shall always, I predict, embrace *creatio ex nihilo*, and is on good ground for doing so . . . [on the other hand] what we know, through experience of God's creative and recreative activity is that God works with the material that is available. This understanding of grace, wherein God gently and lovingly works *with* us, not *above* or *in spite of* us, assuredly bears some consonance with a Whiteheadian cosmology, wherein the same can be said for how God works with the world.[24]

In a Wesleyan-relational view, the uncontrolling kenosis of the Spirit would be the avenue by which God could be the ground of all being.

A Concise Review of Emergence

Philip Clayton's book, *Mind & Emergence*, explicitly covers the revolution brought about by the study of evolution that undercuts both *physicalism* and *dualism*. In it, Clayton argues that emergence is the philosophical

---

Barry L. Callen in his systematic theology titled *God As Loving Grace*. For general readings of relational theology, see Sponheim, *Faith and the Other*; and Jansen, *Relationality and the Concept of God*.

21. Ogden, "Process Theology and the Wesleyan Witness," 42–43.
22. Lodahl, "Creation Out of Nothing?," 238.
23. Lodahl, *God of Nature and of Grace*, 65.
24. Ibid., 102–3.

position that best accounts for the data derived from the study of evolution. Terrence W. Deacon notes that emergence is the "term that is most often used by scientists to describe the spontaneous appearance of unprecedented orderliness in nature."[25] He further notes that the term connotes an image of something coming out of hiding, something without precedent, and a bit surprising.[26] Emergentists argue that the reductionary tendencies within the natural sciences are not tenable. As I mentioned earlier, modern advances in the natural sciences reveal a vastly more complicated world than the reductionist program of the late nineteenth and twentieth centuries ever envisioned.[27] The pompous nature of the physics of former years has been humbled—epistemically and practically—by a series of revelations within nature that place inherent limitations upon what physics can explain, predict, or know. For example, *Heisenberg's Uncertainty Principle* delimits our ability to predict with accuracy the exact location and momentum of subatomic particles, and makes one realize that there exists an inherent indeterminacy within the physical world itself. Moreover, *Chaos Theory* has shown that the future states of complex systems are unpredictable, due to finite knowledge of initial conditions.

In the book entitled *The Re-Emergence of Emergence: The Emergentist Hypothesis From Science to Religion*, Clayton and Paul C. Davies edit contributions from various authors, seeking to introduce readers to emergence theory, outline arguments in its defense, and answer the most powerful objections against it. Emergence, Clayton herein notes, has grown out of the successes and failures of the scientific quest for reduction.[28] Whereas weak emergence is the starting point for most natural scientists, strong emergence has received much support in recent years, and several contributors to this text (including Ellis, Silberstein, Peacocke, Gregersen, and Clayton, e.g.) posit that it is a viable option in the natural sciences. Though coming to the text from disparate disciplines and commitments, the various essayists all agree that emergence theory is potent in its explanatory capacity.

For example, Terrence W. Deacon stipulates that the term "emergence" connotes the image of something coming out of hiding, coming into view for the first time, something that is without precedent and perhaps a bit

---

25. Deacon, "Emergence: The Hole at the Wheel's Hub," 121.
26. Ibid.
27. Clayton, *Mind & Emergence*, 94.
28. Clayton, "Conceptual Foundations of Emergence Theory," 1.

surprising.[29] Arthur Peacocke argues that there are good grounds for reintroducing the concept of emergence in naturally occurring, hierarchical, and complex systems that make up the basic parts of the physical world.[30] Niels Henrik Gregersen stresses that the presence of God must be part of any ultimate explanation of why the course of evolution is moving upwards in the direction of increased complexity, rather than aimlessly bouncing to and fro, generating nothing but evolutionary "noise."[31] Gregersen notes that terming events as emergent processes, means, almost by definition, an "emerging from," or a "growing out of," something that is already established,[32] which upon first viewing, may appear to be in contradistinction to Deacon's above cited statements regarding emergence, that it is "unprecedented." However, emergence is "unprecedented" only in its outcome, not in the means by which it gets there, so the two statements are fully consistent. Gregersen also contends that the world may be explained as a fertile abode created by God for the purpose of self-organization and emergence.[33] This picture of the earth as a fertile abode will become more central in my later highlighting of the possibilities for God present in creation and explored through emergence theory.

Gregory Peterson argues that there are three broad interpretations of emergence: reductive, nonreductive, and radical. Apparently, and in application, though not explicitly stated as such, these three ranges of interpretation are equivalent to those that are more broadly classified as "strong" and "weak" by Clayton. Radical emergentists emphasize both epistemological and ontological openness. Accordingly, Clayton, for example, is a radical emergentist. John F. Haught would be another example of a radical emergentist, even though he does not use the emergent terminology per se. Peterson's goal in this essay is twofold: first, to categorize the primary senses of emergence as they occur in relevant fields of philosophy, theology, and

---

29. Deacon, "Emergence: The Hole at the Wheel's Hub," 121. Interestingly, Jaegwon Kim, being forthright, acknowledges that there are two challenges to emergence: how to show that emergence is not reducible to epiphenomenalism, and to give examples of emergence that go beyond supervenience and irreducibility (Kim, "Being Realistic about Emergence," 201).

30. Peacocke, "Emergence, Mind, and Divine Action," 257–78.

31. Gregersen, "Emergence: What is at Stake for Religious Reflection?," 300.

32. Gregersen, "Emergence in Theological Perspective," 310.

33. Ibid., 315–16.

science; and second, to suggest how these different senses may be useful for the theology and science dialogue.[34]

Peterson suggests that seven elements of the emergentist position need to be explored and enunciated carefully in order for emergentist positions to be coherent. For example, one requirement of an emergent entity is that it be capable of some kind of higher-order description. Second, it is typically claimed that these emergent wholes obey various sorts of higher-order laws. Claims of higher-order description and higher-order laws lead to a third claim for emergent entities, that of unpredictable novelty. Peterson notes, fourth, that emergent positions imply that lower-level parts are necessary for the existence of the whole. Fifth, lower-level entities are insufficient for emergent entities. Sixth, some emergent entities are capable of top-down causation; that is, they are causally efficacious. And finally, emergent entities are characterized by "multiple realizability."[35]

After reviewing and critiquing twentieth century views of emergence, Clayton offers his own view regarding emergence theory in chapter two of *Mind & Emergence*, and in so doing, radicalizes the immanence of God. Clayton defines emergence as "the theory that cosmic evolution repeatedly includes unpredictable, irreducible, and novel appearances."[36] He notes that emergence is "that which is produced by a combination of causes, but cannot be regarded as the sum of their individual effects."[37] Moreover, "emergence is the theory that cosmic evolution repeatedly includes unpredictable, irreducible, and novel appearances."[38]

In chapter three, Clayton notes that particularly within biology, one can see multiple instances of where that which emerges becomes a causal agent in its own right. He states that the biggest question facing scientists today is "how nature obtains order 'out of nothing,' that is, how order is produced in the course of a system's evolution when it is not present in the initial conditions."[39] Emergence in evolution therefore "consists of a collection

---

34. Peterson, "Species of Emergence," 689.

35. Ibid., 693–95. It is important to note here that all seven of Peterson's elements of the emergentists' position are fundamentally relational in character, meaning that without the relation to other parts, they would not exist.

36. Clayton, *Mind & Emergence*, 39.

37. Ibid., 38.

38. Ibid., 39.

39. Ibid., 73.

of highly convoluted processes that produce a remarkably complex kind of combinatorial novelty."[40]

Clayton implies that the resurgence of emergence in the twentieth century has done much to deflate the bottom-up "new synthesis" that resulted from Watson and Crick's discovery of the DNA molecule in 1956 being linked to Neo-Darwinian evolutionary thought.[41] The "new synthesis" is *in process* of being replaced by an "interactionist consensus" in which neither genes nor environmentments, neither nature nor nurture, suffice wholly for the production of phenotypes.[42] Within this interactionist paradigm, "fully adequate explanations of biological phenomena require the constant interplay of both bottom-up and top-down accounts."[43] Genotypes produce phenotypes that interact with specific environmentments, which then reproduce genotypes (*ad infinitum*). Clayton agrees, and states that there "is increasing evidence that emergence represents a fruitful . . . meta-scientific . . . framework for comparing the relations between the diverse realms of the natural world."[44]

A Wesleyan Perspective on Emergence

So, having covered Clayton cursorily in the last section, what does he contribute to our understanding of emergence, particularly from an uncontrolling Wesleyan perspective? I'd like to suggest at least four things: emergence is in direct opposition to reductionism; after all, if reductionism is possible, then emergentism turns into to either mechanism or vitalism. Moreover, Clayton takes very seriously both evolutionary continuity and the increase in complexity of organization. Further, Clayton's strong emergentism focuses more-so upon the whole than upon the parts, yet is inherently monistic. And finally, according to Clayton, emergence theory represents an explanatory ladder of nature that eventually leads outside the natural sciences, to which we now turn.

---

40. Ibid., 85. cf. Deacon, "The Hierarchic Logic of Emergence," 273–308.

41. Note this implication is inferred by his placement of the section describing the "new synthesis" in biology into this chapter. Said "new synthesis" posits that the behavior of organisms—and even *ecosystems*—can be explained solely by referencing the gene reproduction and mutation that underlies them.

42. cf. Robert, *Embryology, Epigenesis and Evolution*, 2.

43. Clayton, *Mind & Emergence*, 95.

44. Ibid., 93.

Implication: Possibilities for God

In his book, *The God of Nature*, Christopher C. Knight offers support for a way of thinking about divine engagement with the world known as emergence. Higher levels of complexity naturally unfold, in this model, as a result of the interplay of chance and natural law upon the possibilities and potentials that God bestowed into creation at its beginning and through his continued panentheistic presence in the world.[45] In agreement, Peacocke asserts that the activity of God's Spirit within creation proceeds by no assured program, but is precarious instead.[46] Similarly, Polkinghorne states that the Spirit is the carrier of divine wisdom, even in chaos.[47] As such, the potential for novelty and relative stability lies between the two poles of order and disorder within chaotic systems.[48] The breath of life enables and empowers emergence of the creation and creatures, insomuch as this Spirit of emergence endows creation with the ability to unfold by "natural" processes according to their inherent possibilities and potentialities.[49]

Creation from a pneumatological standpoint, as Dabney affirms, begins with the Spirit, which in turn means that the world is not defined by necessity, but by possibility instead, for the Spirit is the possibility of God.[50] Welker agrees, and notes that the Spirit works modestly, in a continuous fashion in and through natural processes, as well as in novel occurrences.[51] James E. Huchingson also concurs, and notes that primordial chaos was essential to God's creation because it was the source of innumerable possibilities, potentialities, and novelties, without which the immense variety of

---

45. Knight, *The God of Nature*, 35.

46. Peacocke, "The Cost of New Life," 21. Peacocke's reference here to "spirit" is somewhat compatible to Loder and Neidhard, who define spirit to mean "a quality of relationality, and [a] way to conceptualize the dynamic interactive unity by which two disparate things are held together without loss of their diversity" (Loder and Neidhard, *The Knight's Move*, 10).

47. Interestingly, "The author of Genesis," says Catherine Keller, "assumed that the universe was created from a primal chaos: something uncreated, something Other, something that a creator could mold, form, or call to order" (Keller, *The Face of the Deep*, xvii).

48. Polkinghorne, "The Hidden Spirit and the Cosmos," 174. See also, Lodahl, "Creation Out of Nothing?," 233.

49. Welker, "Introduction," *The Work of the Spirit*, xii.

50. Dabney, "The Nature of the Spirit," 78.

51. Welker, "Spirit in Philosophical, Theological, and Interdisciplinary Perspectives," 227.

nature would not be possible.[52] What he here applies to chaos is merely the means through which the uncontrolling kenotic Spirit derives complexity.

Colin Gunton asserts that just as God the Father "took his time" in dealing with the erring world in Christ, so too did he "take his time" in bestowing creative and causal powers unto the Spirit in creation; thus the created world is a project, of sorts, of the Spirit in that the creation takes time to become what it was intended to be, which is consonant with Oord's viewpoint earlier highlighted..[53] In this view, creation ventures forward by enacting various possibilities that are available to it, the success of which is measured only in the propagation of itself (i.e., in retrospect). In a sense, God is not the "creator" per se, but creativity instead, which is consonant with Gordon Kaufman's view. Indeed, Kaufman advocates that thinking of God as "serendipitous creativity" instead of "the creator" is congenial to conceptions of the term "emergence," as outlined by such thinkers as Morowitz and Clayton.[54] He admits to the profound mystery of conceiving "God" in this manner, but intimates that thinking of God as creativity and not as the "creator" implies that God can—and has!—produce novel things from unknown causes in the evolutionary epic.

According to Kaufman, thinking of God as creativity also enables us to bring theological meanings into significant connection with modern evolutionary thought. For him, the word creativity refers simply to the coming into being of something novel and important. He suggests that instead of taking it for granted that, "God" is the name of a creator who has brought everything into being, it is illuminating to think of God as the religious name for the profound mystery of creativity—that is, the mystery of the emergence, in and through evolutionary processes, of novelty in the world. After rethinking creativity as God, we would be "able to connect the enormously meaningful ancient symbol God with central features of our modern thinking about the origins of the cosmos, the evolution of life and other features of the cosmos, and the emergence and development of human life and culture on planet Earth."[55]

52. Huchingson, "Engaging James E. Huchingson's *Pandemonium Tremendum*," 396–397.

53. Gunton, *The Triune Creator*, 93.

54. Kaufman, *In the Beginning . . . Creativity*, 36.

55. Kaufman, "A Religious Interpretation of Emergence," 918. Note that I am sympathetic with Kaufman's intent, i.e., the equation of God with a concept like creativity. Others also are sympathetic with Whitehead's view of creativity, but stop short of equating creativity with God (see, e.g., Neville, *Creativity and God*).

Arthur Peacocke states that the randomness and lawfulness that are built into creation are what one would expect if the evolving universe is to be able to explore options and to experiment with the fullest range of possibilities.[56] Denis Edwards concurs, and asserts that the Spirit of God is intimately interior to each creature, leading the world into the future of God, to which it is always open, exploring innumerable possibilities through seemingly random processes.[57] Also, in speaking of evolutionary novelty, Edwards is in agreement with Clayton's conceptioning of emergence in stating that, "while the new is completely dependent on its preexisting parts, it is not reducible to its components."[58] Edwards perhaps gives us the method in which the Spirit opens up these possibilities for the "new" in an emergent universe by noting that the Spirit is the communion-bringer in the world (i.e., as the interior presence of God that empowers being and becoming)[59] in ways appropriate to each. Similarly, Harold J. Morowitz argues that the Spirit powers—even empowers— emergence by noting that the Spirit is the selection rules between God's immanence and the development of the earth.[60] Note that Morowitz's contention that the Spirit empowers emergence is consonant with Wesley's claim that God's power is fundamentally an uncontrolling empowerment of the other versus being a controlling factor.[61] As a result of the communion in the universe wrought by the Spirit, the godhead is present to each creature, embracing each in uncontrolling love.[62]

Edwards focuses upon the Spirit's distinct role in creation as being that of "the immanent Life-Giver that enables all creatures to be and to become,"[63] which is similar to how Pannenberg writes that the Spirit "is the principle of the creative presence of the transcendent God,"[64] and who also notes that, "the Spirit of God is the life-giving principle, to which all

---

56. Peacocke, *Theology for a Scientific Age*, 118.
57. Edwards, *Breath of Life*, 44.
58. Ibid., 44–45.
59. cf. Taylor, *The Go-Between God*.
60. Morowitz, *The Emergence of Everything*, 197–98.
61. Wesley, Sermon 66, "The Signs of the Times," 4:43.
62. Edwards, *Breath of Life*, 47–49. See also Lodahl, "Creation Out Of Nothing?," 233.
63. Ibid., 117.
64. Pannenberg, *Systematic Theology*, 2:32.

creatures owe life, movement, and activity."[65] In stating that the Spirit is the immanent life-giver within creation, Edwards also agrees with Moltmann, who writes that the Spirit is the "unspeakable closeness of God."[66]

Former Conceptions of the *Kenosis* and Science Connection

Peterson notes that, "[n]onreductive physicalists, as well as other emergentists, sometimes identify emergent entities with information."[67] Bonting attempts to bring the various activities ascribed to the Spirit (Hebrew *ruach*, Greek *pneuma*) under one heading, which he identifies as the *communicator* of information.[68] The Spirit as God's *energeia*, through which God the Father calls all aspects of creation into being, fits very well with modern cosmological theory.[69] In reference to the Big Bang, the Spirit brings in the information needed to transform the explosion into an orderly process of cosmic evolution.[70] The Spirit is the "executive arm" (i.e., the enacting or effectual arm) of the Trinity in that he was active as the Son spoke each word in the primal creating moments recorded in Gen 1.[71]

Thus, the light that first illuminated the earth was caused by the impartation of information and order by the inspiriting of the Spirit of God. When God inspires formless and chaotic matter with his uncontrolling love, nothing becomes something, and the disorderly becomes orderly. Since the level of order required for the origination of complex life was extremely high,[72] it is especially important to acknowledge that the Old Testament begins by presenting the function of the Spirit as being the giver and communicator of orderly information, and consequently, of complex biological life.

I contend that creation in Genesis is not a creation out of nothing, as a onetime event, but is instead a continuous creation. Indeed, on the third

---

65. Ibid., 2:76.
66. Moltmann, *The Spirit of Life*, 12.
67. Peterson, "Species of Emergence," 702.
68. Bonting, "Spirit and Creation," 713.
69. Ibid., 721.
70. Ibid., 723.
71. After the introduction of energy (or pure information) by the Spirit into the formless, chaotic matter, there was light (Gen 1:3).
72. As per Stuart Kaufman, cited in Popa, *Between Necessity and Probability*, 73.

day[73] of the Genesis account, in the midst of God's creativity, God's creating interacts with that which was created in order to produce further acts of creation, insomuch as the process of *creatio continua* becomes one with the process of *creatio ex creation* (creation out of creation). We read on day three: then God said, "Let the *earth put forth* vegetation: plants yielding seed, and fruit trees of every kind on earth that bear fruit with the seed in it" (1:11). On day five of the Genesis account, God commands, "Let the *waters bring forth* swarms of living creatures" (1:20), and again, "Let the *earth bring forth* living creatures of every kind" (1:24). These statements are reflective of the uncontrolling nature of God's love.

According to Michael Welker, neither Gen 1 or 2 "describes God as a highest being who in pure self-sufficiency does nothing other than produce and cause creaturely being."[74] Moreover, he stipulates that in Gen 1 and 2 God's action corresponds to only a few ways in which we normally construe causation and production.[75] Seven times God is listed as evaluating.[76] Three times God is listed as naming.[77] Three times God is listed as acting upon what is already created in order to separate it and give it order.[78] The latter three instances of God's action give credence to the notion of God acting upon formless matter, and thereby giving it order, structure, and complexity. Thus, the creating God is not merely an actor within creation, but also a reactor to creation. Indeed, God's action is an uncontrolling action that reacts, and is an uncontrolling action that lets itself be determined. Gen 1 and 2 depict a creation that has its own activity, is itself productive, and is itself causative.

In the Genesis narrative, then, one is not able to derive a clear demarcation between God's creativity and the creature's activity. On the one hand, God's activity is clearly active in production and causation. On the other hand, God is equally reactive to that which is created. From this data, an abstract, minimal definition of creation as related within the Genesis narrative follows: "creation is the construction and maintenance of associations

---

73. There is neither time nor space to speculate upon what the term "day" might mean or connote.

74. Welker, *Creation and Reality*, 9.

75. Ibid.

76. Gen 1:4, 1:10, 1:12, 1:18, 1:21, 1:25, and 1:31.

77. Gen 1:5, 1:8, 1:10.

78. Gen 1:11, 1:20, 1:24.

of different, interdependent creaturely realms."[79] The study of creation must, therefore, focus upon the interdependencies of natural and providential processes, because creation as a whole—both the reality and nature of it—continually flow into each other.

Not only did God the Spirit create the world at one point in the past, but he now continually upholds it.[80] Indeed, Paul the Apostle expresses God the Son's creative work as that by which "all things were created" (Col 1:16), which is an act of definitive causation (a "coming to be"). The speaking forth of the word of God, which Paul here has in mind, however, necessarily presupposes the *breath* of God (i.e., *pneuma/ruach*—God the Spirit). Moreover, the very next verse explains that, "in Him all things hold together" (Col 1:17), which connotes the continual creative act of the Spirit.[81] It is important, therefore, to view the Spirit not only as originator of creation, but also as the sustainer of creation, upholding its order, and giving it life through uncontrolling love.[82] As Polkinghorne writes, "Part of a notion of *creatio continua* must surely be that an evolving universe is one which is theologically understood as being allowed, within divine providence, 'to make itself.'"[83]

Rather than bringing into being a ready-made world of unalterable character, the Godhead empowers the creation, kenotically and uncontrollingly by the Spirit, to develop according to its own pace. So, then, the Spirit makes things able to make themselves. Theologians today are correct, then, to perceive this long process of evolutionary emergence as God's continued creation, mediated by the interplay of laws and chance.[84] Note that as a consequence of positing *creatio continua*, one must insist that the Spirit of God's providential power is manifest in the unfolding of creation in evolutionary history.[85] No picture of creation is complete that neglects either the definitive or the continually creative uncontrolling work of the Spirit. Thus, the reality of creation deals with both origins and continual operation.

---

79. Welker, *Creation and Reality*, 13.

80. This statement is adapted from Newton, as cited in Southgate, *God, Humanity, and the Cosmos*, 281. For further support, see Goergen, *Fire of Love*, 114.

81. For support of this notion, see: Ward, *God, Chance, and Necessity*, 78.

82. Bonting, "Spirit and Creation," 724.

83. Polkinghorne, *Serious Talk*, 84.

84. Doncel, "The Kenosis of the Creator," 798.

85. Polkinghorne, "Kenotic Creation and Divine Action," 96. In affirmation of this understanding of the ongoing evolution of the creation as being God's manner of creation from the viewpoint of a theologian, see Goergen, *Fire of Love*, 89–105.

The repeated emphasis within Ps 104 is the notion that God preserves of the world, which presupposes that God creates through the power of the Spirit, as well as that the presence of the Spirit is the condition for both potentialities and realities of creation.[86] So then, the psalmist knows nothing of outright spontaneous generation, for God sends forth his Spirit, and all things are created. The Spirit is repeatedly depicted in Ps 104 as the presence of God, as well as the means by which God acts within his creation.[87]

Further, Christ poured himself into humanity so that it could be reconciled to the Father and that it might become acceptable to the Father (Phil 2:5-11). God the Son enters into the limited, finite situation of humankind, descending into it, thereby embracing the whole of human existence in his being. It needs to be noted that the kenosis of the Son referred to in Phil 2:5-11 cannot be understood as a subtraction of deity, but the addition of humanity instead. I would like to make the argument that the biblical connotations of the term kenosis, just elaborated upon, have potent application to theological constructs regarding God's uncontrolling action within the world. In fact, the science and religion dialogue has long wrestled with the topic of God's action in the world, and models for conceiving divine action heretofore have been unsatisfactory.[88] Classical interventionism should be dismissed as illogical because God's action in the world would be inconsistently intermittent if actualized as pure intervention; God acting only as the creator of the world is deistic, and thereby delimits divine action in perpetuity; Thomistic understandings of God as the primary cause and creatures as secondary causes results in unnecessary bifurcations.[89] The resurgence of kenotic theology has thus been helpful in reformulating divine action in an evolutionary world.

Connection between *Kenosis* of the Spirit into Creation and Emergence Theory

Several years ago, a collection of essays by theologians and scientists explored creation as *The Work of Love*, pointing to divine action as kenosis.[90]

86. Moltmann, *God in Creation*, 10.
87. Bonting, "Spirit and Creation," 715.
88. see Southgate, *God, Humanity, and the Cosmos*.
89. Amos Yong, "From Quantum Mechanics to the Eucharistic Meal." http://www.metanexus.net/Magazine/ArticleDetail/tabid/68/id/9285/Default.aspx.
90. Polkinghorne, *The Work of Love*.

In said book, John C. Polkinghorne adopts the understanding of kenosis that is an affirmation of God's voluntary self-limitation,[91] one that allows creatures to enjoy power and freedom. Classical theology, according to Polkinghorne, envisions God in total control and invulnerable such that there is no reciprocal effect of creatures upon the divine nature. According to Polkinghorne's view of kenosis, however, the kenotic Creator interacts with creatures; the word "interact" is preferable to "intervene," in this volume, apparently because intervene carries connotations of an interruption of natural processes. An uncontrolling perspective on God's contact with the world is also more amenable to "interact" rather than "intervene." For Polkinghorne, kenosis connotes the risk of the creating Spirit in submitting to the quasi-free process of evolutionary creation, which qualifies, in a kenotic way, the operation of the Spirit. Polkinghorne notes that the kenotic Spirit is the exemplar of humility, for he kenotically interacted with the created world, and as such, at least in some qualified sense, limits his eternality and omnipotence.[92] The volume conceives kenosis as God's entirely voluntarily self-limitation. A summarization of this volume's view on kenosis is that God allows the created other to be and to act, insomuch as while all that happens is permitted by God's general providence, not all happenings are in accordance with God's will. Such an understanding is basic to the interpretation of evolutionary history as creation making itself.

I find Polkinghorne's theory of kenosis as found within *The Work of Love* helpful, but incomplete. The kenotic theology posited by my book maintains that the Spirit completely shares and imparts himself *into* creation in an uncontrolling manner. The Spirit "poured himself out" into creation, thereby causing it to leap forth from chaos and become a structured and orderly system of life-bearing entities in due course. So then, the Spirit is the life-giving force that enables and ennobles creation to strive toward becoming its fullness via the process of evolution. The creation of ordered matter has its ontological origin in and through the agency of the Spirit of God. Creation is thus a fully kenotic act of self-offering.

According to Kathryn Tanner, the Spirit has historically been seen to either work immediately (proximately, i.e.) or gradually.[93] So then, the

---

91. Note that although I do not agree with the understanding of kenosis as self-limitation, I nonetheless find much value in the essays contained within Polkinghorne's *The Work of Love* volume.

92. Polkinghorne, "Kenotic Creation and Divine," 106.

93. Tanner, "Workings of the Spirit," 87. The gradual model of the working of the Spirit requires methods of inquiry typical of modern science, and holds great promise

Spirit could be seen just as much at work in the ordinary events of history as in its unusual happenings. Just as God usually works within, rather than overriding, the normal course of human affairs, so too does God work within the natural processes of nature, for "the same Spirit doth not breathe contrary notions."[94] The Spirit works modestly, in a continuous fashion, *in* and *through* natural processes.[95] The notion of emergence is compatible with the impersonal kenotic working of the Spirit in empowering creation from within in an almost hidden manner.[96] This hiddenness of the Spirit comports well with the Orthodox theologian Vladimir Lossky's statements to the effect that the Spirit remains "unmanifested, concealing himself even in his appearing."[97] The hiddenness of the Spirit also is consonant with an uncontrolling love of God perspective. By the Spirit's kenosis into creation, creation itself is then enabled, using Clayton's language, to participate in the processes of production and reproduction. In the following two sections, I will explore further the notion of the Spirit's kenosis into unordered matter in discussing primordial chaos, as well as the potentialities that are inherent within matter.

Kenosis and Primordial Chaos

In an interesting contribution to volume entitled *The Work of the Spirit*, Amos Yong discusses the contributions of pneumatology to the broad notion of divine action.[98] In so doing, Yong invokes the Spirit as acting upon primordial chaos. It is my contention that primordial chaos is the

---

for the theology and science dialogue (Ibid., 105). Moreover, Goergen contends, which I also affirm, that as the source of creative evolution, the Spirit works from *within* creation to generate ever increasing complexity, as opposed to externally compelling and manipulating creation (Goergen, *Fire of Love*, 106).

94. Sibbes, *Works*, 5:427.

95. Welker, "Spirit in Philosophical, Theological, and Interdisciplinary Perspectives," 227.

96. Hiddenness is at the heart of kenosis, notes Ernest Simmons. Further, the Hebrew *ruach*, as well as the Greek *pneuma*, both carry with them a sense of hidden and unseen forces (Simmons, "Towards kenotic Pneumatology," 11–16).

97. Lossky, *The Mystical Theology of the Eastern Church*, 169. Interestingly, Nicola Creegan argues that God's trinitarian nature, God's hiddenness, and God's incarnation give us reason to believe that we should be able to discern divine presence in the natural world, but only within the natural processes and thereby only in a somewhat obscured fashion (Creegan, "A Christian Theology of Evolution," 500).

98. Yong, "*Ruach*, the Primordial Chaos, and the Breath of Life," 183–204.

great confusion of matter out of which the Spirit, by kenosis and in an uncontrolling manner, generated order, structure, and ultimately all of life. Primordial chaos, in and of itself, is incapable to produce the formation of an ordered, structured, and functional collocation of atoms, because it is by definition random processes. Indeed, primordial chaos lacks the favorable environmentment that is requisite for enduring and functional patterns of matter to emerge. In fact, in primordial chaos, matter did not exist as such; rather, there was indeterminate and unconditioned disorder.

According to Yong, the Spirit causes the emergence of order and presides over it from within through the processes of division, distinction, differentiation, and particularization.[99] The Spirit did this creating by infusing the primordial chaos with pure and directed information, which resulted in an evolutionary process that was imbibed with fertility. Morowitz agrees in writing, "Emergence selects the restricted world of the real from the super-immense world of the possible."[100] So then, the Spirit is the intermediate between physical laws and chaotic matter. In this sense, the Spirit acted as a liaison in an uncontrolling manner between the primordial chaos, which was the source of variation and novelty, and the resultant ordered and structured creation of the Genesis account. Thus, the movement from chaos to cosmos was, ultimately, directed by the Spirit. This primordial chaos did not contain its own information (only non-directed energy instead), and therefore had to be—at least partially—infused with such by the Spirit. Thus, one may accurately note that the Spirit is the agent of causation by the interjection of both concretion and specification through information.[101] Primordial chaos without an input of active information by the Spirit of God would remain forever indeterminate and unstructured.[102] Matter's receptivity to spirit, which has form as a requisite, also has as its precondition the creaturely descent of the Spirit, his kenosis into creation. Thus, the Spirit of God seems at first to have generated the elementary principles of all things, creating formless masses of matter, which was without arrangement or distinction of parts.

99. Ibid., 194–95, 202.
100. Morowitz, *The Emergence of Everything*, 197.
101. Polkinghorne, "The Hidden Spirit and the Cosmos," 169.
102. cf. Huchingson, "Chaos, Communications Theory, and God's Abundance," 395–414.

Kenosis and Creation Understood as Potentiality

Primordial chaos, due to its intrinsic unpredictability's, allows the *possibility of God* (i.e., the Spirit[103]) much leeway in action in an uncontrolling mode. This primordial chaos was essential to God's subsequent creation because it was the source of innumerable potentialities,[104] without which the immense variety of nature would not be possible.[105] So, then, the Spirit's kenosis into creation leads to the realization of manifold potentialities. This divine *possibility* swept over the primordial chaotic abyss, and by uncontrolling kenosis into this primal creation, the complex activity of ordering within the chaotic primordial waters was onset. Because of the Spirit hovering over the waters, "the chaos becomes promise."[106]

In creation, the Spirit kenotically bestows both *potentiality* and "being" ("Let there be ... "). In this view, "instead of being daunted by the role of chance in genetic mutations as being the manifestation of irrationality in the Universe, it would be more consistent with the observations to assert that the full gamut of potentialities of living matter could be explored only through the agency of the rapid and frequent randomization which is possible at the molecular level of DNA."[107] The way in which "chance" operates within the world to produce new structures, new entities, and even new species, can only be understood as an actualization of the potentialities that the creating Spirit imbibed within creation in an uncontrolling fashion. Thus, the creating Spirit's intention and purpose is actualized through the operation of "chance" and "random" events. One can perceive God within evolution—and even within chaotic systems—then, as the processes themselves, unveiled by the biological sciences, are God-acting-as-uncontrolling-creator. Chaotic systems, perhaps wrongfully labeled, interlace both order and disorder. If the system is too far on the orderly side, the possibility for novelty is greatly reduced, as the system itself is too rigid for anything

---

103. For justification of this terminology, see Dabney, "Naming the Spirit," 58. Also, creation from a Pneumatological standpoint begins with the Spirit, and thus one should interpret the world as not defined by necessity, but by possibility instead, for the Spirit is the possibility of God (Ibid., 78). Michael Lodahl also notes that the "Spirit of God is identified as the possibility of God" (Lodahl, *From God to Creation*, 4).

104. Note that within this section, the terms potentialities and possibilities are used synonymously.

105. Huchingson, "Chaos, Communications Theory, and God's Abundance," 398.

106. Montague, *The Holy Spirit*, 67.

107. Peacocke, *Creation and the World of Science*, 94.

except a rearrangement of what already exists. Conversely, if the system strays too far on the side of disorder, a random world of proverbial anarchy results.[108] The potential for novelty and relative stability lies *between* the two poles of order and disorder within chaotic systems.

In dialogue with Polkinghorne, I posit that the endowment of potentiality and regularity was instituted by, and relies upon, the uncontrolling kenosis of the Spirit into creation. The Spirit, in this kenotic model, is seen as working within the seeming openness of nature, in conjunction with the unfolding of potentiality, and hence is not what might be called a "Spirit-of-the-gaps" (akin to the God-of-the-gaps). George Gaylord Simpson writes that, "within the framework of the evolutionary history of life, there have been not one but many different kinds of progress," which is a correlate to the notion of the actualization of possibilities.[109] Moreover, Karl Popper points out that the realization of possibilities, which may be random, depends upon the total situation within which the possibilities are being actualized so that there "exist weighted possibilities which are more than mere possibilities, but [at the same time are] . . . "tendencies or propensities to become real."[110] I posit that there is a definitive lure of the Spirit within the propensities of nature, which seamlessly coalesces with the notion of the Spirit's kenosis into creation, for this potential, as it were, is directed by the generative activity of the Spirit.

By creating in an uncontrolling kenotic manner, the Spirit both allows and invites the input of creatures in the activity of creation, and reacts according to that input, which invites creation into a cooperative relationship. Indeed, the Spirit did not create in a manipulative, single act, but instead acts in a process in which creation is allowed to develop. There exists overwhelming evidence of a universe marked by development, which points to creation by uncontrolling kenosis. And it should be noted, again, that the Spirit is present "in, with, and under" the processes of biological

---

108. Polkinghorne, "The Hidden Spirit and the Cosmos," 174.

109. Of which these are examples: the increasing specialization with its corollary of improvement and adaptability; increase in the general energy or maintained level of processes; increasing complexity, and so forth (Simpson, *The Meaning of Evolution*, 236).

110. Popper, *A World of Propensities*, 12. Peacocke suggests that there are propensities in evolution, of the Popperian sense noted above, towards the possession of certain features and characteristics, propensities which are built into the evolutionary process. Among these propensities of evolution, Peacocke notes, are "complexity" and "information-processing and storage-ability" (Peacocke, "The Cost of New Life," 30).

evolution within the created world.[111] So, then, the uncontrolling kenotic creating Spirit is present within the historical contingency of evolution, as well as its lawful regularity.[112] Seen in this manner, the Spirit did not bring about creation through a definitive action, but instead used a process of (macro-)evolution somewhat lured though natural laws.

Preliminary Conclusions

The earth is an active, empowering environmentment—even an empowering agent—that brings forth life by various independent processes of self-reproduction. Evolution is the overall process, but emergence punctuates the steps of the evolutionary epic. At the same time, the earth must be seen as an environment of various heterogeneous life-processes. So, then, the earth brings forth, but it does not bring forth itself. By uncontrollingly releasing the power of the self-directed earth, the Spirit enables—potentially—the continual production, variation, and sustenance of vegetable and animal life.[113] Moreover, in order to be consistent within the causal nexus, the Spirit of God kenotically bestows causal power unto the created order, and in effect thereafter becomes the chief cause amongst causes.[114] However, the created world is docile before the Spirit, and therefore ever open to his causal influence.

The entire mission of the Spirit could be succinctly envisioned as one of uncontrolling kenosis.[115] By extrapolation, one may infer that the Spirit was poured into creation so that it might develop fully in complexity into what the Father had intentioned from the beginning. By focusing on the Spirit, via kenosis into creation, as both originator and operator of creation, one can see that the Spirit is both directly and indirectly involved in the world from beginning to end. Thus, whereas the Spirit is the primary cause of all things, he also works through secondary causes. This implies, therefore, that what may commonly be referred to as the natural processes, or even what may be termed random processes, are in reality the indirect acts of the Spirit through secondary causes. It is the postulate of this chapter that distinctive, seemingly nondependent, actions are in fact Spirit-caused,

111. cf. Peacocke, "The Cost of New Life," 32, 86.
112. Polkinghorne, "Kenotic Creation and Divine," 96.
113. Welker, *Creation and Reality*, 42.
114. cf. Polkinghorne, "Kenotic Creation and Divine," 104.
115. Lucien, *Kenosis and Creation*, 116.

though they may appear to be secondarily caused.[116] In this secondary capacity, the Spirit is the remote, uncontrolling cause, while natural forces are proximate causes of events. Whereas the Godhead created all of the natural processes and laws, the Spirit is God's agent of creation within all of the forces of nature via kenosis.

The Spirit, it is herein affirmed, ennobles creation to possess emergent capabilities, as the Spirit imparted propensities into creation that eventuate the rise of higher forms of life. Thus, the breath of life enables and empowers the emergence of creation and creatures. Moreover, this immanent and uncontrolling Spirit of emergence endows creation with the ability to unfold by "natural" processes according to their inherent potentialities. This radicalization of immanence through uncontrolling love comports well with my advocacy of kenosis of the Spirit *into* creation, for in said notion, the Spirit is *intimately interior* to nature, as its source, sustenance and end. Recognize that if theism is to be more than mere deism, it must allow for some sort of divine involvement in the natural world, which leads to the plausibility of some degree of immanence.

In this chapter, I have reviewed and interacted with Clayton's seminal work, *Mind & Emergence*. In that book, Clayton contends that emergence is a viable option in contrast to the waning explanatory power of both physicalism and dualism. Moreover, I have presented the Biblical basis of kenosis of the Spirit *into* creation, arguing that the Bible presents the Spirit as being the active agent of God in the world, particularly regarding the Spirit as life-giver and animator of all creation. I also have made my own contribution of the connections between the uncontrolling kenosis of the Spirit into creation and emergence theory, which hopefully will make a positive contribution toward a systematic theology of creation.

---

116. Compare this postulation with a Neo-Thomist conception of Divine "double agency," as mentioned by Southgate in *God, Humanity, and the Cosmos*, 281.

4

The *Kenosis* of the Spirit *into* Creation[1]

WHETHER OR NOT CREATION is eternal is certainly not a new question. Apparently as early as written language appeared, the idea of an eternal creation was favored by pagan philosophers. Into this confusion, the Christian doctrine of *creatio ex nihilo* was formulated in the second century to dispel such an idea and to affirm God's transcendence. The question of creation arises anew today in light of the current world view, marked by the scientific notion of evolution, which has compelled new models of divine action to emerge. Recently, a collection of essays by theologians and scientists explored creation as *The Work of Love*, pointing to divine action as kenosis.[2] The resurgence of kenotic theology has been helpful in striving to reformulate divine action in an evolutionary world. The kenotic theology posited by this chapter maintains that the Spirit, who *is* uncontrolling Love,[3] completely shares and imparts himself *into* creation.

The Spirit of God "poured Himself out" into creation, thereby causing it to leap forth from chaos and become a structured and orderly system of life-bearing entities. Theologians as early as Ephraem the Syrian recognized that creation was initiated through the Spirit. Indeed, Ephraem writes in his *Commentary On Genesis 1*,

> [The Holy Spirit] "warmed the waters with a kind of vital warmth, even bringing them to a boil through intense heat in order to make

---

1. A previous version of this chapter appeared in *Crucible: Theology & Ministry* 1 1 (2008).
2. Polkinghorne, ed. *The Work of Love*.
3. 1 John 4:16.

them fertile. The action of a hen is similar. It sits on its eggs, making them fertile through the warmth of incubation . . . Thus we learn that all was brought to perfection and accomplished by the Trinity."[4]

As a result of this *breath* of God imparted, nature gives birth to life, and *life-bearing* creatures burst upon the environment.[5] So then, Ephraem sees the Spirit as the life-giving force that enables creation to strive toward becoming its fullness (via the process of macroevolution). The creating Spirit freely limits his infinite power so as to allow for the existence of non-infinite entities.[6] This chapter affirms the notion that creation was a result of the kenotic act of the Spirit *into* creation. Creation is a kenotic act of *self-offering.*

Kenosis in the Two Testaments

I posit that the kenosis of the Spirit into creation had a similar effect as Rebekah's pouring of the water *into* the trough (cf. Gen 24:20). There is an inherent others'-centeredness in kenosis, as one can see in Rebekah's case, as well as both Christ's kenosis and Paul's kenosis. It may be extrapolated, further, that the same others'-centeredness is present with the Spirit's kenosis into creation. The pre-existent Christ poured himself into humanity so that it could be reconciled to the Father and that it might be acceptable to him (Phil. 2:5-11). God, in the person of the Son, "enters into the limited, finite situation of man. Not only does he enter into it, descend into it, but also he accepts it and embraces the whole of human existence his being."[7] Paul similarly poured himself into the Church and its mission so that the reconciliation to the Father wrought by Christ might be appropriated by the mass of men and women (Phil. 3:7-9, Gal. 2:20, 3:28–29, 1 Cor. 9:16).[8]

The Spirit of God, moreover, kenotically empowered the incarnation, life and death of the Son of God.[9] Indeed, by the kenotic action of the Spirit in baptism, Jesus of Nazareth was endowed with power for his subsequent ministry. Moreover, the kenosis of the Son of God on the cross

---

4. Ephraem, *Sancti Patris Nostri*, 1:117.
5. Ralston III, "Kenosis and Nature," 58.
6. Clayton, "Kenotic Trinitarian Panentheism," 252.
7. Moltmann, *The Crucified God*, 176.
8. Patitsas, "Kenosis According to Saint Paul," 77.
9. Bulgakov, *The Comforter*, 257.

The Kenosis of the Spirit into Creation

offers an analogical understanding to the kenosis of the Spirit of God into creation. The Son of God was *poured into* mankind, became man, and then returned to the Father. Additionally, by the kenotic action of the Spirit in the resurrection, Jesus of Nazareth debilitated the damning effects of sin. In the transfiguration, the kenotic action of the Spirit revealed a portion of the glory of God the Father through God the Son.[10] In reality, all of the works of the Christ from God were actualized by the kenotic action of the Spirit (Christ is the *anointed* one, note). One may properly adduce that the Father sends the Son into the material world *through* the agency of the Spirit, who later gets sent into the world *through* the Son.[11] So then, kenosis is the general way in which God interacts with the world.

It is interesting to ponder that the term kenosis is most frequently linked to Christ's voluntary renunciation of certain divine attributes in order to identify himself with mankind, as recorded in the Pauline hymn found in Phil 2:5-11. However, the kenosis of the Son of God referred to in the passage of Phil 2:5-11 *cannot* be understood to mean a *subtraction* of divinity, but the *addition* of humanity instead. Indeed, in the passage of Phil 2:5-11 itself, the verb often translated as "emptied" is *explained, expanded,* and *extrapolated* by three participles that directly follow it—1) *taking* the form of a servant, 2) *becoming* in the likeness of men, and 3) *being found* in fashion as a man. Clearly, even in this reference to Christological kenosis, the net effect is *addition*. I posit that it is this meaning of kenosis, i.e. "poured out," that is best indicative to the kenosis of the Spirit of God *into* creation. So then, the principle that one may draw from the usage of kenosis in reference to God the Son is illustrative of the kenosis in reference to God the Spirit regarding the divine essence. This kenosis of the Spirit can also be seen, for example, in his descent upon Jesus at his baptism. Indeed, the Spirit was *poured into* Jesus so as to *empower* Jesus for his crucial ministry of imparting life to the masses, which resulted in Jesus' own temporal and bodily death.

Beyond the Two Testaments' Usage of *Kenosis*

This uncontrolling kenosis of the Spirit into creation enables the *finite* creation to coexist with the *infinite* Godhead. Thus, the kenosis of the Spirit into creation is supremely an act of love by the Father of all righteousness.

10. Ibid., 346.
11. Ibid., 263.

The kenosis of the Spirit into creation directly entails the notion that creatures owe their existence to the Spirit's creative energies imparted into creation. So then, the Spirit's most potent role—being *poured into* others and other things—makes possible both the life and the activity of the other.[12] Kenosis is certainly not a picture of a traditional monological act of creation by direct production. Instead, by creating in a kenotic manner, God both *allows* and *invites* the input of creatures in the activity of creation, and *reacts* according to that input. Thus, God has chosen to allow the *other* to act, and has chosen to invite creation into a cooperative relationship. So then, God works with what has already been created to develop the creation still further. The uncontrolling kenotic creating Spirit does not overrule his creation or its creatures, but continuously *interacts* with them instead.

Creation is an act of divine kenosis, an expression exercised by uncontrolling love, through which the Creator allows creatures to be themselves. According to Sergius Bulgakov, God the Father always acts by *persuasion*, and not by compulsion, which is exemplified by the action of the Spirit of God in creation.[13] So then, the kenotic Creating Spirit does not overrule his creatures, but *interacts* with them instead. In an expansive chapter that explicates the "revelation of the Holy Spirit," Bulgakov first highlights the kenosis of the Spirit into Creation. Bulgakov begins his discussion of the Revelation of the Holy Spirit with the kenosis of the Spirit of God into creation, because it is the basis of all subsequent revelation. For Bulgakov, then, kenosis, the divine *self-pouring out*, is the essential revelation of who God is.[14] The implication of the priority of the Spirit in revelation gives credence to the notion of priority of the Spirit in creation, making his uncontrolling kenosis the fundamental basis of the derivation of complexity within creation.

Kenosis and Creation Understood as Potentiality

In creation, the Spirit kenotically bestows both *potentiality* and "being" ("Let there be . . ."). As Michael Lodahl notes, the "Spirit of God is identified as the possibility of God."[15] Moreover, hiddenness is the basis of kenosis,

---

12. Linahan, "Experiencing God in Brokenness," 181.
13. Bulgakov, *The Comforter*, 219.
14. Ibid.
15. Lodahl, *From God to Creation*, 4.

notes Ernest Simmons.[16] So then, creation is, in a sense, *larva dei*, the *mask of God*. We encounter God through masks because that is the only way in which finite beings can associate with the infinite ground of all being. Simmons notes that the Hebrew *ruach*, as well as the Greek *pneuma*, both carry with them a sense of hidden and unseen forces.[17] Being panentheistic in relation, there is both distinction and relatedness between the Spirit and creation. Because the Spirit and creation are intrinsically joined together, there is no need of a "causal joint," as per se, for they are composed of the same potentiality.

Regarding potential propensities in evolution, Simon Conway Morris notes that, "within certain limits the outcome of evolutionary processes might be rather predictable . . . [as] nearly all biologists agree that convergence is a ubiquitous feature of life . . . [for] again and again we have evidence of biological form stumbling on the same solution to a problem."[18] Stephen Jay Gould contends that there can be overall direction and implantation of divine purpose through what may popularly be called "chance" that operates within a rule-obeying context.[19] However, neither Gould nor Peacocke see these "propensities" as a *special* providential action by God, as per se, but rather a consequence of how God continuously creates through the processes that he has made (and hence merely a *general* providential action). Contra Gould and Peacocke, I assert that the Spirit communicates at every moment what Whitehead calls divine "initial aims" to creatures.[20]

In Whitehead's philosophy of organism, an initial aim is the means by which God *influences*, but *not determines*, the outcome of all the world's processes. This *initial aim*, I posit, is provided by the kenotic pouring into matter by the Spirit. Although God has influence over all processes of the universe, "luring" them into the future, every event still has power to exert its own creative influence on its future.[21] The initial aim of God is to always unfold maximum molecular possibilities, potential, novelty and complexity.[22] I posit that God provides the initial aim by uncontrolling kenosis

---

16. Simmons, "Towards kenotic Pneumatology," 11–16.
17. Ibid., 14.
18. Conway Morris, *The Crucible of Creation*, 205.
19. Gould, *Wonderful Life*, 51.
20. Whitehead, *Process and Reality*, 244.
21. Ibid., 346. Note that this assertion has direct implications regarding the possibility of creation (and later, humans) denying and/or resisting the lure of God.
22. Stein, "An Inquiry Into the Origins Of Life On Earth," 1004.

Spirit. This initial aim is then nourished by the lure of fullness. To invoke Tillichian/Oorded language, the uncontrolling kenotic Spirit is the ground of causation of the becoming of all that is.

Emphasis on divine love seems to lie behind process theology's picture of a God, who in Whitehead's moving phrase, is a "fellow sufferer who understands," and who acts only through the power of persuasion.[23] Whitehead held that God and the world have always coexisted, and that God creates by working with what exists. An eternal creation for Whitehead rests on God's relational nature. In agreement with Whitehead's assertion that God only acts through persuasion, the kenotic view of creation that I advocate posits that God acts through *luring* creation and its creatures toward his pre-established goal (greater complexity). Moreover, contrary to what both Peacocke and Gould assert, I posit that there is a definitive *lure* of the Spirit within the *propensities* of nature. So then, it is at least conceivable that the kenotic impartation of the Spirit into creation effects and/or causes these "propensities" in nature.

Kenosis and the Creation of Formless Matter

These propensities and potential, as it were, are directed by the ordering principle of the Spirit, following his kenosis into creation. In Justin Martyr, one finds much credence to the notion that formless matter was ordered by God into a productive and life-bearing creation.[24] For example, Justin Martyr states:

> But we have received by tradition that God does not need the material offerings which men can give, seeing, indeed, that He Himself is the provider of all things. And we have been taught, and are convinced, and do believe, that He accepts those only who imitate the excellences which reside in Him, temperance, and justice, and philanthropy, and as many virtues as are peculiar to a God who is called by no proper name. And we have been taught that He in the beginning did of His goodness, for man's sake, create all things out of unformed matter.[25]

---

23. Whitehead, *Process and Reality*, 350.

24. I interpret the Justin Martyr's statements regarding "God" in general to relate to God the Spirit, note.

25 Justin Martyr, in *The Ante-Nicene Fathers*, 1.165.

The Kenosis of the Spirit into Creation

Justin Martyr, in his Apology I 10.2, states that God created the world out of "formless matter," which in context is a rebuttal of creation *ex nihilo*. However, I am using Justin Martyr's statement in order to posit that indeed formless matter could have existed for a time before God the Spirit ordered it into creation. So then, apparently creation progressed from a state of *nothingness* through a state of formlessness and then into a condition in which the formlessness gave way to form. Matter's receptivity to spirit, which has form as a requisite, also has as its precondition the creaturely descent of the Spirit, his kenosis in creation.[26] For Bulgakov, matter itself is the direct result of the kenotic action of the Spirit of God into creation.[27] Thus, the Spirit seems at first to have created the elementary principles of all things, creating formless masses of matter, which was *without* arrangement or distinction of parts.

Correctly, in my opinion, Ambrose did not posit that God created a fully formed creation by divine fiat. He notes clearly that creating precedes ordering. In his *Hexaemeron*, Ambrose writes that:

> The good architect lays the foundation first and afterward, when the foundation has been laid, plots the various parts of the building, one after the other, and then adds to it the ornamentation ... Scripture points out that things were first created and afterward put in order lest it be supposed that they were not actually created and that they had no beginning, just as if the nature of things had been, as it were, generated from the beginning and did not appear to be something added afterward.[28]

Later in his *Hexaemeron*, Ambrose comments upon the Spirit's role in creation, and notes that, "The Spirit fittingly moved over the earth, destined to bear fruit because by the aid of the Spirit it held the seeds of new birth which were to germinate according to the words of the prophet in Psalms 104:30: 'Send forth thy Spirit and they shall be created and thou shall renew the face of the earth.'"[29]

In his *Confessions*, Augustine notes that the earth, directly following creation, was *formless* matter. He writes, "The earth was invisible and unorganized, and darkness was over the abyss. Formlessness is suggested by these words, so that we might grasp the meaning by degrees, for we are

---

26. Bulgakov, *The Comforter*, 221.
27. Ibid., 345.
28. Ambrose, *Hexaemeron*, 42: 26, 29.
29. Ibid., 42: 32–33.

unable to think cognitively about an absolute privation of form that still does not go as far as nothing."[30] Moreover, Basil of Caesarea similarly notes that creation was not fully complete and formed upon the "first day" (my own words) of creation. Basil writes in his *Hexaemeron*:

> Surely the perfect condition of the earth consists in its state of abundance: the budding of all sorts of plants, the putting forth of the lofty trees both fruitful and barren, the freshness and fragrance of flowers, and whatever things appeared on earth a little later by the command of God to adorn their mother. Since as yet there was nothing of this, the Scripture reasonably spoke of it as incomplete. We might say the same also about the heavens; that they were not yet brought to perfection themselves, nor had they received their proper adornment, since they were not yet lighted around by the moon nor the sun, nor crowned by the choirs of the stars. For these things had not yet been made. Therefore you will not err from the truth if you say that the heavens also were incomplete.[31]

Although it should be noted that Gregory of Nyssa's writings regarding the potentiality of God's creation are akin to Aristotle's ideas of act and potency, Gregory's words here will be interpreted in reference to the Spirit's uncontrolling in-pouring into creation. According to Gregory of Nyssa, all things develop toward a natural order directed by the Creator. He writes,

> just as we say that in wheat, or in any other grain, the whole form of the plant is potentially included—the leaves, the stalk, the joints, the grain, the beard—and do not say in our account of its nature that any of these things has pre-existence, or comes into being before the others, but that the power abiding in the seed is manifested in a certain natural order, not by any means that another nature is infused into it—in the same way we suppose the human germ to possess the potentiality of its nature, sown with it at the first start of its existence, and that it is unfolded and manifested by a natural sequence as it proceeds to its perfect state, not employing anything external to itself as a stepping-stone to perfection, but itself advancing its own self in due course to the perfect state . . . [similarly] "we cannot discern the articulation of the limbs in that which is implanted for the conception of the body before it begins to take form . . . "for even the form of the future man is there potentially, but is concealed because it is not possible that it should be made visible before the necessary sequence of events

30. Augustine, *Confessions*, 21:379.
31. Basil of Caesarea, *Fathers of the Church*, 46:22.

allows it . . . [Moreover] "since it is not from a dead body that the potentiality for conception is secreted, but from one which is animate and alive, we hence affirm that it is reasonable that we should not suppose that what is sent forth from a living body to be the occasion of life is itself dead and inanimate . . . "For in the case of men we consider it an evidence of life that one is warm and operative and in motion, but the chill and motionless state in the case of bodies is nothing else than deadness."[32]

From the comments above from Gregory of Nyssa, one may infer that movement and change are *intrinsic* to creation. So then, *creatio continua*, continuing creation, is an integral concept in the understanding of the Spirit's creative action, and of the Spirit's kenosis *into* creation. The immanent and uncontrolling Creator Spirit is continuously creating and perpetually breathing life into the creation.

Kenosis and *Creatio Continua*

The uncontrolling Spirit of God did not need to create in a single, direct act, but instead was able to create a process in which creation was allowed to develop. This can be seen, for example, by coalescing pneumatology with the modern Big Bang theory, whereby the Spirit can be viewed as the originating principle, creating matter, who sets the Big Bang in motion. So then, instead of creating a finished product by divine fiat, the Spirit empowers the world to *develop*, exerting self-determination. This notion of creation through *development* also leads to an understanding of biological evolution in which the Spirit is seen as using the development of creatures as a type of continuing creation. The uncontrolling kenotic creating Spirit is present within the historical contingency of evolution, as well as its lawful regularity.[33] The Spirit acts within the causal nexus of creation (i.e. natural law, divine providence, and later human action) to input pure informational content by means of the impartation of active energy within creation.[34] So then, the Spirit did not bring about creation in a single, definitive action, but instead used a process of evolution lured by natural laws.

It is important, therefore, to view the Spirit not only as originating principle of creation, but also as *sustainer* of creation, upholding its order,

---

32. Gregory of Nyssa, "On the Making of Man," 421.
33. Polkinghorne, *The Work of Love*, 96.
34. Ibid., 101.

and giving it life out of himself. One may deduce, therefore, that the Spirit indeed makes things able to make themselves, which affirms a panentheistic perspective. Theologians today, then, are correct to contemplate this long process as God's continued creation, mediated by the interplay of laws and chance.[35] As a consequence of positing *creatio continua*, one must insist that the uncontrolling Spirit's power is manifest in the unfolding of creation in evolutionary history.[36]

John Chrysostom also says that God's providence in the world is akin to continuing creation. In Chrysostom's commentary regarding the Gospel according to John, one finds the following statements in reference to God's timely and unfolding actions:

> for the same Evangelist says, 'They could not lay hands on Him, because His hour was not yet come' (8:20); and again, 'No man laid hands on Him, because His hour was not yet come' (7:30); and again, 'The hour is come, glorify Thy Son.' (17:1.) What then do the words mean? . . . He desires to show this; that He works all things at their convenient season, not doing all at once; because a kind of confusion and disorder would have ensued, if, instead of working all at their proper seasons, He had mixed all together, His Birth, His Resurrection, and His coming to Judgment. Observe this; creation was to be, yet not all at once; man and woman were to be created, yet not even these together; mankind were to be condemned to death, and there was to be a resurrection, yet the interval between the two was to be great; the law was to be given, but not grace with it, each was to be dispensed at its proper time.[37]

So then, John Chrysostom here insists that creation "unfolds" continually, and not all at once, which is an antecedent to modern hypotheses regarding *creatio continua*. What Chrysostom here applies to the Son of God, I ascribe to the Spirit of God.

Kenosis and Creation Today

The kenosis of the Spirit into creation is purely voluntary, as it is simply the overflowing of the goodness and uncontrolling love of God. God's loving goodness is forever *pouring out* without running out, as well as *emptying*

---

35. Doncel, *The Kenosis of the Creator*, 798.
36. Polkinghorne, *The Work of Love*, 96.
37 Chrysostom, "Homilies on the Gospel of Saint John," 76.

without getting emptied, and this happens eternally not only within the inner life of the Trinity, but also with the created world. God reveals his inner Triune life in creating the world thereby. In fact, creation is the first outflowing of the divine goodness within the Trinity, and God saw that this creation was "very good."[38] As implicitly derived from the creation of the vast universe, this chapter affirms that the action of the Spirit of God knows no limits, for the Spirit is supra-spatial.[39] Because of the Spirit's kenosis into creation, the *absolute* God is able to establish a relationship with the *relative* creatures, of which humanity is exemplar.

The uncontrolling Spirit was, as it were, "taking a risk" in creating a world kenotically, for it necessarily involves both chance and randomness through the processes of evolution.[40] However, the Spirit imparted propensities into creation that eventuate the rise of information-processing systems, as well as information-storage systems, which were both necessary for the realization of higher forms of life.[41] Moreover, the Spirit is the very power of being this chapter posits. Although the Spirit of God's omnipotence has been *self-limited* in that the Spirit chose freely and uncontrollingly to give partial self-determinative power over to creation, this does not mean that the Spirit is incapable of doing whatever he wills; instead, it is not in accordance with his uncontrolling love to insist on total control. So then, the Spirit limits himself, giving *genuine* freedom, and thus *genuine* power, to that which has been created. It may be deduced, then, that the Spirit created a type of world in which he is not the only agent. Indeed, the Spirit creates entities that are truly "other" than himself, and part of that otherness is agency. The Spirit enables creation to be itself by bestowing freedom to creation, as well as by enabling creation to become itself through bestowing authentic causal powers within material matter. Creation, then, needs to be understood dynamically as a process.

In the kenotic paradigm of the Spirit's presence in the creation of the world herein presented, one should recognize that Gen 1 involves the ministerial use of the created order in the forming of other created things. Creation is a series of acts done by the luring Spirit of creation that is done "in time," as well as a series of acts done by the luring Spirit of creation that, "takes time." Just as God the Father "took his time" in dealing with an erring

---

38. Gen. 1:31.
39. Bulgakov, *The Comforter*, 276.
40. Peacocke, *The Work of Love*, 27.
41. Ibid., 30.

world in Christ, so too did he "take his time" in bestowing creative and causal powers to the Spirit in creation. Thus, the created world is a project, of sorts, of the Spirit in that the creation takes time to become what God kenotically enspirited it to become.[42]

Preliminary Conclusions

As God did his work of creating by means of the Spirit, so believers are to do their work by the Spirit. It may be deduced that the kenosis of the Spirit in the form of self-*limiting* makes possible the kenosis of the Spirit in creation in the form of self-*giving*. Indeed, that which is the fullness of God (i.e., the Spirit) enters into "unfullness" so that it may later be made full. Thus, the overall purpose of this kenosis by the Creating Spirit into creation is theosis by means of enosis.[43] This idea supports the notion of Aquinas, who intimated that resemblance to God is the ultimate end of all things. That is, the purpose of *kenosis* is *theosis*, or union with God, by means of *enosis*, or the infilling by God.

---

42. Gunton, *The Triune Creator*, 93.
43. Ellis, *The Work of Love*, 109.

5

Thomistic Personalism in Dialogue with *Kenosis*[1]

> Man cannot live without love. He remains a being that is incomprehensible for himself, his life is senseless, if love is not revealed to him, if he does not encounter love, if he does not experience it and make it his own, if he does not participate intimately in it ... In this dimension [of love] man finds again the greatness, dignity and value that belong to his humanity.[2]

POPE JOHN PAUL II recounts in *Crossing the Threshold of Hope*, "As a young priest, I learned to love human love. This has been one of the fundamental themes of my priesthood ... If one loves human love, there naturally arises the need to commit oneself completely to the service of 'fair love,' because love is fair, it is beautiful."[3] Writing as Karol Wojtyla, the Pope committed himself intellectually to this task in his important work, *Love and Responsibility*, in which he presents a holistic vision of love based upon a personalist framework. Love cannot exist but between two self-possessing persons; only if one is in possession of himself can he give himself away. For this reason, in committing himself to "the service of fair love," Wojtyla simultaneously committed himself anew to the study of the person, albeit in another, further dimension. Ultimately, Wojtyla believed, one must attempt

---

1. A greatly revised form of this essay previously appeared in *Studia Elckie* 19 1 (2017) 21–32.
2. John Paul II, *Redemptor Hominis*, § 10.
3. John Paul II, *Crossing the Threshold of Hope*, 123.

to understand the human person in terms of love, because it is love alone that reveals the meaning of the person.

That, "love reveals the meaning of the person" can be understood in a couple of different ways. On the one hand, we can begin with the experience of love and investigate it in all its fullness, and thereby come to know all those aspects of man that are truly defining of his personhood. According to Wojtyla, "the experience of love, properly understood, remains a simple and universal gateway through which everyone can pass in order to gain an awareness of what makes a person a human being: reason, affection and freedom."[4] In this way, love can serve as the basis for coming to understand the full meaning of the person. On the other hand, we can first endeavor to develop a comprehensive anthropology of humanity as both metaphysical and personal subject, and from there work our way to the level of love as the highest end and good of humanity, that which most perfectly fulfills him and most fully reveals who he is. As Wojtyla states elsewhere, "Love is the fullest realization of the possibilities inherent in man . . . The person finds in love the greatest possible fullness of being, of objective existence. Love is an activity, a deed which develops the existence of the person to its fullest."[5] Love can and does serve, then, in a double capacity, as both the source and summit of our understanding of the human person.

In the following chapter, one will find five distinct parts. In the first section, I depict Thomistic Personalism as expressed in Karol Wojtyla's *Love and Responsibility*. In that particular work, Wojtyla characterized love as the inherent affirmation of the value of the person. One can notice the influence of Thomistic Personalism on Wojtyla's thought in part in the objectivism of his ethics, which held that people are to pursue things and activities as means of fulfillment, and not simply subjective pleasures. Yet, there is a form of love that is pre-eminent, which Wojtyla refers to herein as betrothed love, the defining characteristic of which is self-donation.

In the second part of this chapter, I build on Wojtyla's characterization of betrothed love as self-donation, noting that the bible gives good grounds for illustrating the Spirit as the active agent of God in the world, particularly regarding the Spirit as *life-giver* and *animator* of all creation through self-donation (or self-giving). In this section, I note that the Spirit is the

---

4. John Paul II, "Address to Members of the Pontifical John Paul Institute," http://www.vatican.va/holy_father/john_paul_ii/speeches/2001/documents/hf_jp-ii_spe_20010531_istituto-jp-ii_en.html, § 2.

5. Wojtyla, *Love and Responsibility*, 82.

effectual arm of the Trinity that was active as the Son spoke each word in the primal creating moments. The Spirit, I postulate, is ultimately responsible for both the conditions for life, as well as life itself. I note further that the Greek verb *kenoó*, from which the term kenosis is derived, can mean either "to empty," or "to pour out," and contend that the Spirit's uncontrollingly "pouring of himself out" into creation enables the derivation of life itself.

In section three of this chapter, I correlate Thomas Jay Oord's essential kenosis and uncontrolling love of God theology and Wojtyla's depiction of love as self-donation. I note that in various works over the last decade, Oord has sought to supplement the recent resurgence in the natural sciences upon the import of "love." Fundamental to all of the titles therein surveyed, with slight variation, is Oord's definition of love—to love is to act intentionally, in sympathetic/empathetic response to others (including God), to promote *overall* well-being. I note that Oord highlights how love is depicted in the biological sciences, where it is often encompassed under the heading of altruism, which pictures love, in effect, as self-donation. The picturing of altruism as a form of love is significant because it highlights the import of cooperation, even at the most fundamental levels of creation.

In part four of this chapter, I take note of a collection of essays written several years ago, edited by John Polkinghorne, which pictured divine action and love as kenotic self-donation. Therein, kenosis is pictured as an affirmation of God's voluntary self-limitation, a limitation that allows creatures to enjoy their own power and freedom, which results in the kenotic Creator *interacting* with creatures. While I find much value in that collection of essays, my own view departs from theirs, as the kenotic theology set forth in this chapter maintains that the Spirit is completely imparted *into* creation. The Spirit of God, thereby, *inspirits* formless and chaotic matter, and "nothing" thereby becomes "something"—that is, as a result of this *breath* of God imparted, nature eventually gives birth to life.

A Characterization of Thomistic Personalism as Expressed in Wojtyla's *Love and Responsibility*

If one looks at Wojtyla's *Love and Responsibility*, they can see a number of different ways that he applies Thomistic Personalism. To begin with, one can observe with Wojtyla that, "In dealings between persons of different sexes, and especially in the sexual relationship, the woman is always the object of activity on the part of a man, and the man the object of activity on the part of the woman."⁶ Man-as-person is not simply an object in the world but above all a subject, and as such is *dominus sui*, or master of himself. Each of us is in possession of free will and therefore capable of self-determination. Because a human is self-determining, he can never be used as a mere means to another's end, for as Wojtyla says, "This is precluded by the very nature of personhood, by what any person is."⁷

According to Wojtyla, the personalistic value intrinsic in each of us reveals a deeper personalistic norm which should always govern our actions with others: "This norm, in its negative aspect, states that the person is the kind of good which does not admit of use and cannot be treated as an object of use and as such the means to an end. In its positive form the personalistic norm confirms this: the person is a good towards which the only proper and adequate attitude is love."⁸ One preliminary way in which one might understand love, then, is as the opposite of use. Conversely, one might say that love is the affirmation of the value of the person: "love for a person must consist in affirmation that the person has a value higher than that of an object for consumption or use."⁹

In order to prevent objectification, Wojtyla believes the individuals involved must seek joint fulfillment in a common good, for "when two different people consciously choose a common aim this puts them on a footing of equality, and precludes the possibility that one of them might be subordinated to the other," since both are "subordinated to that good which constitutes their common end."¹⁰ One can notice the influence of Thomism on Wojtyla's thought in the strict objectivism of his ethics in that people are to pursue real goods as means of fulfillment, and not simply subjective pleasures, which will never make one truly happy.

According to Wojtyla, sexual attraction between man and woman points to the value of unity and complementarity: "Sexual attraction makes obvious the fact that the attributes of the two sexes are complementary, so that a man and a woman can complete each other . . . The urge to mutual completion which accompanies this division [of the sexes] indicates that

---

6. Wojtyla, *Love and Responsibility*, 24.
7. Ibid., 26.
8. Ibid., 41.
9. Ibid., 42.
10. Ibid., 28–29.

the attributes of each sex possess some specific value for the other."[11] There are two aspects essential to true love according to Wojtyla, namely the willingness to never make the other an object of use, and the affirmation of the essential value of the other.

In *Person and Being*, W. Norris Clarke makes the insightful observation that one interacts with others not only because they are limited and contingent, and thus in need of the goods which they possess, but also because they have goods which they naturally desire to share:

> For Aquinas, finite, created being pours over naturally into action for two reasons: (1) because it is poor, i.e., lacking the fullness of existence, and so strives to enrich itself as much as its nature allows from the richness of those around it; but (2) even more profoundly because it is rich, endowed with its own richness of existence, however slight this may be, which it tends naturally to communicate and share with others.[12]

At the level of the person, this desire to communicate the good manifests itself as good will, which is an essential aspect of personal love.

Like the person, true personal love must include both an objective and a subjective dimension. Indeed, it needs to be grounded in the practice of virtue and the choosing of real goods; yet, it must also be grounded in the concrete subject-hood of the person with all of his physical and emotional aspects. Experiences teach us that if either dimension is lacking, so too is love, for love must be an integrated whole. As worthy a love as integrated friendship is, according to Wojtyla, it is not the highest form of love. True love between persons must include elements of affirmation, attraction, desire and goodwill. Yet, there exists a level of love beyond all these that Wojtyla refers to as betrothed love. The defining characteristic of betrothed love is self-donation: "Betrothed love differs from all the aspects or forms of love analyzed hitherto. Its decisive character is the giving of one's own person (to another). The essence of betrothed love is self-giving, the surrender of one's 'I.'"[13]

At first glance, this notion of self-donation or self-gift seems rather incomprehensible in light of the incommunicable nature of the person. The person, as an intrinsically self-possessing being, cannot be reduced to an object for another. For this reason, "in the natural order it makes no sense

---

11. Ibid., 48.
12. Clarke, *Person and Being*, 10.
13. Wojtyla, *Love and Responsibility*, 96.

to speak of a person giving himself or herself to another . . . The person as such cannot be someone else's property, as though it were a thing."[14] Yet, "what is impossible and illegitimate in the natural order . . . can come about in the order of love."[15] This statement concerns a real mystery in the order of being, but one which Christ gave voice to when he said, "Whoever seeks to gain his life will lose it, but whoever loses his life will gain it" (Luke 17:33). Christ here indicates the mysterious nature of the gift of self: it is mysterious not only in that it is a real possibility for the human person, but even more so because it is a necessity in order to attain the fullness of life. Self-donation is thus "doubly paradoxical: first in that it is possible to step outside one's own 'I' in this way, and secondly in that the 'I' far from being destroyed or impaired as a result is enlarged and enriched."[16] Wojtyla refers to this mystery as "the law of ekstasis," according to which the lover "'goes outside' the self to find a fuller existence in another."[17] I submit that this understanding of ekstasis is fundamental to the concept of God's uncontrolling love.

A Characterization of *Kenosis* as Self-Donation

Picking up on Wojtyla's characterization of betrothed love as self-donation, the bible gives good grounds for illustrating the Spirit as the active agent of God in the world, particularly regarding the Spirit as *life-giver* and *animator* of all creation through self-donation (or self-giving).[18] Indeed, just as the Spirit kenotically entered into the chaotic seas through which the Jews passed in their exodus and parted them (Ex 14:21), so too was the Spirit of God parting the chaos of the primordial waters, thereby preparing creation to progress through the long processes of evolution thereafter. The Spirit of life hovered over the primordial waters and transformed the *chaos* into the *cosmos*. In Gen 1:2, the Spirit moved upon the face of the waters, which constitutes an obvious creative act. The verb used in Gen 1:2 depicts the Spirit hovering mysteriously over the waters, preparing for the acts of creation to follow. It is interesting to note that the Hebrew verb is here has been translated "hovering" (as a bird over her young; see Deut 32:11),

14. Ibid.
15. Ibid.
16. Ibid., 97.
17. Ibid., 126.
18. cf. Paul's assertion that the Spirit "gives life" in 2 Cor 3:6.

whereas the Syriac cognate term means "to brood over" or "to incubate." That the Spirit was hovering like a mother stork might hover over her nest is a portent of life to come from the dark, murky depths of the chaos below. The Spirit, one may postulate, is ultimately responsible for both the conditions for life, as well as life itself. The Spirit is the effectual arm of the Trinity that was active as the Son spoke each word in the primal creating moments.

A Correlation Between Oord's Essential *Kenosis* and Love as Self-Donation

Thomas Jay Oord's intention in *Defining Love: A Philosophical, Scientific, and Theological Engagement* and in *The Nature of Love: A Theology* is to supplement the recent resurgence in the natural sciences upon the import of "love." Fundamental to both titles, with slight variation, is Oord's definition of love: to love is to act intentionally, in sympathetic/empathetic response to others (including God), to promote *overall* well-being.[19] In *Defining Love*, Oord looks at the general forms of love—historically speaking—and thereby attempts to decide what love requires. He then explores how love is depicted in the biological sciences, where it is often encompassed under the heading of altruism, which pictures love, in effect, as self-donation. In the final chapter of *Defining Love*, Oord offers his constructive proposal of a theology of love informed by the sciences, which he terms an "essential kenosis" theology.[20]

Oord expands his "essential kenosis" theology in *The Nature of Love*, first by asserting—and defending—the primacy of love, which is followed by a depiction of *agape, eros,* and *philia* love in the bible. In order to flesh-out his theology of love, Oord explores Augustinian love theology, noting its positive contributions as well as its deficiencies. *The Nature of Love* reaches its apex in the last chapter, wherein Oord proposes his promising "essential kenosis" theology, a theology that presents God as steadfastly loving.[21] Throughout both texts, Oord highlights the relational nature of God—to love is to be mutually related. Love is depicted as multiform, multiexpressive, multivarious, and multifaceted, which provides both the promise of (expansionality) and the problem with (ambiguity, lack of precision) of the research regarding love. Noting the often overlooked characteristics

---

19. Oord, *Defining Love*, 29; and Oord, *The Nature of Love*, 17.
20. Oord, *Defining Love*, 199.
21. Oord, *The Nature of Love*, 129.

of *philia* love, Oord intentionally promotes the importance—perhaps even primacy—of it, as *philia* is essentially the form of love that requires *cooperative* relations between two things to promote what is good. In my opinion, *philia* love, if we are to use these terms at all, is the most important in dialogue with the natural sciences; *philia* is the love of co-laborment, so to speak. Oord's essential kenosis theology, as well as his recovery of the import of *philia* love, has potent application to picturing love as self-donation.

In *The Uncontrolling Love of God: An Open and Relational Account of Providence* (2015), Oord offers a culmination of nearly a decades' worth of work.[22] Indeed, one finds herein footprints of his *Relational Holiness: Responding to the Call of Love* (2005), undertones of his *Creation Made Free: Open Theology Engaging Science* (2009), traces of his *Defining Love: A Philosophical, Scientific, and Theological Engagement* (2010), and whispers of his *The Nature of Love: A Theology* (2010). In *The Uncontrolling Love of God*, we find the pinnacle of Oord's work thus far in an expanded notion of his "essential kenosis" theology.[23] His depiction of "essential kenosis" herein makes numerous asseverations that are constructive for depicting love as self-donation: first, God's uncontrolling love is preeminent, as it logically precedes any other divine attribute; second, existence teems with randomness interlaced with order; third, the most helpful definition of kenosis is "self-giving;"[24] fourth, God necessarily loves the "other;" and fifth, God's love is full-orbed—expressing *agape*, *philia*, and *eros*. Moreover, because God's nature is self-giving love, he cannot prevent genuine (read random) evil. All of these aspects of essential kenosis theology, I posit, have import to a modern depiction of love as self-donation. Moreover, it is my contention that all of these aspects are also relevant to a modern relation of theology and science.

Picturing Divine Action and Love as Kenotic Self-Donation

The kenotic theology set forth in this chapter maintains that the Spirit is completely shared and imparted *into* creation. The Spirit of God is "poured into" creation, *inspiriting* formless and chaotic matter, with "nothing" thereby becoming "something," that is, a system interlaced with order.

22. Oord, *The Uncontrolling Love of God*.
23. Ibid., 151.
24. Ibid., 159.

As a result of this *breath* of God imparted, after much groaning and even more time, nature eventually gives birth to life-bearing creatures billions of years later.[25] So then, the Spirit is the life-giving force that enables creation to strive toward becoming its fullness via the long and grueling process of evolution. As such, the complexification of matter has its ontological origin in and through the agency of the Spirit of God. Creation is thus a kenotic act of uncontrolling *self-offering*, which affirms a depiction of love as self-donation.

A pneumatological rereading of Gen 1 and 2 shows that creation is not a creation out of nothing, as a onetime event, but is instead a continuous creation, a transformative process of producing higher aggregate conditions from lower. There exists overwhelming evidence of a universe marked by development, which points to creation by kenosis. *Creatio continua* operates as an enabling condition for all that occurs thereafter. As Polkinghorne elsewhere writes, "Part of a notion of *creatio continua* must surely be that an evolving universe is one which is theologically understood as being allowed, within divine providence, 'to make itself.'"[26] Rather than bringing into being a ready-made world of unalterable character, the Godhead allows creation, kenotically empowered by the Spirit, to develop according to its own pace over the course of billions of years.

I do find, however, some valuable insights in *The Work of Love*. For example, Ian Barbour contends that the Spirit usually works by *persuasion*, that is, from within, in ways that inspire, renew, and empower.[27] Moreover, Arthur Peacocke asserts that the rules within the evolution game can only be regarded as a feature that has been endowed by God. The creating Spirit's intention and purpose is actualized through the operation of chance and random events. We see God in evolution, Peacocke asserts, for "the processes themselves, as unveiled by the biological sciences, are God-acting-as-Creator, God qua Creator . . . God gives existence . . . to a process that itself brings forth the new: thereby God is creating."[28] However, the activity of the Spirit within creation proceeds by no assured program, but is precarious instead.[29] In dialogue with Polkinghorne, I suggest that the endowment of both potentiality and regularity was instituted by, and relies upon, the

---

25. cf. Rolston III, "Kenosis and Nature," 58.
26. Polkinghorne, *Serious Talk*, 84.
27. Barbour, "God's Power," 9.
28. Peacocke, "The Cost of New Life," 23. Emphasis in the original.
29. Ibid., 21.

kenosis of the Spirit *into* creation. The Spirit, in this uncontrolling kenotic model, is seen as working *within* the seeming openness of nature, in conjunction with the unfolding of potentiality.

By creating in a kenotic manner, the Spirit both allows and invites the input of creatures in the activity of creation, and reacts according to that input. Thus, God has chosen to allow the other to act, and has chosen to invite creation into a *cooperative* relationship, which coalesces with Wojtyla's conception of love as self-donation. Indeed, the Spirit did not create in a manipulative, single act, but instead onset a process in which creation was allowed to develop over a large amount of time.[30]

Preliminary Conclusions

So then, whereas the Spirit is the *primary* cause of all things, the Spirit also works through *secondary* causes. This implies, therefore, that what may commonly be referred to as the natural processes, or even what may be termed random processes, are in reality the indirect acts of the Spirit through secondary causes. As such, distinctive, seemingly nondependent, actions are in fact Spirit-caused, though they may appear to be secondarily caused. The apparent secondary causation is due in large part to the fact that the Spirit is the agent of discovery within the various possibilities of God.[31] In this secondary capacity, the Spirit is the remote cause, while natural forces are proximate causes of events.

In this chapter, I have noted that there are two aspects essential to true love according to Wojtyla, namely the willingness to never make the other an object of use, and the affirmation of the essential value of the other. I have also presented the biblical basis of kenosis of the Spirit *into* creation, arguing that the bible presents the Spirit as being the active agent of God in the world, particularly regarding the Spirit as life-giver and animator of all creation. In my kenotic model, the uncontrolling Spirit is seen as working *within* the seeming openness of nature, in conjunction with the unfolding of potentiality, allowing and inviting the input of creatures in the activity of creation. Thus, God has chosen to allow the other to act, and has chosen to invite creation into a *cooperative* relationship, which coalesces with Wojtyla's conception of love as self-donation. I have contended that the kenosis

---

30. Instead of creating a *finished* product by divine fiat, the Spirit allows the world to *develop* within the framework the Godhead generated.

31. Dabney, "Naming the Spirit," 58.

of the Spirit *into* creation makes otherness possible and actualizes it, which amounts to betrothed love through self-donation.

I have also highlighted Oord's contentions that expand the idea of depicting love as self-donation. Indeed, his essential kenosis asserts that God's uncontrolling love is preeminent, that existence teems with randomness interlaced with order, that the most potent definition of kenosis is self-giving, that God necessarily loves the other, and that God's love is full-orbed—which I have dubbed full-Oorded—comprised of *agape*, *philia*, and *eros*. I have further interacted with John Polkinghorne's conception of kenosis that depicted creation as *The Work of Love*, both critiquing and building on his views. Finally, I have contended that the entire mission of the Spirit could be envisioned as kenosis through betrothed self-donated love.

Ultimately, the essence of both the person and personal love gives way to, or better yet, is transcended by, uncontrolling self-giving. In the final analysis, we are given the capacity of self-possession in order to be able to give ourselves away. Only in doing so can we achieve the highest form of love, and only in doing so can we truly be fulfilled. Thus, the essence of the self is to transcend the self through betrothed self-donated love.

Part Three

Teleology
&
Theology

6

Divine Action in an Evolutionary World
Toward a Teleological Model of Causality in the Theology & Science Dialogue

Divine Action in Nature

THE PROBLEM TO BE addressed in this chapter relates to the God-world relationship and portrayals of divine action that necessitate a causal joint between them. Succinctly, the problem is a God who acts within a world marked by evolution in which the discussion is dominated by efficient causality, thus disallowing *a priori* the actions of an immaterial deity. Causality has troubled philosophers at least since the time of Aristotle; the quest to clarify causality is due to its implications for other philosophical issues, as clarity regarding causation is intrinsically vital for clarity in the areas of metaphysics, epistemology, and the philosophy of science.[1]

Probably the most radical change in the meaning of "cause" occurred during the seventeenth century, in which there emerged a strong tendency to understand causal relations as instantiations of deterministic laws. In the seventeenth century, the topic of causation was prominent in large part because of the need to reconcile mechanistic physics with traditional beliefs regarding the relation between God and creation. During this early modern period many philosophers questioned the intelligibility of causal interactions and the notion of causation itself.[2] As a consequence of this

---

1. Brand, ed., *The Nature of Causation*, 1.
2. Loeb, *From Descartes to Hume*, 17.

debate, causes were no longer seen as the active initiators of a change, but as inactive nodes in a law-like implication chain. Natural philosophers, thus, attempted to explain causation in terms of matter and motion alone; causation and determinism became virtually equivalent.

At the beginning of the debate regarding causation in the seventeenth century, there were four types of causes: material, efficient, formal, and final. Also, at the beginning of the early modern debate, God was seen to be the total efficient cause of all things.[3] According to Clatterbaugh, three major transitions occur during the roughly seventy years, 1671–1739, of the early modern debate regarding the nature of causation. First, the notion of causation was simplified. Second, the notion of causation was secularized. Third, the concern of the causation debate was changed from the metaphysical problem of causation to the attempt to identify true causal connections.[4]

The discussion regarding causation culminates with the reduction of all causation to mere efficient causation, as apparent in Hume. The early modern philosophers almost wholesale discard talking about the Aristotelian four causes, and reduce what we can epistemically be aware of regarding causation to efficient causation only. Contemporary discussions of causation are invariably influenced by Hume's views on the subject, as the relationship between causes and effects is seen as a purely *external* affair. Another aspect of this influence is that all we can definitively know of causation is regular succession; the cause of an event, after Hume, is almost universally supposed to be some condition or set of conditions that temporally precedes some other in time.

The contemporary crisis concerning the reality of God's action in the world is largely due to a particular view of science inherited, largely, from the Humean and Enlightenment periods (this view is sometimes called scientism), and not science per se. T. A. Smedes's recent book analyzes the problem concerning talk about God's action in the world today; he argues that scientism's view of divine action is narrow, and its criticisms are aimed only at interventionist models of divine action.[5] It is this scientism that challenges the notion that God acts within the causal nexus of the world. According to the scientistic interpretation, the universality of laws implies the impossibility of a divine being acting within the universe from "outside"

---

3. Clatterbaugh, *The Causation Debate in Modern Philosophy 1671–1739*, 15.
4. Ibid., 4.
5. Smedes, *Chaos, Complexity, and God*, 1.

Divine Action in an Evolutionary World

without breaking or temporarily suspending the laws of regularity.[6] Thus, there is a logical argument employed by scientism to dispute the possibility of divine action within the physical world.

Incompatibilist Views of Divine Action

Incompatibilist views of divine action presuppose that, "acts of God make sense only if there are realms of physics where the behavior of bodies is not determined by physical law: then and only then is there room for objective acts of God . . . Attributions of an event to an act of God and to deterministic explanation by physical law are taken to be mutually exclusive."[7] The idea of providence is intimately connected to *creatio continua*, as the former flows from the later. According to Smedes, the notion of providence can be analyzed in the following three concepts: conservatio, concursus, and gubernatio.[8] He avers that causality applies only to the created order, and since God is transcendent in his immanence, he is not a part of the created order, so he is likewise then not limited by its causality.[9] Smedes recognizes three possible starting points from which to consider divine action. First, one could posit an interventionist view in which God works contrary to, or temporarily suspends, natural laws. Second, one could postulate that God acted singularly at one point in the past, setting in motion all that has happened thereafter. Third, one could view God as working in accordance to the laws of nature, continuously acting and interacting with the world in order to accomplish his aims and desires.[10]

Many scholars in the current theology-science dialogue view God as being continuously at work in a way consistent with the known laws of nature insomuch as the term "intervention" is refused with reference to speaking of divine acts.[11] While being noninterventionist in these models, God is nevertheless able to respond to events in the world *through* the laws of nature, using them in a way analogous to that in which other agents use tools.[12] The postulation of non-intervention is critical to the discussion of

---

6. Ibid., 15.
7. Porter, *By the Waters of Naturalism*, 4.
8. Smedes, *Chaos, Complexity, and God*, 21.
9. Ibid., 25.
10. Ibid., 27.
11. See, e.g., Polkinghorne, *Scientists as Theologians*, 41.
12. cf. Knight, "Theistic Naturalism," 533–42.

the God-world relation and theologies of divine action, as "The one who is faithful must show reliability in his relationship with his world. He will not be an arbitrary intervener in its processes but they will have about them a consistency which reflects his character."[13]

There are many, often competing and contrary, theories of the God-world relationship and divine action currently being posited within the theology and science interplay.[14] Some of the more notable include the guidance of the laws of nature through some sort of temporal causal joint (or perhaps a whole range of such joints), according to which the laws of nature may be manipulated by God for particular providential ends; candidates for such a joint range from the "unpredictabilities of physical process . . . [seen as] the sites of ontological openness,"[15] to the concept of "whole-part constraint"[16] both of which, among others, will be cursorily examined in what follows.

Let me begin, briefly, with the thoroughly naturalistic representation. The Dutch theologian and philosopher Willem B. Drees makes a lucid point in saying that, "naturalism cannot, and should not, categorically exclude the possibility of . . . a reversal of our ideas about the most fundamental structure and relative ordering of phenomena and disciplines."[17] Drees is

---

13. Polkinghorne, *Science and Creation*, 51.

14. The following description of the God-world relation and divine action draws heavily—with some substantial modification provided by Clayton (see Clayton, *God and Contemporary Science*, 167–231)—from Christopher Southgate, who offers a lucid classification of four views on divine action: 1) theistic naturalism, 2) general providential action without gaps in the causal order, 3) particular providential action without gaps in the causal order, and 4) particular providential action employing particular gaps in the causal order (Southgate, *God, Humanity, and the Cosmos*, 271–76). According to Clayton, Thomas F. Tracy allows for five types of divine agency, in addition to the initial creation. First, God could act directly in every event to sustain the existence of each entity that has a part in it, which Tracy refers to as *conservation*; second, God could act directly to determine various events which occur by chance on the finite level, which Tracy calls *quantum-level intervention*; third, God could act indirectly through causal chains that extend from God's initiating direct actions, referred to as *amplification of effects at quantum level* by Tracy; fourth, Tracy contends that God could act indirectly in and through the free acts of persons whose choices have been shaped by the rest of God's activity in the world, which he calls *persuasion*; and fifth, God could also act directly to bring about events that exceed the natural powers of creatures, i.e., the traditional notion of *miracle* (Clayton, *God and Contemporary Science*, 215).

15. Polkinghorne, *Scientists as Theologians*, 40.

16. Peacocke, "God's Interaction with the World," 263–87.

17. Drees, *Religion, Science, and Naturalism*, 258.

committed to the adequacy of naturalistic explanations, and is reluctant to speak of particular divine action.[18] He contends that the search for a causal joint in the God-world relationship neglects—even undermines—the self-sufficiency of nature, and thus should be avoided, also arguing that Polkinghorne's proposal for divine action through information input is inadequate, in part because it does the very thing that it purports not to do: intervene.[19]

Particular Divine Action Exploiting Inherent Gaps

Some theists employ a model of particular divine action that exploits inherent gaps within nature, with John C. Polkinghorne being a representative of the view based on chaotic systems, along with advocates of quantum-based theories of divine action.[20] In order to avoid what he thinks may lead to deistic connotations, Polkinghorne seeks to locate a causal joint mechanism in chaos theory, one in which it is possible to construe God's "creatorly action in a more personal mode."[21] In *Science and Providence: God's Interaction with the World*, Polkinghorne locates the *causal joint* of particular divine action and also suggests the *means* by which God might effect such action. The postulations upon which Polkinghorne bases his argument are that (chaotic) non-linear systems are highly sensitive to initial conditions, they are genuinely unpredictable, and therefore God can influence the chaotic systems by an input of active information, which does not entail energy input. Although the physical laws of nature are marked by regularities, God is free to work through the indeterminacies of chaos.

In particular, Polkinghorne avers that the epistemological limitations of chaos theory "signal that ontologically much of the physical world is open and integrated in character."[22] Thomas F. Tracy agrees, writing that the central "concern that is addressed by the idea of divine action [occurring] through natural indeterminacies, [is] namely, the concern to provide a means by which God can affect the course of events once history

18. Ibid., 12–21. See also: Görman, Drees, and Meisinger, eds. *Creative Creatures*; Meisinger, Drees, and Liana, eds. *Wisdom or Knowledge?*; and Drees, Meisinger, and Smedes, eds. *Creation's Diversity*.
19. Drees, *Religion, Science and Naturalism*, 96.
20. Smedes, *Chaos, Complexity, and God*, 33.
21. Polkinghorne, *Science and Christian Belief*, 78–79.
22. Polkinghorne, "The Metaphysics of Divine Action," 153.

Part Three: Teleology and Theology

is underway without disrupting the natural causal order."[23] Polkinghorne is persuaded that science does not belie the idea of God acting within the world, because the causal nexus of the world is not closed, but open and indeterministic instead. Polkinghorne chooses a middle-way concerning divine action between a single act of providence and interventionism, and posits that there is a continual interaction between God and the world.[24]

The most distinguished feature of chaotic systems is their sensitivity to initial conditions, which means that even the minutest changes are amplified, and thereafter can alter the trajectory of the entire system. Polkinghorne does not agree with the common conceptioning of chaotic systems in that he denies that they are thoroughly deterministic. Instead of determinism, Polkinghorne accedes to a version of critical realism, which is characterized by the colloquial saying that epistemology models ontology.[25] In Polkinghorne's model of chaotic systems, the unpredictability that is apparently inherent therein indicates that our world is open. In a later title, Polkinghorne affirms the "gap" offered by non-linear systems, writing:

> It is important to recognize that... the significance of the sensitivity of chaotic systems to the effects of small triggers is *diagnostic* of their requiring to be treated in holistic terms and of their being open to top-down causality through the input of active information. It is not proposed that this is the localized mechanism by which agency is exercised. I do not suppose that either we or God interact with the world by the carefully calculated adjustment of the infinitesimal details of initial conditions so as to bring about a desired result. The whole thrust of the proposal is expressed in terms of the complete holistic situation, not in terms of the clever manipulation of bits and pieces. It is, therefore, a proposal for realizing a true kind of top-down causality. It may fittingly be called *contextualism*, for it supposes the behavior of parts to be influenced by their overall context.[26]

In an essay from 1996, Polkinghorne adds that, "It seems entirely conceivable that God also interacts with the creation through the input of active information into its open physical process. We glimpse, in a rudimentary way, what might lie behind theology's language of God's 'guiding' and 'drawing

---

23. Tracy, "Divine Action and Quantum Theory," 894.
24. Polkinghorne, *Belief in God in an Age of Science*, 6.
25. Smedes, *Chaos, Complexity, and God*, 47.
26. Polkinghorne, "The Metaphysics of Divine Action," 154.

on' creation, language often associated with talk of the Spirit working immanently on the inside of creation."[27]

To summarize Polkinghorne regarding divine action, one may say that he argues that the infinite number of possible paths reflects the infinite number of possible initial conditions. He argues that no system is entirely isolated, as every change within the universe will eventually influence everything else therein. Chaotic systems should be interpreted as consisting of ontological openness. Thus, he argues that God's action should be conceived as acting upon the whole of the system, and not the parts of it, because "the behavior of parts . . . [is] influenced by their overall context."[28] Further, Polkinghorne asserts that the Spirit's active information has the ability and potential to alter the evolution of the universe as a whole in accordance with God's will. And as a result of the trickle-down effects inherent within top-down causal systems, even the most elementary levels of the cosmos can be influenced by his will.[29]

Models of divine action within chaos theory are riddled by problems, however, because chaos theory is seen to be intrinsically deterministic in current understandings. Amos Yong contends that Polkinghorne's attempt to turn chaos theory "from a deterministic to an indeterministic science is less than persuasive to DAP [Divine Action Project] researchers."[30] It should be noted, however, that the problems associated with interventionism are truly only problematic if in fact the causal nexus of the world is closed. Smedes stipulates that Polkinghorne takes science and the scientific worldview seriously, which means that interventionist divine action is unacceptable to Polkinghorne, as the natural order demands its own integrity; however, this does not mean that the order found therein is rigidly deterministic or closed.[31]

Peacocke is notably skeptical regarding claims that God works through the apparent "gap" that chaotic systems offer in reference to God's action, because it raises the question of whether or not God himself knows the outcome of situations/systems that are unpredictable to humans.[32] Peacocke also argues against divine action through chaotic systems because

---

27. Polkinghorne, "Chaos Theory and Divine Action," 248.
28. Polkinghorne, "The Metaphysics of Divine Action," 154.
29. Smedes, *Chaos, Complexity, and God*, 62–63.
30. Yong, "The Spirit at Work in the World," 126.
31. Smedes, *Chaos, Complexity, and God*, 44.
32. Peacocke, *Paths From Science Towards God*, 102.

it renders God an interventionist in nature, which he finds theologically and theoretically unacceptable. Peacocke contends that if he were to defend such chaotic intervention by God, that it "would then be no different in principle from that of God intervening in the order of nature, with all the problems that [position] evokes for a rationally coherent belief in God as the Creator of that order."[33] Peacocke's argument against chaotic systems being the mode of divine action is clear in the following passage:

> Since God can only know what it is logically possible to know ("omniscience") and that is confined to the probabilities of the outcome of any measurement, God cannot, logically, know definitively the precise outcome of any particular measurement. Furthermore, if God were to alter one such event in a particular way, then, for the overall probabilistic relationships that govern the quantum events to be obeyed, many others—absurdly many—would also have to be changed. Only thus would we, the observers, detect no distortion of the overall statistics, as the hypothesis assumes. So this is certainly no neat, tidy way to solve the problem and one wonders where the chain of necessary alteration would end.[34]

Micro-level Particular Divine Action

Other scholars have moved away from macro-level particular divine action toward divine action on micro-levels that exploits inherent gaps within nature and instead. Proponents of this position include Robert John Russell, who in a relatively recent contribution entitled *Cosmology: From Alpha to Omega*,[35] spends several chapters covering divine action in nature. Therein, Russell argues for quantum level divine action, and posits that a quantum-based model of divine action would not disrupt any laws of nature, since quantum theory states that quantum events are intrinsically indeterminate; thus, Russell sees quantum divine action to be non-interventionist.

Russell favors quantum-based divine action over and above competing theories that may entail God to work in chaotic systems, or in a top-down manner, as with the metaphorical picture of the world as the body of God. There is near universal agreement that quantum events are genuinely non-deterministic. Notably, for those of this persuasion, Wildman classifies

---

33. Ibid., 103.
34. Ibid., 106.
35. Russell, *Cosmology*, 110–225.

three possibilities for quantum divine action, grounded in the indeterminism of quantum events:

1. God could initiate measurement events;
2. God could adjust probabilities to make an outcome state more likely; and
3. God could select an outcome state.[36]

Wesley J. Wildman later notes that the third option is seemingly the most coherent, which would seemingly comport well with the notion eschatological (i.e., teleological) causation.[37] In opposition to the notion that God could adjust the probabilities to make outcomes more likely, Wildman states that presumes a "strong-ontological interpretation of stochastic laws of quantum mechanics and thus is interventionist."[38]

In quantum divine action, however, it would not be enough merely to alter a state or two, and then leave the system "be," for then no significant change would ensue; God would have to alter and/or select several successive state-changes to enact a significant change within the quantum realm, which would necessitate continuous monitoring.[39] In principle, quantum divine action is impossible to detect, may not be amplifiable to the macroscopic level, may often be easily thwarted, is insufficient for many historical events, and does not alleviate theological problems. I agree with Sansbury, who argues that the theological problem of divine action remains, for even at its most promising, quantum mechanics offers insufficient resolution. He notes that the "limitations of such minute systems reintroduce the same problems they are expected to solve . . . God's knowledge of the future is restricted to causally determined future events and probabilities of contingent future events."[40]

The causal joint in quantum-based proposals on divine action seems to outline a promising proposal as to how God might act in the world science describes; however, both Peacocke and Polkinghorne reject quantum indeterminacy as a candidate for the causal joint.[41] Among Peacocke's

36. Wildman, "The Divine Action Project, 1988–2003," 31–75.
37. Ibid., 60.
38. Ibid., 56.
39. Ward, *Divine Action*, 121.
40. Sansbury, "The False Promise of Quantum Mechanics," 112; that is, the effects of quantum fluctuations tend to cancel out.
41. Southgate, *God, Humanity, and the Cosmos*, 275.

several objections to quantum-based divine action are that God could not logically have the knowledge to determine the precise result of a quantum event, and if God were to alter such an event, God would have to alter a great number of others simply in order to hide divine activity behind the observed statistics; moreover, he is convinced that a quantum-based view of God continually determining the outcome of processes is at variance with the emphasis in the scientist-theologians have historically placed on the notion that God has created processes which *themselves* can give rise to novelty, diversity and complexity in the natural environment.[42] Polkinghorne disputes the micromanaging that is required by the divine agent in reference to quantum systems being the method of divine action, commenting that, "if quantum theory does have a role to play in solving the problem of agency, it will only be because its effects are amplified in some way to produce an openness at the level of classical physics."[43] This is one reason why Polkinghorne favors chaos theory over quantum theory in reference to the methodology of God's action in the world.

Particular Providential Action *without* Gaps

Still other theists allow for particular providential action *without* gaps in the causal order; in different ways this is proposed by Neo-Thomists, world-as-body-of-God theologians, and Arthur R. Peacocke.[44] Largely, Neo-Thomists speak of "double agency," a concept originally developed by Aquinas, having been revived and furthered by contemporary theologian Austin Farrer.[45] In this double-agency model, God is the primary cause of all that is; however, in effecting the divine purposes God works through secondary causes (e.g. the laws of the universe and the activities of human agents). Nevertheless, God can—and does!—work through these secondary causes to bring about *particular* results. However, double agency has been much criticized. For example, Tanner contends that double agency both profits from the strengths of that system and suffers from its weaknesses, with the largest weakness concerning the relation of God and time; if God brought the entire time-space continuum about in a "moment,"

---

42. Peacocke, "Biological Evolution," 357–76.
43. Smedes, *Chaos, Complexity, and God*, 47.
44. Southgate, *God, Humanity, and the Cosmos*, 271.
45. Farrer, *A Science of God?*

great difficulty results with regard to describing freedom.[46] Moreover, for the neo-Thomist, we cannot know anything definitive regarding causality because divine causation differs from any other kind, and we cannot expect to be able to characterize it in human terms.[47]

The use of the image of the world-as-the-body-of-God is heavily dependent on the analogy of human action, with particular reference to mental causation.[48] But immediately it runs into problems. For example, in the case of human action, mental intentions are grounded in the *physical*; the mind is not an autonomous entity existing independently of the central nervous system. Further, Polkinghorne points out that this analogy could render God unable to act autonomously of the world, as God could be dependent on the inputs from God's body; this model—in its logical extension, then—causes substantial theological problems.[49]

Peacocke uses world-as-the-body-of-God analogy, but with caution—"in a human body, the 'I' does not transcend the body ontologically in the way that God transcends the world."[50] He is also very cautious about explicating the causal joint, explaining that such a concept does not do "justice to the many levels in which causality operates in [the] world."[51] He does not find any theologically-relevant gaps in the causal order, and is reluctant to contemplate divine intervention in the natural order;[52] as such, Peacocke follows Kaufman and Wiles in postulating that God's action is on the-world-as-a-whole, but also offers a metaphor for divine action in terms of the way in which the properties of a whole system affect the behavior of individual parts; the nature of the whole, then, exerts constraints on the behavior of the parts. Peacocke originally called this "top-down causation" but now prefers to call it "whole-part influence."[53] The material world, in this model, has God as its boundary.[54]

---

46. Tanner, *God and Creation in Christian Theology*, 90–98. cf. Southgate, *God, Humanity, and the Cosmos*, 271.

47. See Stoeger, SJ, "Describing God's Action in the World," 239–61.

48. McFague, *The Body of God*, 41–42. cf. Southgate, *God, Humanity, and the Cosmos*, 272. Also see Murphy, "Introduction," xii–xv.

49. Polkinghorne, *Science and Providence*, 18–21.

50. Peacocke, "God's Interaction with the World," 285.

51. Ibid., 282.

52. Peacocke, *Theology for a Scientific Age*, 183.

53. Peacocke, "The Sound of Sheer Silence," 221.

54. Southgate, *God, Humanity, and the Cosmos*, 272.

Part Three: Teleology and Theology

Whereas Polkinghorne employs chaos theory as the means of divine action, Peacocke posits that complexity and self-organization fill that role. Particles of matter have the tendency, as self-organizing systems have shown, to organize into systems that cannot be explained by reference to its component parts.[55] The Creator, as Peacocke has written, unfolds "the potentialities of the universe . . . by a process in which the creative possibilities inherent, by his own creative intention, within the fundamental entities of that universe and their interrelations, become actualized within a temporal development shaped and determined by those self-same inherent potentialities."[56] He asserts that theology cannot ignore science, but "must have intellectual integrity and take into account the realities unveiled by twentieth century science."[57] Instead of ignoring science, theology should seek consonance with science.[58] God cannot know the indefinite future. This does not mean that future possibilities are not known by God, or even future probabilities. However, even granted that God may know future possibilities and probabilities, this would not allow him to intervene within the causal nexus of the universe, according to Peacocke, because that would be akin to God being a "semi-magical arbitrary Great Fixer," which is theologically unacceptable.[59]

A case could be made, then, that Peacocke's God is the entire environmentment of the cosmos. In his model, God's interaction with the world is by means of the input of active information; God is radically and totally immanent in the world, as well as transcendent (i.e., panentheistic).[60] As Drees points out, speaking of God and nature in this way is only a metaphor, but it is a strong metaphor.[61] Thomas Tracy criticizes Peacocke for stretching this panentheistic analogy too far, pointing out that the examples of "top-down" causation of which we aware are all analyzable in strictly "bottom-up" terms.[62]

Polkinghorne and Peacocke, though both Anglicans, operate within different scientific traditions, and thus reflect two different theological

---

55. Smedes, *Chaos, Complexity, and God*, 42.
56. Peacocke, *Creation and the World of Science*, 106.
57. Peacocke, *Paths From Science Towards God*, 9.
58. Peacocke, *Theology For a Scientific Age*, 21.
59. Peacocke, *Paths From Science Towards God*, 57.
60. Peacocke, *Creation and the World of Science*, 148–49.
61. Drees, "Gaps for God?," 236.
62. Tracy, "Particular Providence and the God of the Gaps," 307.

trajectories. Polkinghorne is a physicist, and theologically conservative, being influenced greatly by Jürgen Moltmann. Peacocke is a biologist, and theologically liberal, influenced greatly by Geoffrey Lampe.[63] This difference can be best seen in their approaches to *panentheism*: Polkinghorne is suspicious of the concept, his theology stressing divine transcendence; panentheism *will be* the condition of the creation at its culmination at the eschaton.[64] In contrast, Peacocke stresses divine immanence; the creativity of the world, elaborated by biology, is a sign of divine omnipresence. However, it should be noted that both contend that God has no definitive knowledge of future events, and both also allow for particular divine action.

Peacocke's views of law and chance coalesce, however, with Polkinghorne views of order and disorder within chaotic systems. Peacocke writes,

> This givenness [i.e., the interchange of chance and necessity that results in self-organizing systems], for a theist, must be regarded as one of the God-endowed features of the world. The way in which what we call 'chance' operates within this given framework to produce new entities, structures and processes, can then properly be seen as an eliciting of the potentialities that the physical cosmos possessed from the beginning. Such potentialities a theist must regard as written into creation by the Creator's purpose and as gradually being actualized by the operation of chance stimulating their coming into existence. One might say that the potential of the 'being' of the world is made manifest in the 'becoming' that the operation of chance makes actual. God is the ultimate ground and source of both law and chance."[65]

For Peacocke, then, the world is not governed merely by either chance or necessity, but an interaction of the two instead. For Smedes, this is evidence of divine purpose governing the universe (or teleology).[66]

The largest difference in Peacocke and Polkinghorne regarding God's relation to created matter is Peacocke's open embrace of an explicit panentheism, whereas Polkinghorne rejects the panentheistic understanding of the relationship between God and creation (as ably represented by Clayton[67]). Peacocke writes that, "Panentheism is the belief that the Being of

---

63. Southgate, *God, Humanity, and the Cosmos*, 276.

64. Polkinghorne, *Science and the Trinity*, 166.

65. Peacocke, *Paths From Science Towards God*, 77. It seems that Peacocke here uses the term "theist" in reference to what is more often called "panentheist."

66. Smedes, *Chaos, Complexity, and God*, 113.

67. See, e.g., Clayton, "On the Value of the Panentheistic Analogy," 699–704.

Part Three: Teleology and Theology

God includes and penetrates all-that-is, so that every part of it exists in God and (as against pantheism) that God's being is more than it and is not exhausted by it . . . God is the immanent creator creating in and through the processes of the natural order . . . [insomuch as] God can influence the world in its totality, as a System-of-system."[68] This last statement—that God can influence the totality of the world—is an invocation of top-down causality, or in Peacocke's terminology, whole-part influence.

For Peacocke, this top-down causation is not interventionistic because God does not set aside the natural order, but uses the causal nexus located therein in order to realize his purposes. Peacocke notes that, "this maintaining and supporting interaction is a continuing one as well as an initial one, and can be general or particular in its effects."[69] Peacocke also claims that the top-down causal model depicts God as "continuously interacting . . . with the world-as-a-whole but without infringing and of its natural relationships, so that no 'interventions', in the sense of rupturing previously observed regular relationships, occur to our observation."[70] Additionally, the freedom of God to affect the world, according to Peacocke, is retained—even furthered—in his model of top-down causation. In fact, Peacocke makes the assertion that some events "would not otherwise have happened had God not so specifically intended."[71] He does not see God's action as a Humean-type miracle, and thus not an overriding of a law of nature. Instead, Peacocke views God as *using* the laws of nature to actualize his intentions. I submit this view is consequential to the posit of the uncontrolling love and kenosis of God.

Peacocke desires a model of divine action that does justice to the rationality of our world, to human freedom, and to freedom of God to do intentional, particular actions.[72] He suggests that God should be regarded "as continuously creating, as the eternal Creator, for God continues to give existence to processes that are inherently creative and producing new forms."[73] In an important note regarding potentialities, Peacocke writes, "The Creator unfolds the created potentialities of the universe through a process in which its possibilities and propensities become actualized

---

68. Peacocke, *Paths From Science Towards God*, 57.
69. Peacocke, "God's Interaction with the World," 287.
70. Peacocke, *Theology For a Scientific Age*, 164.
71. Peacocke, *Paths From Science Towards God*, 110.
72. Smedes, *Chaos, Complexity, and God*, 131.
73. Peacocke, *Paths From Science Towards God*, 67.

... The processes are not themselves God, but the action of God as Creator. God gives existence in divinely created time to a process that itself brings forth the new—thereby God is creating. This means we do not have to look for any extra supposed gaps in which, or mechanisms whereby, God might be supposed to be acting as Creator in the living world."[74] As a result of this assertion, one may discern that Peacocke sees the increasing complexity of the universe since the Big Bang entirely naturalistically in proximate terms. Indeed, "chance operat[es] within a lawlike framework [as] the basis of the inherent creativity of the natural order, its ability to generate new forms, patterns and organizations of matter and energy."[75] In this conceptioning, "God creates *through* what we call 'chance'" operating within the natural order, each stage of which builds upon the former,[76] with God exploring the inherent potentialities *within* the cosmos.[77] Again, I posit that Peacocke's view is consonant with the uncontrolling love of God.

Theologically speaking, as Smedes notes, this means that the eschaton in Peacocke's theology is possibly open to numerous potential outcomes that are congruous to God's intentions, or even to some that might be contrary to his intentions.[78] Nicholas Saunders, in a recent book, claims that Peacocke's position of divine action appears more promising than does Polkinghorne's position of divine action.[79] Smedes disagrees, and says that, "if Peacocke's model is the most viable today, Christian theology is in dire straits."[80] As a consequence of Peacocke's theology, heavily kenotic in character, the eschaton is not predetermined, in contrast to classical theology and some advocates of modern theology. And although the trustworthiness of God is "a generator and basis for hope," Peacocke cannot give a guarantee that God will eventually realize his intentions at the eschaton.[81] Peacocke notes that eschatology is underdetermined by the facts of the Christian religion, writing, "All speculation on detailed scenarios of this consummation,

---

74. Ibid., 136f.

75. Peacocke, *Theology For a Scientific Age*, 65.

76. Ibid., 119. Also see Peacocke, *Paths From Science Towards God*, 77.

77. Note that Peacocke regularly describes himself as a "theistic naturalist" (see, e.g., Peacocke, *All That Is*, 11.

78. Smedes, *Chaos, Complexity, and God*, 131. (Peacocke, *Paths From Science Towards God*, 48).

79. Saunders, *Divine Action & Modern Science*, 213.

80. Smedes, *Chaos, Complexity, and God*, 171.

81. Peacocke, *Creation and the World of Science*, 351.

the theological exercise called 'eschatology,' surely constitutes a supreme example of attempting to formulate a theory underdetermined of the facts. As such, it seems to me a fruitless and unnecessary exercise—for the source of Christian hope rests only on the steadfastness and faithfulness of the God who is revealed as Love."[82] I submit that Peacocke's insights above are highly applicable to a modern relation of theology and science assisted by both emergence and kenosis, understood from an uncontrolling love perspective.

General Providential Action *without* Particular Gaps

Nevertheless, there are some theists who advocate general providential action *without* particular gaps in the causal order that reject particular divine action. For example, Gordon Kaufman rejects particular divine action, and contends instead that God's interaction is to-the-world-as-a-whole, sustaining the cosmos from moment to moment. There is no particular causal joint, only the overall creator-creature relation.[83] According to Maurice Wiles, arguing in a manner similar to Kaufman, God's final choice cannot be deterred, but the precise form of the fulfillment of things will be contingent upon the response of the natural world as well as by the creativity of the Godhead; he suggests the analogy of the improvised drama in which God sets the plot-outline, but then leave the "actors" free to improvise their parts within the epic.[84] Again similar to Kaufman, Wiles sees God's relation as to-the-world-as-a-whole. There is no particular causal joint, only the overall creator-creature relation. Thomas F. Tracy points out, this is essentially to subsume providence into creation, and this position pays a heavy theological price in so doing.[85]

Perhaps more so than Polkinghorne or Peacocke, Kaufman or Wiles, Keith Ward is hesitant to proclaim that the "where and how" of God's causation could ever be known by humans, for God's causality cannot be

---

82. Peacocke, *Theology For a Scientific Age*, 17.
83. Kaufman, *God the Problem*.
84. Wiles, *God's Action in the World*, 37–38.
85. Tracy, "Particular Providence and the God of the Gaps," 301–04. Tracy has also written numerous essays in the last decade that classify theories of divine action, all in the same manner, largely. See, e.g., Tracy, "Scientific Perspectives on Divine Action?," 196–201; Tracy, "Theologies of Divine Action," 596–611; and Tracy, "Evolutionary Theologies and Divine Action," 107–16.

reduced to or identified with some set of causal physical processes.[86] Ward points out five different types of divine action. First, there is an originative act; second, there are particular acts; third, there are acts in response to chances permutations of matter or to free choices of humans; fourth, there are acts of relation by God to persons; and fifth, there are acts of shaping redemptive good from destructive evil.[87] That God can do absolutely anything at any moment is an extreme that needs to be ruled out just as much as the extreme that God cannot act within the universe contingently at all. A commitment to the intelligibility of the universe allows one to posit the hiddenness of divine causation within specific points of physical processes that are laden with creative choices, all the while conforming to general regulative laws.[88]

God may indeed choose the outcome of some particular processes, but leave others to mere creative "chance." As Michael J. Langford has written, "it must be the case that there be several possibilities within the natural order at any one time . . . God's action is the steering along one of these possible routes."[89] So then, God can bring into natural world many creative possibilities that permit him acting "in a way that is analogous to the use of opportunities by the human artist."[90] Thus Peacocke concludes, perhaps "the creator [could] be imagined to unfold the potentialities of the universe which he himself has given it, selecting and shaping by his redemptive and providential action those that are to come to fruition."[91] Bishop Montefiore posits that, "the Holy Spirit is infused into the very elements of matter itself, enduing them with this tendency which is consonant with the Divine plan."[92] If the universe is part of God, Ward is careful to assert, he is a "directing power" within it.[93]

---

86. Ward, *Divine Action*, 72.
87. Ibid., 111.
88. Ibid., 112.
89. Langford, *Providence*, 87. Langford indicates herein three methods of divine action: the creative activity of God, the sustaining activity of God and God's action as final cause; they are listed in order of increasing involvement of God in the created order.
90. Langford, *Providence*, 90.
91. Peacocke, *God and the New Biology*, 97.
92. Montefiore, *The Probability of God*, 138.
93. Ward, *Divine Action*, 117.

PART THREE: TELEOLOGY AND THEOLOGY

Preliminary Conclusions

Even in view of the difficulties—covered heretofore—regarding both God's relation to and action within the natural world, Christian theology is, nevertheless, committed to the view that there is a God who acts in history.[94] But the scientific worldview seems to leave no place for a God who acts; there are, bluntly, no God-shaped gaps within the world, as science seems to continually close them. We Christian thinkers of today are in a potential quandary, then, as we do not seemingly like the idea of a God acting frequently (thereby disrupting regularity), or a God who acts infrequently (thereby being dispassionate). After all, according to William Alston, the Christian God is, preeminently, a God who acts.[95]

In view of the deficits in notions of the God-world relation and divine action noted above, "It would now appear, at least at first blush, that either God acts as the Divine Architect, who created a finely tuned machine and left it to function in a perfect manner expressive of its Designer, *or* God becomes the Divine Repairman, whose imperfect building of the machine in the first place requires him, like an inept refrigerator repairman, to return from time to time to fix up errors he made the first time around."[96] However, things are not that simple. The clear goal in the current debate, nevertheless, is to avoid an interventionist approach.[97] Although Clayton acknowledges that, "it would be metaphysical prejudice to rule out any chance of direct divine action in the natural world," he adds that, "the evidence is on the side of regularity."[98] Crain seemingly agrees, writing that, "both the divine presence in the world and divine action in the world are nonintrusive, noninvasive, and noninterventive."[99]

This is where a Peircean-influenced "evolutionary developmental teleology" will come into play, whereby the *telos* of evolution is seen to be, broadly, increased complexity, a position which was formerly explicated in chapter 2, and to be elaborated upon in chapter 8. Analogically and correlatively, I propose a Pneumatico-teleological notion of uncontrolling kenotic divine action that empowers cosmological causes within the

---

94. Ibid., 1.
95. Alston, "Divine Action," 41–62.
96. Clayton, *God and Contemporary Science*, 190.
97. Sansbury, "The False Promise of Quantum Mechanics," 113.
98. Clayton, *God and Contemporary Science*, 191–92.
99. Crain, "God Embodied In, God Bodying Forth the World," 670.

general parameters of God's eschatological intentions. Indeed, contemporary theology should strive to understand how "God empowers the world from within" and how God is "continuously sustaining and energizing" from within.[100]

---

100. Ibid., 671; cf. Clayton, "Emergence From Physics to Theology," 685.

7

Aquinas, Teleology, and the Modern Evolutionary Synthesis[1]

THE TELEOLOGY OF THOMISM maintains that a substance—that is, a living organism—must possess a palatable function in order to subsist. In fact, Aquinas writes, "It is impossible for a substance to exist that has no operation."[2] In the modern synthetic theory of evolution, however, many overly naturalistic adherents posit that the concept of function is no longer apropos to speak of in science. Functions (read purposes), they contend, must be applied by an intentional agent, and the derivation of species by natural selection is not the result of an intentional agent. More strongly, evolution itself is not intentional. Furthermore, any discussion of agency or intention is inconsistent with the modern perspective of science.

The modern evolutionary synthesis (also known as the new synthesis, the modern synthesis, the evolutionary synthesis, or the neo-Darwinian synthesis) is a twentieth century integration of ideas in biology that offers an account of the evolution of species, the acceptance of which is still predominate. This synthesis, produced between 1936 and 1947, reflects the consensus garnered during that time frame about how evolution occurs.[3] In the middle of the nineteenth century, evolutionary ideas by Charles Darwin were first generated (he published his work in 1859). Concurrently, though relatively unknown except in closely-related circles, the monk Gregor Men-

---

1. A previous version of this essay appeared in *Man in Culture* 26 (2016) 375–95.
2. Aquinas, *Summa Contra Gentiles*, II.80.1618.
3. Mayr, *The Evolutionary Synthesis*, 13.

del laid down the principles of discreet genetics. These developments of Mendel were rediscovered in the early twentieth century by a broad audience, and between 1918 and 1932, it was shown that Mendelian genetics were consistent with natural selection and gradualistic evolution.

The modern evolutionary synthesis is still, to a large extent, the paradigm in modern evolutionary biology.[4] Is Thomistic teleology[5] inconsistent with the modern synthetic theory of evolution? This is the large meta-question that this chapter will investigate. Aristotelian philosophy will be employed in this investigation, since Aristotle is the father of teleology[6] and his philosophical system relies on the concept of function, yet he does not posit an intelligent agent explicitly.[7] Instead, he maintains that, "It is absurd to suppose that ends are not present [in nature] because we do not see an agent deliberating."[8] He furthermore maintains that species, or rather essences, are descriptive manifestations in nature. Aquinas is faithfully Aristotelian in his metaphysics; however, he is also a theist. Thus, one must discern if Aquinas's teleology requires—or necessitates—his God. If this is the case, one has to further discern whether an intentional agent is compatible with the modern synthetic theory of evolution. If the two are incompatible, it may require a revision of Thomistic philosophy. I aver that Thomistic teleology is dependent on an intentional agent, but his division of the disciplines[9] allows for the modern synthetic theory of evolution to be cogently adhered unto.

Aquinas Employs Aristotle's *Physics*

Contrary to views that Thomistic commentaries on Aristotle's *Physics* are literal, and that Aquinas should be thought of as merely expounding

---

4. Mayr, *What Evolution Is*, 270.

5. Teleology, for Aristotle, can be summed up as "'That for the sake of which' is a thing's purpose, its end, the goal at which it aims." cf. Owens, "The Teleology of Nature in Aristotle," 159–73.

6. Aristotle conceived of teleology in the following manner: "nature is among the causes which act for the sake of something." Cf. Aristotle, *Physics* 2.8, 198b10.

7. Aristotle does not see final causality, or teleology, as a kind of preexistent, quasi-efficient cause pulling things toward certain goals (O'Rourke, "Aristotle and the Metaphysics of Evolution," 35).

8 Aristotle, *Physics* 2.8, 199b27-9.

9. Aquinas, "On Natural Science, Mathematics, and Metaphysics," 7.

Aristotelian views,[10] I contend that his "philosophical commitments and interests—the very problems posed for him by philosophy—differ radically from those of Aristotle."[11] Aquinas adapted Aristotelian teleology by applying his distinct theological and philosophical flavors. Indeed, it is the position of Helen Lang that Aquinas inverts the teleological formula of Aristotle, in effect reversing its ends. In his *Physics*, Aristotle begins with a definition of nature; what follows therein is an argument for the "broadest subject of physics."[12] He ends with the unmoved mover in order to elucidate motion.[13] Arguments in regard to the unmoved mover are asserted so as to be an explanatory factor of nature. As such, nature is presented as the eventual subject of physics.[14] Aquinas reads Aristotle's arguments in a reverse manner, insomuch as where Aristotle delineates the purpose of the argument—nature—first, Aquinas advocates that the *Physics* reaches its pinnacle in God.[15] In doing this, Aquinas produces an inversion of the Aristotelian sequence, as Lang explains:

> For Aristotle, the books of the *Physics* do not progress toward an end; rather, the main thesis of each book is first; later books refer to what precedes because arguments become progressively narrower and more specialized. Physics is the science of things which are by nature; Aristotle intends within physics to establish his definition of nature, to develop the concepts required by it, and to solve objections which might be raised against it. But for Thomas, physics sets out from the most general effect in order to arrive at its most important cause. Thus, physics sets out from what Thomas calls mobile being... and culminates in the proof of an unmoved mover, called God.[16]

Aquinas reverses the intent of Aristotle's *Physics*, noting that it begins with the general and works toward the specific (as Lang says, "progressing toward an end"[17]) "in order to reach the first cause of motion in the

---

10. Gilson, *The Philosopher and Theology*, 210–11.
11. Lang, "Aristotelian Physics," 570.
12. Lang, *Aristotle's Physics and Its Medieval Varieties*, 163.
13 Lang "Aristotelian Physics," 574.
14. Ibid., 573.
15. Ibid., 576.
16. Ibid., 579.
17. Lang, *Aristotle's Physics and Its Medieval Varieties*, 165.

universe, the unmoved mover of *Physics* 8, whom Thomas identifies as God."[18] Aquinas depicts motion, the subject of physics, as created. Creation should be studied in regard to its first cause principally, which is God.[19] So then, the study of physics concludes in and with God; further, the center of physics is to "reach God within the bounds of natural philosophy."[20] As such, Aquinas's physics—and his teleology—are inseparable from God.

Among Medieval philosophers, there is no unanimity on whether God created the universe in stages over a linear period of time—that is, in succession—or all at once (but with some things, organic life specifically, being created "in potency").[21] Dun Scotus, for example, held to the view of "in potency." Indeed, he writes,

> Something is said to be in potency in two ways: in one way, because it is the end term of a power [*potentia*], or is that to which the power is directed, and this is said to be objectively in potency (as the Antichrist, or whiteness that is to be generated, is said in one way to be a being in potency). In the other way, something is said to be in potency as the subject of a potency, or as that in which the potency is. And in this way something is said to be in potency subjectively, because it is in potency to something but not yet perfected by it (as a surface that is to be made white).[22]

Aquinas believed that these two views—succession or in potency—could be reconciled with each other, and even accepted them both. His intellectual perspective in this matter serves as a model to follow for contemporary scholars' approach to the putative "war" between science and religion. We would do well to follow his lead.[23]

---

18. Ibid., 164.
19. Lang, "Aristotelian Physics," 581.
20. Ibid., 582.
21. Cross, "Dun Scotus and Divine Necessity," 130.
22. Dun Scotus, *Lect.* II, d. 12, q. un., n. 30, 191–192.
23. "A positive dialogue is necessary, not least because the way each subject answers its own questions must bear some fitting relationship to the answers offered by the other, if it is indeed the one world of reality that both are seeking to speak about. There will be no strict logical entailment between the two sets of answers, but there certainly needs to be a certain degree of consonance. How? and Why? are distinct questions, but the forms of their answering must fit compatibly together" (Polkinghorne, *Theology in the Context of Science*, 97–98).

PART THREE: TELEOLOGY AND THEOLOGY

Teleology: Existence and Operation

As mentioned earlier, Aquinas's teleology is essential to understanding his science. He writes, "no substance is deprived of its proper operation"[24] because of the order in nature. He says further, "Nothing is idle or pointless in nature"[25] because, as Pasnau notes, "nature wouldn't consign a substance to idle existence."[26] Nature, according to Aquinas's teleology, has no "reason to allow idle substances, extant but incapable of actually functioning."[27] Therefore, existing substances must have a function.[28]

Aquinas here is directly applying Aristotle's teleology. He states, "The Philosopher says in De caelo II (268a8) that every thing is for the sake of its operation; hence, if a thing remains, its operation remains. This is also what Damascene says, that no substance is idle."[29] Aquinas stipulates that this means "the operation of any thing serves at its end, being what is best in it [and that] nature will bring about the best possible result."[30] This seemingly means that if something cannot continue to operate, it cannot continue to exist—which appears contrary to the modern evolutionary synthesis, as things like organs and structures persist long after their function is exasperated, as long as they do not have an associated biological cost.

For Aquinas, extricating existence from life is absurd, because things do not simply exist—they exist as certain types of things, with particular types of operations. Indeed, "To live just is to exist in a certain way . . . to function in a certain way."[31] Consequently, if an entity or thing's operation cannot be implemented, it cannot exist, because existence is not a property entities and things have in addition to their other characteristics and capacities. He writes, "For a thing to exist just is for it to act in one way or another;"[32] accordingly, ceasing to function means ceasing to exist for substances. And note that an organism is a substance, when substance is understood as something that subsists, as an underlying subject of acci-

---

24. Aquinas, *Quaestiones Quodlibetales*, 3.9.1c.
25. Aquinas, *Summa Theologiae of St. Thomas Aquinas*, 88.1 obj 4.
26. Pasnau, *Thomas Aquinas and Human Nature*, 370.
27. Ibid., 371.
28. Aquinas, *Summa Contra Gentiles*, II.97.1823.
29. IV *Sent* 50.1.1 sc I.
30. *QDV* 19.1c.
31. Pasnau, *Thomas Aquinas and Human Nature*, 370.
32. Ibid.

dents.³³ As the subject of accidents, substance is an indispensable notion to any theory of change, including that of the modern evolutionary synthesis.

Aquinas uses Aristotle's notion of hylomorphism, which means "matter" (*hylos*) and "form" (*morphos*)—terms that Aristotle borrowed from Plato and his parable of the cave in *The Republic*. Aristotle contended that no matter exists without corresponding to a form, and no form can exist without having a presence in matter. Thus, Aristotle taught that the body cannot persist without the soul, and the soul cannot persist without the body, which in effect means there is no afterlife. Aquinas was not as emphatic regarding form and matter's inseparability. As a Dominican priest, Aquinas held high regard for Scripture, which seems to indicate that a separation of soul and body is possible.³⁴ Nevertheless, Aquinas uses the concept of hylomorphism to explain change in general, which entails a potentiality to become an actuality.

While Aquinas's understanding of hylomorphism accounts for accidental change, the biological concept of evolution necessitates substantial change. In the event of accidental change, there is a basic substance that remains the same, allowing for the accidents to vary. It seems to me as if this method could be cogently applied to substantial change. For substances, there is no underlying thing which remains while allowing for change. A substance, therefore, may come into existence or cease to exist, but it cannot change, as per se, since it has no subject of the change. Living bodies have substance because of their substantial form. Substantial forms change in accident, but they cannot change their very essence, according to Aquinas. Indeed, "In a substantial change, the substance itself simply comes to be, or ceases to be."³⁵ Thus, there is no possibility for a form to change within Aquinas's hylomorphic system.

However, with Pasnau, it is my contention that hylomorphism provides the avenue for a Thomistic explanation of biological evolution.³⁶ "[A] thing's mode of operation follows its mode of existence," ³⁷ which indicates that a change in operation causes a change in mode, because "how a thing

---

33. Ibid., 48.

34. For example, Matthew 10:28 avers that the body and soul are not mutually dependent.

35. McInerny and O'Callaghan, "Saint Thomas Aquinas," http://plato.stanford.edu/archives/win2010/entries/aquinas.

36. Pasnau, *Thomas Aquinas and Human Nature*, 370.

37. Ibid., 373.

operates depends on how it exists."[38] Therefore, to have a different mode of existence is to undergo an alteration of what a thing is. When a biological organism, for example, morphs so much that it no longer has any consistency with its ancestral line, and has a profoundly different function of life as well, then a different species emerges.[39]

Aquinas's theory of universals, and how it navigates the notion of vagueness, is instructive for biological evolution. He accepts the Aristotelian definition of a universal, which indicates that a universal (that is, an essence or substantial form[40]) is something that is naturally appropriate to exist in many things and which is also predicated of many different things. Aquinas accepts that universals are dependent on mind, as they are made by intellect and therefore exist only in the intellect, but they also maintain a truth about the world by corresponding to what exists in the world.[41]

Teleology and Intention

Thomistic philosophy is fundamentally teleological, a view that some scholars of science and philosophy argue is incompatible with our understanding of the natural environment. Teleology, assumed to be intentional, is "purposive or goal-directed activity," which when applied to nature means that, "purposive activity is present and asks how the activity is to be identified and described."[42] Nature itself is—for the purposes of study—"mobile things."[43] Motion is a kind of change, and within the Aristotelian system of thought, explanation of change requires matter and form. These two components, matter and form, are "constituted by nature."[44] Aristotle notes, "And since 'nature' means two things, the matter and the form, of

---

38. Ibid., 372.

39. Note that I am here using the term "emerge" in a distinctly philosophical sense to refer to the biological concept of emergence theory, as delineated by Clayton, *Mind & Emergence*.

40. Cohen, "Aristotle's Metaphysics," http://plato.stanford.edu/archives/sum2012/entries/aristotle-metaphyics.

41. Pasnau and Shields, *The Philosophy of Aquinas*, 73–74.

42. Owens, "The Teleology of Nature in Aristotle," 159.

43. Ibid.

44. Ibid., 160.

which the latter is the end, and since all the rest is for the sake of the end, the form must be the cause in the sense of 'that for the sake of which.'"[45]

Within the hylomorphic system, form is the final cause, as it "in its structural role is the intelligible content of the thing, and in its primary or basic occurrence in the thing it serves as the focal point towards which all else is directed."[46] Aristotle uses the example of mind when recounting nature, because mind coordinates activity by means of intention. "For nature, like mind, always does whatever it does for the sake of something, which something is its end."[47] Nature acts hierarchically, leading, if you will, all individual organs within a body toward the whole of the body, and an individual human toward reproduction of another individual.[48] Aristotle stipulates that nature is akin to an intelligent entity, "Yet for him nature as such is not endowed with intelligence, nor is there any outside demiurge or world soul or creator to do the directing."[49] Francisco J. Ayala states that, "Final causes, for Aristotle, are principles of intelligibility."[50] Aristotle does not think that final causation requires justification, since it is a fundamental feature of the natural world.

Aristotle states that final causes are inherent in the natural order, but these do not require explanation by reference to some divine designer, as they are immanent within nature.[51] Aquinas disagrees with Aristotle, as he contends that final causes[52] do in fact require ultimate explanation, and he argues that the explanation for these final causes is a divine intellect. The evidence that Aquinas provides for this claim is cause-effect relationships. Thomistic teleology is straightforward, as "Every agent acts for an end: otherwise one thing would not follow more than another from the action of the agent, unless it were by chance."[53] By agent, Aquinas means anything that serves as an efficient cause, insomuch as that within the agent there is

---

45. Aristotle, *Physics* 2.8; 199a30-34; cf. Johnson, *Aristotle on Teleology*, 64.
46. Owens, "The Teleology of Nature in Aristotle," 161.
47. Aristotle, *De Anima* II, 4,415b16-20.
48. Owens, "The Teleology of Nature in Aristotle," 162.
49. Ibid., 170.
50. Ayala, "Teleological Explanations in Evolutionary Biology," 14.
51. Shields, *Aristotle*, 82.
52. The present-day crisis in divine action results from a shift in the notion of causation. In premechanistic science, that which was dominated by Aristotle, a component of final causation was included in every event, in addition to that of efficient, formal, and material causes (Clayton, *God and Contemporary Science*, 189).
53. *ST* I, Q 44, Art. 4.

Part Three: Teleology and Theology

some potentiality to cause a specific effect. Whenever cause-effect relationships are evident in nature, Aquinas posits a final cause as the producer of the effect. So then, Aquinas necessitates an explanation whereas Aristotle does not; indeed, Aquinas states that the effect produced by the cause needs to actually subsist in some way. This effect does not subsist in the natural world—it is simply pointed to by the cause—and it does not exist in the world of forms, so it must exist in an intellect, which could be seen to be as outside[54] of the natural world[55].

When Aquinas argues for the existence of God based on both the order of and purpose in nature, he points out that natural things have intrinsic intelligibility and directedness in behavior. We can understand nature because of its order. The reason that nature is cognizable, the reason we can trust our use of empirical evidence and the reason we can detect natural laws that explain the physical, is because of its internal purpose, which is present due to its source in God. God builds from within. Nature is cognizable by causes discoverable in it, and these causes necessitate divine agency. Indeed:

> The evidence for God's Creation of the natural universe is the known fact—a fact that we know on the basis of our scientific research—that natural things are intelligible. If they are intelligible, they are so as the products of nature—that is, they are intelligible in terms of their natural causes. If this is true of the totality of natural things, then there must be some ultimate source of this intelligibility—there must be some ultimate cause for the being of any and all natural things. This ultimate source for the being and intelligibility of nature cannot be yet another natural thing. It must be something outside of nature that has the power to produce the totality of nature and does not itself require a cause. Both the existence and intelligible order of the natural universe, therefore, show that it exists because of an ultimate cause: God the Creator.[56]

However, Aquinas also depicts that there are aspects of the world in general that are immaterial and necessitate non-physical explanations.

---

54. Feser, *Aquinas*, 112.

55. I cannot agree with this point made by Feser, since I adhere to a panentheistic metaphysic which pictures God as inherently immanent within the world; in the thought of Arthur Peacocke, God is seen, in the panentheistic vision, as working "in, with, and under natural processes."

56. Tkacz, "Out of Nothing at All," http://www.catholic.com/magazine/articles/aquinas-vs-intelligent-design.

Atheistic Evolution and the Problem of Teleology

It is sometimes stated that all things natural will ultimately be explained by physics. Indeed, various philosophers of science maintain that scientific forms of explanation are the "whole story," adequate to explain the entirety of human experience.[57] Thomas Nagel, akin to Aristotle, poses teleology without a divine agent. Instead, he avers there are things that cannot be explained physically. He does acknowledge that evolution occurs and that consciousness evolved from non-conscious life. Nagel contends that the area of the intentional cannot be accounted for by what he calls "scientific naturalism"[58] and others call "Darwinist materialism."

Nagel posits a natural teleology (one in which he explains is "a cosmic predisposition to the formation of life, consciousness, and the value that is inseparable from them"[59]) that offers a non-reductionist account of non-physical things such as consciousness and reason. This account avers that, "in addition to the laws governing the behavior of the elements in every circumstance, there are also principles of self-organization or of the development of the complexity over time that are not explained by those fundamental laws," which is a form of a variety emergence.[60] This natural teleology contains laws that describe "the development of an organization over time."[61] Teleological explanation is applicable to this world, and supplies principles that constrain "temporally extended development," and are "an irreducible part of the natural order."[62] In contrast, non-teleological accounts furnish explanations that are in terms "of how each state of the universe evolved from its immediate predecessor."[63]

Natural teleology explains the existence of life as not being a cosmic accident but rather "something to be expected, or at least not surprising ... [something] made likely by physical law."[64] It is a directed course toward an outcome. Nagel contends that this hypothesis is "congruent with atheism" but is also available for a theist. Nagel claims that, "a theist who believes

---

57. Reiss, *Not By Design*, 147.
58. Nagel, *Mind and Cosmos*, 68.
59. Ibid., 123.
60. Ibid., 59.
61. Ibid., 66.
62. Ibid., 93.
63. Ibid., 92.
64. Ibid., 89.

God is ultimately responsible for the appearance of conscious life could maintain that this happens as part of a natural order that is created by God, but that does not require further divine intervention."[65] In my opinion, this is what Aquinas also held. Indeed, Thomistic philosophy also makes claims regarding the limits of causal explanations. His teleological concept that, "nature does nothing in vain" explains this conception, and according to him, there are certain things which must be explained teleologically. One example is human consciousness, which is a quandary to naturalism as it is intentional. Can evolutionary processes explain what consciousness is? In review of the current state of the philosophy of science, the answer is no.

For Aquinas, "the inviolable unity of mind, brain, and body" is a foundational conception of intention.[66] Freeman maintains that intention is necessary to "fill the explanatory gap between electrophysiological data" and goal-directed behavior.[67] Thomas recognized this gap in his work on cognition, positing:

> the distinction between matter, which has unique and individual forms, here and now, that are not accessible to knowledge versus the intellect, which has classes of forms that are abstracted from matter, and that do not exist in matter. It is precisely the forms of material things that the intellect knows: it knows what each material being is, and each material thing is what it is because of its form.[68]

Although Aquinas recognized the necessity of accounting for the immaterial aspects of human life, he was able to reconcile the existence of randomness within the creation of his God.

Chance and Teleology

Physicalist philosophers of science argue that evolution cannot be described as teleological, contending this is true because of the random nature of evolution by natural selection. Moreover, some contend that the foundational concept of chance[69] within evolution is contrary to the notion

---

65. Ibid., 95.
66. Freeman, "Nonlinear Brain Dynamics," 207.
67. Ibid., 210.
68. Ibid., 213.
69. William Wallace describes chance as "an interference between, or an intersection of, two lines of natural causality not determined, by the nature of either, to interfere

of a divine plan. Random—read chance—events are responsible for genetic modification, which along with natural selection is the means by which evolution occurs, and it appears that randomness is incompatible with Thomistic philosophy. However, Aquinas accepts the presence of chance within his system, and considers it consistent with God's design. Indeed, Aquinas maintains that God intends the existence of chance within the natural environmentment, and that it provides the opportunity for variation. As such, the source of genetic mutation, which is derived by chance, is consistent with the idea of divine intention. Aquinas sees chance as an accidental cause (*causa per accidens*), not a proper cause (*causa per se*).[70] Chance is a real feature of the world, according to Aquinas. Indeed, he thinks that, "it would be contrary to the character of divine providence if nothing were to be fortuitous and a matter of chance in things."[71] Aquinas contends that chance at a lower level creates intention at a higher level.[72] Causation at one level "emerges" from chance at a lower one, as in the case of evolution, wherein chance at the molecular level of genetics causes variation in species.[73] This produces an ordered progression toward more complex organisms. The random element of chance mutation in this context is constrained by natural selection, which determines the derivation of those traits and drives evolutionary change. Natural selection can be said to "preserve what is useful and eliminate the harmful," and this provides for the natural teleology Aquinas and Nagel need.[74]

Division of the Disciplines

As discussed earlier, Aquinas recognizes that different disciplines are looking for different types of answers to questions about causes, and different disciplines have differing domains. Creation is within the domain of metaphysics and theology, whereas the natural world is within the domain of the natural sciences. Aquinas understands, for example, that theology, philosophy, and natural science will search for various causes and explanations. Science and philosophy, as well as theology have different aims: The

---

with one another" (Wallace, *Elements of Philosophy*, 47).
70. Dodds, *Unlocking Divine Action*, 38.
71. SCG III, 74, no. 2.
72. Peacocke, *Theology in an Age of Science*, 117.
73. Dodds, *Unlocking Divine Action*, 103.
74. Ibid., 83–4.

philosopher of nature considers creatures as natural beings, and aims to comprehend their causes and properties. The natural sciences, in contrast, seek to discover "real causes in the world."[75] The theologian attempts to understand creatures by means of the first principle and as aimed at the ultimate end of God. Despite all this diversity of domains, there is only one truth, and all disciplines relate to God, regardless their deviating subject matter.

Aquinas finds the apparent conflict between the natural world and the revealed word is due to uncertainty "regarding the nature of creation and natural change."[76] He would, seemingly, explain the controversy over teleology in evolution in terms of this confusion. That is, evolution is a kind of change, whereas God's creation is not a kind of change, because change has natural cause or passive potency of some kind. Although it is a cause, it is a cause of a different kind than change. Aquinas distinguishes here between causes that are existential and operational. That is, evolution is an operational cause for Homo *sapiens sapiens*, while God is their existential, final cause. Aquinas distinguishes between the existence of natural beings and their operations, insomuch as God causes natural beings to exist in such a way that they are the agents of their own operations. In the Thomistic account of creation, God does not work from "outside" of his creation to advance things in the way he proposes. Instead, as the order of everything is from God, this prevents him from having to "intervene" in nature to ensure things proceed according to his general plan.

God is a cause within nature, but not just *another* cause. Aquinas thinks of causes in regard to creation in two ways: The first is primary (divine), and the second is creaturely, but both are present at all times in creation.[77] God's causation, furthermore, does not reduce the explanatory power of science.[78] One might contend that ascribing a cause to nature correspondingly entails taking that cause from God's power. Doing this, however, is confusing the fact of creation with the "order or mode" of natural development within the world.[79] Science often makes claims with theological implications. Misunderstanding in regard to those implications is

---

75. *ST* 1.105.5 sol.

76. Tkacz, "Aquinas vs. Intelligent Design." http://www.catholic.com/magazine/articles/aquinas-vs-intelligent-design.

77. Goris, *Free Creatures of an Eternal God*, 304.

78. Aquinas, *Quaestiones Disputatae De Potentia Dei*.

79. *ST* I, Q85, A1.

often the result of the confusion between the types of causes. Science gives a natural explanation, while theology offers teleological explanations.[80]

In response to the tension between disciplines, Aquinas posits two creations: God is transcendent, on the ontological level, which is a different level than the contingent world. According to Aquinas, Godly creation is original and outside of time in a sense, and is the source of all causal connections. Earthly creation, in contrast, is continuous and in time. As there are multiple levels of causation, so there are various levels of creation. Different metaphysical levels of creation involve different metaphysical levels of causation. The first is the most basic, fundamental understanding of creation, which is accessible through reason, and in this regard, no faith is required. The second, which contains all of the first creation, plus revelation, includes ideas that seem unlikely in view of science, which can be known by faith only. An example Aquinas gives is of the temporal finiteness of the universe.

Preliminary Conclusions

Aquinas interprets Aristotelian naturalism to fit his theological worldview; he accounts for nature by means of natural explanation, and his concept of teleology—which links function to operation—contributes to the philosophical understanding of the natural world, including the modern evolutionary synthesis. He is able, for example, to account for randomness in the world without undermining his theology. However, he also posits that immaterial concepts, such as consciousness, exist and offers for them immaterial explanations. An adherent to Thomistic philosophy can indeed accept evolution, and even use Thomistic hylomorphism to explain the evolution of species; however, the ultimate order of existence depends entirely upon the final cause of the universe, which is God. Thomistic philosophy is strong enough to withstand the tension between modern science and theology, and provides philosophical accounts for scientific concepts. Its strengths are unparalleled in that regard.

---

80. Carroll, "Creation, Evolution, and Thomas Aquinas," 319–47.

8

Charles Sanders Peirce's Evolutionary Developmental Teleology

CHARLES SANDERS PEIRCE WAS a novel thinker, in terms of both originality and in application. One area of his originality was his evolutionary developmental teleology. Another area of originality is his novel conceptioning of evolutionary causation, which is founded upon his foundational and fundamental three categories of Firstness, Secondness, and Thirdness. In what follows, I will argue the notion of a "developmental teleology" is applicable to Peirce's idea of teleology in general. Seen as such, final causes evolve, and they are not static. This contention means that teleology emerged out of the increasing complexification of life on earth, and continues to be general, not specific in its derivation. Moreover, in Peirce's agapasm, as explicated in part two of this chapter, God gives himself away in act of love without any conditions as to the potential responses to that love, as well as to what responses may fulfill that love. Rather, it is merely a display of completely reckless, overflowing, and uncontrolling love. Seen as such, the many and varied manifestations of complexity that macroevolution has given rise to are to be seen as a fulfillment of the teleological goals of God.

Peirce's Evolutionary Developmental Teleology

Charles Sanders Peirce's evolutionary philosophy was not bounded by classical determinism, as he stressed its illogicality. He notes, "We must therefore suppose an element of absolute chance, sporting, spontaneity, originality, freedom, in nature."[1] In what follows, I will explicate three models of evolution as presented by Peirce. His threefold description of evolution, comprised of tychism, anancasm, and agapism provides a plausible account of evolution that is explainable by reference to teleology. Moreover, I will explain how Peirce, by virtue of his developmental teleology, brought a unique understanding of reality to philosophy. Furthermore, I will dialogue with Peirce, drawing from him a developmental teleological view, which will then be applied to a modern rendition of teleology that may be palatable for the evolutionary sciences. An "evolutionary developmental teleology," based upon the implicit arguments found within Peirce's seminal writings, will be proposed, whereby the telos of evolution is seen to be, broadly, increased complexity, a telos of which is ever growing.

Final causation, though being constantly neglected and forgotten since the onset of modernity, remains the hidden foundation of all causal explanations, and thus of mechanism itself. In order for this hidden foundation to come to light, we need first have a closer look at the inherent unity of four kinds of causes and the constant conjunction of efficient causation and final causation.[2] Peirce interprets the inter-dependence of efficient and final causation in this way:

> Final causation without efficient causation is helpless: mere calling for parts is what a Hotspur, or any man, may do; but they will not come without efficient causation. Efficient causation without final causation, however, is worse than helpless, by far; it is mere chaos; and chaos is not even so much as chaos, without final causation: it is blank nothing.[3]

At the same time, Peirce compares the relationship between efficient and final causation to that between the sheriff and the court. Final causation cannot be imagined without efficient causation just as "the court cannot be imagined without a sheriff." On the other hand, "an efficient cause, detached from a final cause in the form of law, would not even possess efficiency."[4] In an unpublished manuscript, Peirce fiercely criticizes the neglect of final causation in the modern era, stating "the non-recognition of final causation

---

1. Peirce, "One, Two, Three," 243.
2. More detailed and insightful discussion of the complementary relation between efficient and final cause can be found in Short, "Peirce's Concept of Final Causation," 376–79; and in Hulswit, "Teleology," 188–91.
3. Peirce, *The Essential Peirce*, 124.
4. Ibid., 121.

... has been and still is productive of more philosophical error and nonsense than any or every other source of error or nonsense. If there is any goddess of nonsense, this must be her haunt" (MS 478, ca. 1903).

Peirce's Three Cosmological Principles

For Peirce, there are three cosmological principles: tychism or chance,[5] agapism or love,[6] and synechism or continuity.[7] Peirce's objective idealism involves a developmental teleology (a position between nominalism and realism), a view wherein final causes are not future certainties, but present possibilities that may be attained in the future. Hence there is no fixed end of the world; rather, all things are marked by continual growth and change. Regarding his conception of evolution, Peirce writes, "Three modes of evolution have thus been brought before us: evolution by fortuitous variation, evolution by mechanical necessity, and evolution by creative love. We may term them tychastic evolution, or tychasm, anancastic evolution, or anancasm, and agapastic evolution, or agapasm."[8] The first kind of evolutionary theory discussed is represented by the Darwinian view, which views evolution proceeding "heedlessly" by discontinuities (or chance variations) appearing with no reason whatsoever.[9] Chance—for the tychistic-type of evolution—is not associated with any particular "direction."

The second type of evolution discussed within Peirce's essay entitled "Evolutionary Love," is anacasticism, which Peirce characterizes as deterministic. He writes, "diametrically opposed to evolution by chance are those theories which attribute all progress to an inward necessary principle, or other form of necessity."[10] The necessity herein referred to is mechanical in nature. This anacasticism is deterministic; indeed, whether internal or external, the necessity works so that evolution proceeds through a succession of events from which they cannot deviate. Nothing is due to chance.[11]

---

5. Peirce, *The Collected Papers of Charles Sanders Peirce*, eds. Hartshorne and Weiss, 6.102.
6. Ibid., 6.287.
7. Ibid., 6.173.
8. Ibid., 6.302.
9. Ibid., 6.287–97.
10. Ibid., 6.298.
11. Hausman, *Charles S. Peirce's Evolutionary* Philosophy, 174.

The third type of evolution written of in "Evolutionary Love" affirms the presence of a form of love that plays a role in development.[12] Agape—which Peirce calls the operative principle of "evolutionary love"—is inherently open to variations and deviations to the laws and agencies of laws. This third type of evolution—also known as agapasm—incorporates the other two types of evolution described within "Evolutionary Love." Agapasm is a form of evolution, then, that incorporates chance and necessity, but is not reducible to either, or merely the sum of the two together; it is a synthesis of these aspects with "something else," which I take as being a reference to, presumably, telos. For Peirce, developmental teleology prevails at all levels and all stages of evolution.[13]

Peirce's Perspective Upon Chance & Final Causality

Peirce contends that spontaneity will not be overcome by some final end or telos.[14] As such, Peirce notes that the universe will always contain some irregularity in it--in essence there will always be an expression of both freshness and brute fact in the universe. Indeed, for Peirce, there must be some "absolute chance" in the universe and "at any time . . . an element of pure chance survives and will remain until the world becomes an absolutely perfect, rational and symmetrical system, in which mind is at last crystallized in the infinitely distant future."[15] It is important to the point of this chapter that Peirce notes that this will occur in the infinitely remote future, not in the near future. For Peirce, "no final cause is actual; every final cause is a general type."[16] Like Aristotle, Peirce avers that final causes work with efficient causes;[17] he argues for more than that, however, as "final causes tend to create or find the efficient causes that are necessary for their realization."[18] Entities, whether animate or not, attempt to "actualize in their own way the same general type or possibility actualized in the fullest possible way in God . . . a general type is a final cause because of

---

12. Ibid.
13. Ibid., 16.
14. Ibid., 17.
15. Peirce, *Collected Papers*, 6.33.
16. Short, "Peirce's Concept of Final Causation," 369.
17. Peirce, *Collected Papers*, eds. Hartshorne and Weiss, 1.220.
18. Peirce, *Collected Papers*, eds. Hartshorne and Weiss, 2.149.

the goodness that would characterize any actualization of it."[19] In fact, in Darwinian evolution, "random variation & tautology cooperate to produce order . . . [and] if a final cause is a general type, then it might be actualized in any number of different ways."[20] In this view, then, no matter what chance variation produces, God can work it into his overall telos.

In agreement, working from a Peircean view, Hulswit defines final causes as "general types that tend to realize themselves by determining processes of mechanical causation. Final causes are not future events, but general (physical) possibilities which may be realized in the future."[21] Employing Peirce's category of tychism, Hulswit notes that chance is central to teleology, and thus teleology is creative, exhibiting an irreducible novelty;[22] this unpredictability and irreducibility "is the reason why final causes cannot specify exact results."[23] It is for the same reasons that end states can be reached in different ways. By denying that final causes are static, unchangeable events, Peirce avoided the problems attached to classical essentialism, which beset the Aristotelian perspective on teleology in the Enlightenment—wrongly or rightly—and thereby provides a way to reintroduce final causation in a scientifically respectable manner in today's environment.[24]

A Presentation of Peirce's View of Evolutionary Causation

This second part of the chapter will transition to focus upon Peirce's view upon evolutionary causation, and how it complements his view upon evolutionary, developmental teleology, and could, in fact, be seen as an application of his thoughts upon the former issue. Peirce contends that bodies indeed obey the laws of mechanics, but it may be that if our means of measurement were better, or if we were able to wait inconceivable ages, exceptions to any law may be found. In fact, it may be that chance, in the Aristotelian sense of there being the absence of a necessitating cause, has to be admitted as being relevant in our universe. The terms causation and causality are often used as synonyms. In *From Cause to Causation: A*

---

19. Short, "Peirce's Concept of Final Causation," 371.
20. Ibid., 372.
21. Hulswit, "Teleology," 188.
22. Hulswit, "Peirce's Teleological Approach to Natural Classes," 746.
23. Hulswit, "Teleology," 195.
24. Hulswit, "Peirce's Teleological Approach to Natural Classes," 766.

Peircean Perspective, however, Hulswit makes a distinction between *causation*—or the production of an effect by its cause(s), and *causality*—which is defined as the relationship between cause and effect. Although Peirce never explicitly made this distinction, he implicitly did so by criticizing the principle of causality, and by elaborating a constructive theory of causation. In Peirce's conception, there is a triple *interdependence* of final causation, efficient causation and chance.[25] It was to Peirce's merit to have stated the problem succinctly: "The great principle of causation which, we are told, it is absolutely impossible not to believe, has been one proposition at one period in history and an entirely disparate one [at] another and is still a third one for the modern physicist. The only thing about it which has stood ... is the *name* of it."[26]

This confusion is at least partly due to the complex evolution of the concept of cause. The modern concept of cause is the result of the interplay between the Aristotelian-Scholastic conception—according to which causes are *active initiators of a change*, and the modern scientific conception—according to which causes are the *inactive nodes in a law-like implication chain*. Although the Aristotelian-Scholastic conception of cause has remained an aspect of our common-sense idea of "cause," the modern scientific view is without question the most predominant in philosophical discourse. According to the latter view, causation means some sort of *law-like relation* between cause and effect, rather than the *production* of an effect by its cause. Peirce's conception of causation, however, is different, according to which each act of causation involves a *teleological*, an *efficient* and a *chance* component. Peirce's conception of an efficient cause in fact holds a middle way between the Aristotelian-Scholastic conception of cause and the modern scientific conception of cause.

Peirce's Highly Original View of Causation

In his 1902 paper "On Science and Natural Classes," Peirce developed an original view of causation according to which each act of it involves an efficient component, a final component, and a chance component.[27] The efficient aspect of causation is that each event is produced by a previous event (the efficient cause), whereas the teleological aspect is that each event

25. Hulswit, *From Cause to Causation*, 44–45.
26. Peirce, *Reasoning and the Logic of Things*, 197.
27. Peirce, *The Essential Peirce*, vol. 2, 115.

is part of a chain of events with a definite tendency. The chance component is that each event has some aspect that is determined neither by the efficient nor by the final cause.

According to Peirce, *final causes* are general types that tend to realize themselves by determining processes of efficient causation. Final causes are basically habits: they direct processes toward an end state. The habits of nature (which we refer to as the laws of nature) are final causes because they display tendencies toward an end state. Moreover, these habits are not static entities because they may evolve in the course of time. Peirce called the possible evolution of final causes "developmental teleology."[28] Thus, final causes are not future events, but general possibilities, for the end state of the process to which the act of causation belongs can be reached in different ways. It is therefore a mistake to contend that a *telos* is referent to a future state of affairs influencing the present state of affairs. In fact, Peirce says this much in writing:

> we must understand by final causation that mode of bringing facts about according to which a general description of result is made to come about, quite irrespective of any compulsion for it to come about in this or that particular way; although the means may be adapted to the end. The general result may be brought about at one time in one way, and at another time in another way. Final causation does not determine in what particular way it is to be brought about, but only that the result shall have a certain general character.[29]

The idea that *efficient causation* can only be understood within the context of final causation is central to Peirce's conception of causation. According to him, "efficient causation . . . is a compulsion determined by the particular condition of things, and is a compulsion acting to make that situation *begin* to change in a perfectly determinate way; and what the general character of the result may be in no way concerns the efficient causation."[30] The efficient cause functions as a *means* for the attainment of the end. Thus, "final causality cannot be imagined without efficient causality."[31]

Moreover, according to Peirce, every event is characterized not only by an aspect of final causation and an aspect of efficient causation, but also

---

28. Peirce, "The Law of Mind," 331.
29. Peirce, *Collected Papers*, 1.211.
30. Peirce, *Collected Papers*, 2.120.
31. Peirce, *Collected Papers*, 1.213.

by an aspect of objective *chance*. Each natural process involves an aspect of objective chance at every stage of the process, which *cannot* be reduced to efficient or final causation. Above, I explained that Peirce's conception of causation is characterized by a triple *interdependence* of final causation, efficient causation, and chance. Keeping in mind that we earlier distinguished two mutually incompatible conceptions of cause—the Aristotelian-Scholastic conception and the modern scientific conception—I conclude that Peirce's conception of causation forms an ingenious middle way between these two conceptions. On the one hand, Peircean causes are the active initiators of a change (rather than the inactive nodes in a law-like implication chain). On the other hand, however, the action of a *cause* is essentially a case of the operation of a law, and in fact directly implies a law.

An Explication of Peirce's Three Categories

This section begins by highlighting the three original, yet fundamental categories as outlined by Peirce. Peirce's entire system of thought, it could be said, rests upon his notion of three fundamental categories, which he called Firstness, Secondness, and Thirdness.[32] He derived these categories by two independent methods, one deductive and the other phenomenological. He summarized the categories as follows: "The First is that whose being is simply in itself, not referring to anything nor lying behind anything. The Second is that which is what it is by force of something to which it is second. The Third is that which is what it is owing to things between which it mediates and which it brings into relation to each other."[33]

Expanding on his category of Firstness, Peirce emphasized that because its nature is to be independent in origin from anything else, it can never be adequately grasped or described:

> The idea of the absolutely First must be entirely separated from all conception of or reference to anything else; for what involves a second is itself a second to that second. The First must therefore be present and immediate, so as not to be second to a representation. It must be fresh and new, for if old it is second to its former state. It must be initiative, original, spontaneous, and free; otherwise it is second to a determining cause. It is also something vivid and conscious; so only it avoids being the object of some sensation. It

32. Peirce, *The Essential Peirce*, 2.272–73.
33. Peirce, *The Essential* Peirce, 1.246.

> precedes all synthesis and all differentiation: it has no unity and no parts. It cannot be articulately thought: assert it, and it has already lost its characteristic of innocence; for assertion always implies a denial of something else. Stop to think of it, and it has flown![34]

So then, once we conceive of any phenomenon that manifests something of the nature of otherness, we meet the category of Secondness:

> The Second is precisely that which cannot be without the first. It meets us in such facts as Another, Relation, Compulsion, Effect, Dependence, Independence, Negation, Occurrence, Reality, Result. A thing cannot be other, negative, or independent, without a first to or of which it shall be other, negative, or independent ... We find secondness in occurrence, because an occurrence is something whose existence consists in our knocking up against it ... The idea of second must be reckoned an easy one to comprehend. That of first is so tender that you cannot touch it without spoiling it; but that of second is eminently hard and tangible. It is very familiar too; it is forced upon us daily: it is the main lesson of life.[35]

Finally, Thirdness is the category that introduces the possibility of mediation, which cannot arise from either Firstness or Secondness alone:

> First and Second, Agent and Patient, Yes and No, are categories which enable us roughly to describe the facts of experience, and they satisfy the mind for a very long time. But at last they are found inadequate, and the Third is the conception which is then called for. The Third is that which bridges over the chasm between absolute first and last, and brings them into relationship.[36]

Whereas the category of Firstness is characterized by an "airy-nothingness" and Secondness is characterized by the "Brute Actuality of things and facts," Thirdness "comprises everything whose being consists in active power to establish connections between different objects."[37] In this view, Thirdness is the source of meaning and intelligibility in the universe.[38] Peirce speculated that the order (Secondness) and intelligibility (Thirdness) of the universe evolved from a primordial condition of indeterminate chaos (Firstness):

---

34. Peirce, *The Essential Peirce*, 2.248.
35. Ibid., 1.248–49.
36. Ibid., 1.249.
37. Ibid., 2.435.
38. Corrington, *An Introduction to C. S. Peirce*, 135.

> In the beginning,—infinitely remote—there was a chaos of unpersonalised feeling, which being without connection or regularity would properly be without existence. This feeling, sporting here and there in pure arbitrariness, would have started the germ of a generalising tendency . . . Thus, the tendency to habit would be started; and from this with the other principles of evolution all the regularities of the universe would be evolved.[39]

Peirce developed his system of three categories into a highly original evolutionary cosmology. In fact, he proposed that there are three possible modes of evolutionary change, which parallels his three categories. The first mode of evolutionary change is "tychastic" evolution, which he regarded as the basic form of Darwin's theory. For example, he writes, "Natural selection, as conceived by Darwin, is a mode of evolution in which the only positive agent of change in the whole passage from moner to man is fortuitous variation."[40] Evolution by strict chance is a manifestation of Peirce's category of Firstness, because Firstness is the category in which a lack of determination by other events or entities is the chief characteristic. Peirce, ultimately, found Darwin's scheme—considered alone—as unsatisfactory.[41]

The second possible mode of evolution—"anancastic"—is that which is constrained completely by necessity, constraint, and determination by something other than itself. In contradistinction to this view, and in support of Peirce's own position, many current positions regarding macroevolutionary theory argue that the process of evolution reflects a balance of chance and necessity.[42] In Peircean terms, they argue for a balance between Firstness and Secondness. However, Peirce rejected the idea that such a balance—by itself—offers an adequate explanation of the world as we know it, proffering instead that a complete explanation of evolution requires the category of Thirdness beyond the categories of chance (Firstness) and necessity (Secondness).[43]

Peirce also regarded Thirdness as the category that gives to the universe "a vital freedom which is the breath of the spirit of love."[44] Therefore, he referred to this third mode of evolution as "agapistic" evolution, build-

---

39. Peirce, *The Essential Peirce*, 1.297.
40. Ibid., 1.358.
41. Ibid., 1.357.
42. cf. Bartholomew, *God of Chance*; see also Ward, *God, Chance, and Necessity*.
43. Peirce, *The Essential Peirce*, 1.331.
44. Ibid., 1.363.

ing upon the Greek term *agape*, which translates into English as "love." He commented, regarding this mode of evolution that, "Everybody can see that the statement of St. John [i.e., "God is love," 1 Jn 4:8] is the formula of an evolutionary philosophy, which teaches that growth only comes from love ... The philosophy we draw from John's gospel is that this is the way mind develops; and as for the cosmos, only so far as it yet is mind, and so has life, is it capable of further evolution."[45]

Peirce's Categories Interpreted Pneumatologically

I would like to suggest that pneumatology could add an important element to this depiction of Peirce's category of Thirdness. Indeed, the Spirit may be understood as manifesting the characteristics of Peircean Thirdness. According to a Christian re-reading of Gen 1:2, the Spirit (*ruach*), while sweeping over the formless void, brings order (Secondness) to the primordial chaos (Firstness). Furthermore, in the Old Testament the Spirit, again alike unto Thirdness, is described as the source of all life (e.g., Ps 104:29-30), with regard to both human (e.g., Gen 2:7) and nonhuman entities (e.g., Gen 6:17; Ps 104:25). In the New Testament, a shift occurs to the emphasis on the role of the Spirit as the source of *new* creation (e.g., Rom 8:11). Nevertheless, I contend that the Spirit, like Thirdness, brings the life-giving power of God to other entities.

In addition to the similarities between the Spirit and Thirdness as the source of life, there is a parallel in that the Spirit may be regarded as the source of openness to the future, which coheres with Peirce's notion that it is the category of Thirdness upon which freedom depends.[46] Yet another aspect of this parallel is that in Peirce's concept of *agapasticism*, openness to the future is closely connected with the nature of love. In historic trinitarian theology, there is an understanding of the Spirit in terms of love, notably in Augustine's infamous identification of the Spirit as the bond of love between the Father and Son.[47]

These minimal considerations demonstrate that there are significant parallels between the characteristics of the Spirit and those of Peirce's category of Thirdness. A further question is whether it is justifiable to claim that, like Thirdness, if the identifying characteristic of the Spirit is the

---

45. Ibid., 1.354.
46. Pannenberg, *Systematic Theology*, vol. 2, 97–98.
47. Augustine, *The Trinity*, 43.

function of mediation? Whereas neither scripture nor tradition has consistently made such an identification, I contend that such a connection is at least plausible. Some support can be found for an identification of the Spirit with the phenomenon of mediation, for example, in John's Gospel, wherein Jesus promises that the Father will give the disciples the Spirit as an "advocate" (cf. John 14:16), who will act as a mediator between Christ and the world. In pre-Christian Greek literature, the word *paraclete*, usually translated as "advocate," can also mean "mediator."[48]

The apostle Paul uses the language of mediation when he declares that God's love has been poured into our hearts through the Holy Spirit (cf. Rom 5:5) and that the Spirit "intercedes" for the saints (cf. Rom 8:26). Augustine suggested that, "the Holy Spirit is a kind of inexpressible communion or fellowship of Father and Son."[49] The idea that the primary characteristic of the Spirit is that of mediation is summed up well by Taylor and Wood when they call the Spirit "the Go-Between God."[50]

As I indicated above, the scriptural and traditional understanding of the Spirit has significant parallels with Peirce's category of Thirdness. I suggest further that the role of the Spirit in creation may therefore be regarded as that of mediating between God and the world, bringing into relationship that which would otherwise be separated. This coheres well with the scriptural witness, according to which God enters the world in the Incarnation through the mediation of the Spirit (see e.g., Matt 1:20) and the reconciliation of the world to God is regarded as a function of the Spirit (e.g., Rom 8:1-27). According to Karl Rahner, a symptom of the isolation of the doctrine of the Trinity from the rest of Christian theology, including the doctrine of creation, has been a recalcitrance to consider the possibility that the world may exhibit actual vestiges of the triune creator.[51] A model of the trinitarian creation informed by Peirce's categories and evolutionary philosophy offers a new way of developing this neglected theological concept.

Preliminary Conclusions

So what does this proceeding analysis of Peirce's thoughts upon evolutionary developmental teleology, in conjunction with a presentation of his

---

48. Bauer and Danker, *A Greek-English Lexicon of the New Testament*, 623.
49. Augustine, *The Trinity*, 12.
50. Taylor and Wood, *The Go-Between God*, 22.
51. Rahner, *The Trinity*, 13-14.

views upon evolutionary causation mean? I suggest several things in what follows. First, Peirce's teleology is "more than a mere purposive pursuit of a predetermined end; it is a developmental teleology."[52] Although Peirce used the term "developmental teleology" only in his discussion of the development of human personality, Hulswit points out that it is also "applicable to [his] idea of teleology in general: learning from the developmental aspect of our own human purposes, we can inductively infer that all final causes in nature are, at least in principle, subject to evolution."[53] Thus—as a second point—final causes evolve, and they are not static. The developmental teleology of Peirce is characterized by the continuity of the evolutionary process, and this principle of continuity is essential for his developmental teleology and his understanding of reality.[54]

Third, I maintain that a significantly revised conception of teleology must be developed, if it is to see a resurgence of widespread plausibility in today's somewhat scientifically literate populace. Moreover, I contend—fourthly—that the conception of teleology may need serious revision for it to even be maintained as a viable theological category. One contribution of Peirce's view is that it pictures teleology as evolving and it is to be seen as a general goal versus having a definite end-state or goal predetermined. In dialogue with Peirce, I argue—fifthly—that teleology emerged out of the increasing complexification of life on earth, and continues to be general, not specific. Teleology is grounded in the physical realm via the kenosis of the Spirit *into* the natural world, but cannot be reduced to it, as the Spirit operates within the natural world as its empowerment.

Furthermore, as a sixth point, in dialogue with Peirce's insistence on the absence of teleology in anancasm and the inclusion of it in agapasm, I conceive of teleology as at least partially self-determining. Self-determination is, in fact, fundamental to evolutionary developmental teleology and an uncontrolling kenotic love. In his agapasm, Peirce has a condition that is permissible of future growth, and this condition does not negate any tendency that may seem at odds with it. As such, seventh, the "directedness" of the condition, then, may be characterizable in terms of the God that gives of himself in act of love without any conditions of potential responses to that love, and what responses may fulfill that love; it is merely a display of

---

52. Peirce, *The Essential Peirce*, 1.331.

53. Hulswit, "Teleology," 197.

54. cf. Peirce, *The Collected Papers of Charles Sanders Peirce*, eds. Hartshorne and Weiss, 5.436.

completely reckless overflowing, uncontrolling love. This viewpoint comports well with a Wesleyan perspective on the uncontrolling love of God, as has been recently argued for by Thomas Jay Oord in various titles.[55] Seen as such, this leads to a Wesleyan view that stipulates that the many and varied manifestations of complexity that macroevolution has given rise to can be seen as a fulfillment of the teleological goals of God. What's more, causation is a multifaceted event, comprised of previous actions which are determined, future developments which are at least projaculately anticipated by a final (teleological) component, and current effects which are affected and perhaps even effected by chance events, which are comprised by Peirce in his view that each act of causation involves an upon efficient component, a final component, and a chance component.

---

55. See, e.g., Oord, *The Uncontrolling Love of God*. Also see the multi-author text entitled *Uncontrolling Love: Essays Exploring the Love of God, with Introductions by Thomas Jay Oord*, eds. Michaels et al. Note that I am one of about fifty contributors to this text.

9

Evolution, Emergence, and Final Causality
A Proposed Pneumatico-Theological Synthesis[1]

THERE IS AN UNPRECEDENTED challenge and opportunity for philosophy today: to mediate the ever-emerging dialogue between science and religion. Indeed, the times are ripe for genuine science-religion dialogue seeking possible complementarity between the findings of science with philosophical insights and religious experience, without succumbing to reductionist methodologies that compromise distinct realms of inquiry. Douglas Futuyma suggests that, "creation and evolution, between them, exhaust the possible explanations for the origin of living things. Organisms either appeared on the earth fully developed or they did not. If they did not, they must have developed from pre-existing species by some process of modification. If they did appear in a fully developed state, they must have been created by some omnipotent intelligence."[2] However, this chapter will suggest that a pneumatological (re-)interpretation of emergence, one that, "reads" the philosophical concept of emergence through theological lens, is *at least* plausible, and *possibly* fruitful for further research. Herein one will find a pneumatico-theological hypothesis that "reads" the evolutionary epic—and the long periods of stasis that it exhibits—in such a manner that is consistent with contemporary understandings of the philosophical construct of emergence theory.

---

1. A previous version of this essay appeared in *Wesleyan Theological Journal* 52 2 (2017) 148–64.

2. Futuyma, *Science on Trial*, 197.

Evolution, Emergence, and Final Causality

This chapter offers a new theological interpretation of the evolutionary advance, accepting and incorporating elements of a Neo-Darwinian understanding of macroevolution, while supplementing those with insights from the budding studies of emergence. Sudden "jumps" in complexity—everywhere present, yet rarely explained—may be the result of emergence working within God's *telos*, insomuch as emergence may be the means through which the Godhead actualizes the evolutionary advancement. Despite the insistence on gradualistic evolution by many contemporary biologists, I argue in this chapter—in part—that whereas the empirical evidence might not support a gradualistic view of (macro-)evolution, it may very well support a view of (macro-)evolution informed by a pneumatological "reading" of emergence.

This chapter contends, pointedly, that the Godhead creates and refines his "creation" in and through the process(es) of evolution; however, it also affirms that the evolutionary process is marked by long periods of stasis, followed by sudden increases in complexity—with these sudden appearances of complexity being attained in and through instances of emergence in an uncontrolling manner. Intimations of this chapter's position were alluded to over four decades ago; indeed, noted biologist Niles Eldredge agrees—in principle—with this concept, in saying, "Expectation colored perception to such an extent that the most obvious single fact about biological evolution—non-change—has seldom, if ever, been incorporated into anyone's scientific notions of how life actually evolves. If ever there was a myth, it is that evolution is a process of constant change."[3]

Again drawing on sources from the last forty years, it can be surmised that many evolutionists agree that the empirical evidence for evolution includes two features particularly *inconsistent* with the gradualism promoted by orthodox Darwinism: stasis and sudden appearance. Species appear in the physical world looking much the same as when they disappear, and a particular species appears at once and nearly fully formed.[4] This ubiquitous absence of intermediate forms is true not only for major morphologic transitions, but even for most species-level variations. Jacques Monod, a supporter of gradualistic, Neo-Darwinian evolution, posits that chance suddenly gave rise to the first organism—perhaps a bacterium, alga, or protozoan—which later evolved into complex invertebrates and plants,

---

3. Eldredge, *The Myths of Human Evolution*, 8.
4. Eldredge and Gould, "Punctuated Equilibria," 13–14.

followed by fish, amphibians, reptiles, birds and, finally, mammals.[5] However, the proof of such a gradualistic sequence requires at least one of two kinds of evidence: either an unbroken chain of transitional forms or surviving intermediates, neither of which has been produced heretofore.

One would think that in the one hundred and fifty years following Darwin, with thousands of trained biologists studying the problem while using complex lab equipment, someone would have filled these gaps within the gradualistic Darwinian paradigm. However, each phyletic group, generally speaking, suddenly appears within the geological strata as a unique individual, relatively unlinked by intermediates.[6] In order to arrive at the intended goal—which is to argue for the coherency of a triangulation between evolution, emergence, and final causality—this chapter will dialogue extensively with current proponents of emergence theory in the following sections, attempting to garner what such a position entails, and will then conclude by suggesting what may be the uniting factor between evolution and emergence: kenosis, understood theologically as a pouring of the Divine Spirit *into* primal matter, which provides emergence theory with explanatory power and thus expands its fecundity, particularly by opening up the *possibility* of final causality. Note that this chapter is intended to contribute, at least minimally, to the constructive interface between evolutionary theory and emergence. In the long-run, we need a robust theory of divine providence,[7] because we need a theological and metaphysical account regarding how divine agency is more effective than that of nature alone, and the place to reconcile providence and evolution is theology, not science. Moreover, it is up to theologians, not scientists, to show how this robust theological account is consistent with biological explanation.

A Short Explication of Emergence Theory

In *Mind & Emergence*, Clayton offers his own view regarding emergence theory, which radicalizes the immanence of God within the natural world.

---

5. Monod, *Chance and Necessity*, 110.
6. Denton, *Evolution*, 290.
7. Note that Karl W. Giberson and Donald A. Yerxa acknowledge that God's action in the world poses a challenge for the Christian scholar, because invocations of divine *providence* as an explanatory category are usually considered unacceptable (Giberson and Yerxa, "Providence and the Christian Scholar," 123). Thus, it would be wise to explore models of congruence in reference to divine action and naturalistic evolution.

Clayton's radicalization of immanence also comports well with this book's advocacy of kenosis of the Spirit into the natural environment, for in said notion, the Spirit is intimately present to nature, as its source and end (a point which will be argued for later in a latter part of this chapter). In a recent attempt to picture God as immanent within nature, Stuart A. Kauffman avers that the concept of God could be the "shared name for the true creativity in the natural universe."[8] Kauffman believes that thinking of God as the natural, awesome creativity in the universe could help not only the dialogue between science and religion, but also work toward the construction of a global ethic that would shape global civilization. He, it should be noted, does not believe in a transcendent God; rather, he thinks of God as the immanent principle of creativity within the cosmos. Kauffman discusses, rudimentarily, a new scientific worldview—beyond reductionism to emergence and radical creativity in the biosphere and human world. I find Kauffman's theory to be illuminative, for as Kauffman notes, this view pictures God not as transcendent, not as an agent, but as the very creativity in the universe itself.[9] Support for this conception of God's immanence in nature can also be found in Arthur Peacocke, who argues that God—being immanent within nature—could affect holistically the state of the world system because the ontological gap between the world and God is located everywhere in space and time.[10] Thus, God's activity cannot, in principle, be detected and labeled as such, for God is active within and *through* nature's natural operations.

In his popular introductory college biology textbook, Neil A. Campbell writes, "with each upward step in the hierarchy of biological order, novel properties emerge that were not present at the simpler levels of organization. These emergent properties arise from interactions between the components . . . Unique properties of organized matter arise from how the parts are arranged and interact . . . [insomuch as] we cannot fully explain a higher level of organization by breaking it down to its parts."[11] That is, emergent phenomena are dependent upon, but irreducible to, lower levels.

---

8. Kauffman, "A Religious Interpretation of Emergence," 903.
9. Ibid., 905.
10. Peacocke, *Paths from Science Towards God*, 110.
11. Campbell, *Biology*, 23.

PART THREE: TELEOLOGY AND THEOLOGY

The *Kenosis* of the Spirit into the Natural World

In an important insight, Davis and Hays posit that reading Scripture in today's environmentment requires one to move beyond the Enlightenment's ideal of a detached objectivity, and view reading Scripture as an art, one that requires both discipline and imagination.[12] Applying Davis and Hays' thoughts, one may envision that the uncontrolling Spirit of life hovered over the primordial waters and transformed the chaos into the *cosmos*. One could perceive this creative activity of the Spirit as being either inside the chaos (picturing God as uncontrollingly immanent within nature), or as the Spirit reaching down to create order according to the laws of nature, picturing God as transcendent above the natural world, with this chapter being near(er) to the previous category.[13] The recent trend toward picturing God as immanent will now be supplemented by resurrecting a view of God's action given by Aquinas in his *Summa theologiae*, wherein he writes:

> Some have understood God to work in every agent in such a way that no created power has any effect in things, but that God alone is the ultimate cause of everything wrought; for instance, that it is not fire that gives heat, but God in the fire, and so forth. But this is impossible. First, because the order of cause and effect would be taken away from created things: and this would imply lack of power in the Creator: for it is due to the power of the cause, that it bestows active power on its effect. Secondly, because the active powers which are seen to exist in things, would be bestowed on things to no purpose, if these wrought nothing through them . . . In order to make this clear, we must observe that as there are few kinds of causes; matter is not a principle of action, but is the subject that receives the effect of action. On the other hand, the end, the agent, and the form are principles of action, but in a certain order. For the first principle of action is the end which moves the agent; the second is the agent; the third is the form of that which the agent applies to action (although the agent also acts through its own form) . . . Thus then does God work in every worker, according to these three things. First as an end . . . Again it is to be observed that where there are several agents in order, the second always acts in virtue of the first; for the first agent moves the second to act. And thus all agents act in virtue of God Himself: and therefore He is the cause of action in every agent. Thirdly, we must observe that God not only moves things to operated, as it

---

12. Davis and Hays, *The Art of Reading Scripture*, xv.
13. Crain, "God Embodied In," 666.

were applying their forms and powers to operation, just as the workman applies the axe to cut, who nevertheless at times does not give the axe its form; but He also gives created agents their forms and preserves them in being . . . and because in all things God Himself is properly the cause of universal being which is innermost in all things . . . [it follows that] in all things God works intimately."[14]

Ian Barbour elucidates four different typologies by which one may view God's activity with and within the natural world.[15] The classical Monarchial model views God to be a ruler within his kingdom in terms of the relation between himself and nature. Barbour notes that the Deist model depicts God as a sort of clockmaker who allows nature (i.e. the clock) to work itself out according to the design by the maker. The Neo-Thomist model pictures God as the worker and the world as a tool used by the worker. Barbour stipulates that the Kenotic model can be characterized as the world being like a child, and God being like a parent. Using Barbour's typologies, a pneumatological interpretation of emergence, as advocated by this chapter, would be best categorized as a variant of the Neo-Thomist model in that the Spirit creates both the world (i.e. the "tool"), as well as the processes by which the tool is used.[16] Because the uncontrolling Spirit created all of the natural processes and laws, it is not demeaning that he sometimes uses wind, fire, earthquakes and floods (along with other processes) to create and recreate the earth; the Spirit is God's creative agent within *all* of the forces of nature.[17] Just as God usually works within,[18] rather than overriding the normal course of human affairs, so too does God work within the natural processes of nature; the uncontrolling Spirit works modestly in a continuous fashion, in and through natural processes.[19] By the Spirit's

---

14. Aquinas, *Summa theologiae*, Ia q.45 a.8.

15. Barbour, *Religion in an Age of Science*, 243–70.

16. cf. Peacocke, *Theology for a Scientific Age*.

17. Compare this postulation with a Neo-Thomist conception of Divine "double agency," as cited in Southgate, *God, Humanity, and the Cosmos*, 281.

18. Goergen contends, which I also affirm, that as the source of creative evolution, the Spirit works from *within* creation to generate ever increasing complexity, as opposed to externally compelling and manipulating creation (Goergen, *Fire of Love*, 106). This comports well with Oord's position of God's uncontrolling love, note.

19. Welker, "Spirit in Philosophical, Theological, and Interdisciplinary Perspectives," 227.

kenosis into the natural world, it itself is then enabled, using Clayton's language, to participate in the processes of production and reproduction.

Rather than bringing into being a ready-made world of unalterable character, the Godhead allows the natural world, uncontrollingly and kenotically empowered by the Spirit, to develop according to its own pace. This evolving fertility is not a linear progression, but is staggered instead, as the Spirit is not the manipulator of the natural world, but its director. In support of this assertion, the Spirit is seen at various junctures within the bible to operate via proximate causation. For example, Ps 104:30 (NKJV) states, "When you send your Spirit, they are created, and you renew the face of the earth." Here the term create (*bara*) is used, not of the initial generation of life, but of its continual regeneration, as the context speaks of the Spirit causing "the grass [to] grow for the cattle, and plants for man to cultivate" (vs. 14). It is "He [the Spirit, who] makes springs pour water into the ravines; [and flow] between the mountains" (vs. 10) . . . and who "bring[s] darkness, [and] it becomes night" (vs. 20). Further, it is the Spirit that continually provides food for all living things (vs. 28). The repeated emphasis within Ps 104 is the notion that God works *with* and *within* the world, which presupposes that God creates through the power of the Spirit, as well as the notion that the presence of the Spirit is the condition for both potentialities and realities of nature (cf. Moltmann 1993, 10). So then, the psalmist knows nothing of outright spontaneous generation, for God sends forth his Spirit, and they (i.e., all things) are created. Interestingly, Moltmann gives the Spirit a near monopoly in "creation." From Ps 104:30, which speaks of the life-giving action of the Spirit, Moltmann concludes: "This presupposes that God always creates through and in the power of his Spirit.[20] The Spirit is repeatedly depicted in this psalm as the presence and power of God, as well as the means by which God acts within creation.[21]

Kenosis of the Spirit Into Nature and Emergence Theory

One can perceive God within evolution, then, for the processes themselves, unveiled by the biological sciences, are God-acting-as-co-creator. Indeed, the Spirit enables emergence by endowing nature and the creatures therein with the ability to unfold by apparent natural processes according to their

20. Moltmann, *God in Creation*, 9.
21. Bonting, "Spirit and Creation," 715.

own inherent potentialities and possibilities. This chapter posits that there is a definitive uncontrolling lure of the Spirit within the propensities of nature, which seamlessly coalesces with the notion of the Spirit's kenosis into nature, for this potential, as it were, is actualized by the Spirit. This advocation of "lure" is quite similar to the one used by the process theologian Peacocke, who argues that God is the co-creator with finite agents, luring them without coercion and *without* pre-determining the outcome of the lure.[22]

This notion of creation through development also leads to an understanding of biological evolution in which the Spirit is seen as using a type of continuing creation. There exists overwhelming evidence of a universe marked by development, which points to a "creation" by kenosis. The kenotic creating Spirit is present within the historical contingency of evolution, as well as its lawful regularity.[23] Thus, the Spirit did not bring about "creation" in a single, definitive action, but instead used a process of evolution guided by natural laws.

Emergence and Final Causality

In his *Physics* (ca. 350 BCE), Aristotle sought to determine the number of causes or accounts for why something is what it is. Based on his observation and logical analysis, Aristotle concluded that four causes were necessary for a complete explanation of an object:

1. the formal cause, the principle that makes a thing what it is;
2. the material cause, the principle out of which a thing comes to be;
3. the efficient cause, the principle responsible for the motion of a being; and
4. the final cause, the principle for the sake of which something is done.[24]

Based upon these four causes, Aristotle developed a philosophical system to explain the universe. Beginning with Aristotle, and throughout the late-nineteenth century, philosophers generally accepted the sufficiency of the four causes. However, many modern scientists and philosophers dismiss the notion of a final cause, arguing that these types of 'causes' are not justifiable, since they cannot be verified empirically. As Frederick Copleston

---

22. Peacocke, *Creation and the World of Science*, 306.
23. Polkinghorne, "Kenotic Creation and Divine Action," 96.
24. McKeon, *The Basic Works of Aristotle*, 240.

puts it, since the time of Descartes, "explanation by means of final causes, of 'souls', of occult vital principles, and of substantial forms [did] nothing to promote the advance of physical science and were therefore discarded."[25] Consequently, modern science only grapples with material and efficient causes in its explanations. Yet this same science can now be the basis for a reasonable argument for the consideration of final causes in philosophical modeling.

In relation to emergence, Clayton elsewhere notes that, "God could guide the process of emergence by introducing new information (formal causality) and by holding out an ideal or image that could influence development without altering the mechanical mechanisms of evolution or adding energy from the outside (final causality)."[26] It may indeed be likely that final causality has more import in this discussion of emergence than Clayton seemingly allows for it, especially in light of a pneumatic understanding of the lure/woo of God toward eschatological fulfillment, and when viewed from the kenotic position argued by this current chapter. In recounting the emergence theories within the twentieth century, Clayton notes that Conway Lloyd Morgan anticipated, by some sixty-five years, Niles Eldredge's postulation of "punctuated equilibrium." Morgan perceived that emergence entails an evolution that is punctuated; he resisted his contemporary's view that an *e'lan vital* (vital energy) was introduced from a force outside of nature. In contrast, Morgan advocated a position in which the underlying forces driving evolution toward greater emergence are thoroughly immanent within the natural world. Clayton relays that perhaps "punctuated equilibrium" could be thought of in terms of final causation.[27] If so, the big transitions in "punctuated equilibrium" are signs of divine intervention.

Preliminary Conclusions

Evolution is the overall process, but emergence punctuates the steps of the evolutionary epic. At the same time, the earth must be seen as an environmentment of various heterogeneous life-processes. So then, the earth brings forth, but it does not bring forth itself. By releasing the power of the self-directed earth, the uncontrolling Spirit enables—potentially—the

---

25. Copleston, *A History of Philosophy Vol. IV*, 138.
26. Clayton, "Divine Causes in the World of Nature," 273.
27. cf. Clayton, *Mind & Emergence*, 13–14.

continual production, variation, and sustenance of vegetable and animal life.[28] By focusing on the Spirit, via its kenosis into nature, as both originator of and (co-)operator with the created world, one can see that the Spirit is both directly and indirectly involved in the world from beginning to end.[29]

Clayton asserts that God as the primary cause never conflicts with secondary causes. In view of this assertion, it is important to realize that Clayton's form of emergence is predominantly bottom-up, as opposed to top-down. Is Clayton's God entirely stripped of divine power and divine alterity by being immanent within the causal structure of the world? Apparently not: "one can accept an epistemic presumption in favor of naturalistic interpretations and still hold that it is metaphysically possible that . . . the regularities of the natural world are occasionally, or perhaps frequently, broken by direct interventions of God."[30] Moreover, Clayton states that emergentists must "give up" the principle of causal closure, which is common to modern physics.[31] Whereas this chapter agrees with Clayton's dismissal of a thoroughly fixed notion of finalistic causes in biology, it suggests that instead of the organs/isms being guided by the potentialities that are open to it, that they are instead lured by the potentialities that are open to it. The concept of lure instead of guide would entail the Spirit to be ever-before the evolutionary advancement of organs/isms, wooing them toward their eschatological fulfillment in Christ. These statements regarding finalistic causes are reminiscent of Whitehead, who posits that the divine lure is at work since the moment of the initial creation of the world.[32]

---

28. cf. Welker, *Creation and Reality*, 42.

29. In personal communication on 6 June, 2007, Clayton said that he holds the assumption that final causation conflicts with the explanatory paradigm of the biological sciences. So then, if he argues that God does something biologically impossible, then Clayton opens up a chasm between himself and biological scientists. Clayton said that he follows Thomas Aquinas, with God being the primary cause, and with creation being the secondary cause(s).

30. Clayton, *Mind & Emergence*, 163.

31. Ibid., 56.

32. Samuel Alexander stated that there is a principle of development *within* evolution, i.e., something that drives the whole process, which he terms the "nisus" (Alexander, *Space, Time, and Deity*) Alexander noted this was a creative metaphysical principle that bore resemblance to Whitehead's principle of Creativity. If we could perhaps wed Whitehead and Alexander together, it could be very effective because Whitehead has a theory of agency and lure whereas Alexander has various evolving levels of agency.

PART THREE: TELEOLOGY AND THEOLOGY

The Spirit, it is herein affirmed, ennobles nature to possess emergent capabilities.[33] The Spirit imparts propensities into nature that uncontrollingly eventuate the rise of higher forms of life.[34] The *breath of life*, thus, enables and empowers the emergence of nature and the creatures that inhabit it. Moreover, this uncontrolling Spirit of emergence endows nature with the ability to unfold by "natural" processes according to their inherent potentialities. A pneumatological interpretation of emergence easily allows for the notion of common descent, granting that it is a (more than) probable inference, based upon homology, fossil progression, embryological similarity, and rudimentary organs.[35] In this aspect, the complexity seen everywhere within the biotic world is ultimately the result of the Spirit, but evolution is an intricate—if not the most important—part of the mechanism of its derivation.

In this chapter, the ever-present call for dialogue between religion and science has been taken seriously, in part by interacting with Clayton's seminal work, *Mind & Emergence*, wherein Clayton contends that emergence is a viable option in contrast to the waning explanatory power of both reductionistic physicalism and substance dualism. Moreover, this chapter has presented the biblical basis of kenosis of the Spirit into nature, arguing that it presents the Spirit as being the active agent of God in the world, particularly regarding the Spirit as life-giver and animator of all of the natural world. In using Clayton's text as the source of its extrapolations, this chapter has also made a contribution toward a systematic theology of creation by elucidating the connections between kenosis of the Spirit into the natural world, emergence theory and final causality. God, in the person of the Spirit, is uncontrollingly at work within natural processes, luring, wooing, and awaiting the ever-increasing complexity within the natural environment.

---

33. cf. Welker, *The Work of the Spirit*, xii.

34. Peacocke, for example, suggests that information-processing systems, as well as information-storage systems, are examples of necessary things that arise as evolution proceeds, and are necessary for higher forms of life (Peacocke, "The Cost of New Life," 30).

35. Gould, "Evolution and the Triumph of Homology," 66–69.

Part Four

Pneumatology,
Philosophy,
&
Science

10

A Modern Depiction of Natural Theology in Dialogue with Aquinas, Darwin, and Whitehead

ACCORDING TO EMIL BRUNNER it is the task of our theological generation to "find its way back to a proper natural theology."[1] He argues that, since God "leaves the imprint of his nature upon what he does," it follows that it is fundamentally a Christian belief that the "creation of the world is at the same time a revelation, a self-communication of God."[2] It is relevant to my argument in this chapter that Brunner here does not consider his natural theology as *proof* of God, but rather as consistent with belief in God. Natural theology, fortunately, is enjoying a renaissance, catalyzed both by the intellectual inquisitiveness of natural scientists and the reflections of Christian theologians.

Natural theology can be broadly understood as the systematic exploration of a proposed link between the everyday world of our experience and another asserted transcendent reality, an ancient and pervasive idea that achieved significant elaboration in the thought of the early Christian fathers.[3] It offers, for example, an important conceptual framework for the exploration of Christian theology as a rational enterprise and a clarification of how the Christian faith relates to scientific postulates. Natural theology mandates a principled engagement with reality that is theologically

---

1. Brunner, "Natur und Gnade," 375.
2. Ibid., 343.
3. McGrath, *The Open Secret*, 2.

and scientifically informed. It has the potential to open up new vistas of understanding between scientific and religious cultures. There remains, however, a widespread perception that Charles Darwin's theory of natural selection marked and continues to mark the end of any viable natural theology, particularly in its classic formulation. But I shall argue in this chapter that there is a "wider natural theology" that remains untouched by Darwinian formulations of evolution by natural selection. It is my intention to provide the basic outlines of a workable natural theology that is in dialogue with the biological sciences, particularly the theory of evolution by natural selection.

Aquinas's Depiction of Natural Theology

In *Summa Theologica* I.2.3, Aquinas argues that the "existence of God can be proved in five ways." Aquinas's fifth way:

> is taken from the governance of the world. We see that things which lack intelligence, such as natural bodies, act for an end, and this is evident from their acting always, or nearly always, in the same way, so as to obtain the best result. Hence it is plain that not fortuitously, but designedly, do they achieve their end. Now whatever lacks intelligence cannot move towards an end, unless it be directed by some being endowed with knowledge and intelligence; as the arrow is shot to its mark by the archer. Therefore some intelligent being exists by whom all natural things are directed to their end; and this being we call God.

Thomas' fifth way hinges on the Aristotelian understanding of final causality. In such a view, it is believed that efficient causation, such as A causing B, cannot be understood except in light of final causation, that is, that there is a natural end in A that causes it to produce B. For if in A there was no inherent end towards B, it would be impossible to account for why A is always or nearly always the efficient cause for B, rather than C or D. Thus, B acts as a final cause for A. It is on this understanding of causal regularities that exist in nature that Aquinas formulates his proof.

In *Aquinas*, Edward Feser states that a match that is struck generates fire and heat rather than frost and cold; moreover, an acorn grows into an oak rather than a rosebush or a dog; further, "the moon goes around the earth in a smooth elliptical orbit rather than zigzagging erratically; the heart pumps blood continuously and doesn't stop and start several times a day; condensation results in precipitation which results in collection which results in evaporation which in turn results in condensation and so forth." He goes on, noting that in each of these cases there are regularities that, "point to ends or goals usually totally unconscious, which are built into nature and can be known through observation to be there whether or not it ever occurs to anyone to ask how they got there. In particular, one can know that there are these ends, goals, purposes in nature whether or not it ever occurs to anyone to consider the purposes, or even the existence, of a designer of nature."[4]

A Darwinian Natural Theology

What impressed Thomas Henry Huxley most forcibly on his first reading of Darwin's *Origin of Species* was his "conviction that teleology, as commonly understood, had received its deathblow at Mr. Darwin's hands."[5] This has sometimes been misunderstood to imply that it was the notion of teleology in general which Huxley contended was discredited by Darwin, rather than a specific form of teleology. This is clearly not the case. Huxley's comments refer to teleology "as commonly understood," a veiled reference to the specific form found in classical or traditional formulations such as that of Aquinas which seeks to *prove* the existence of God. This is made clear in his 1887 lecture "On the Reception of the Origin of Species," in which Huxley rebutted three common criticisms of Darwin's theory of natural selection, each of which he held to be based on a misrepresentation of Darwin's views.[6]

For example, Huxley writes, "It is said that he [Darwin] supposes variations to come about 'by chance', and that the fittest survive the 'chances' of the struggle for existence, and thus 'chance' is substituted for providential design."[7] Huxley argues that this is not at all the case, and that Darwin was grossly misunderstood on this point. In fact, Darwin declared that he did not know what had caused certain things to happen, yet located these events firmly within the context of the laws of nature. Moreover, Huxley writes, "A second very common objection to Mr. Darwin's views was (and

---

4. Feser, *Aquinas*, 116.
5. Huxley, *Lay Sermons*, 301.
6. Darwin, ed. *The Life and Letters of Charles Darwin*, vol. 2, 179–204.
7. Ibid., 199.

is), that they abolish Teleology, and eviscerate the argument from design."[8] This view is often repeated, even in the twenty-first century, but is without merit. Huxley is quite clear that the traditional approaches to teleology, those that seek to *prove* the existence of God, face a direct challenge from Darwin's evolutionary account. However, the theory of evolution, he argues, bears witness to a "wider teleology" that is rooted in the structure of the universe.[9] Indeed,

> The teleological and the mechanical views of nature are not, necessarily, mutually exclusive. On the contrary, the more purely a mechanist the speculator is, the more firmly does he assume a primordial molecular arrangement of which all the phenomena of the universe are the consequences, and the more completely is he thereby at the mercy of the teleologist, who can always defy him to disprove that this primordial molecular arrangement was not intended to evolve the phenomena of the universe.[10]

The idea of teleology originates in Aristotle's discussion of natural generation, and in this discussion, he argues that explanatory priority must be given to what lies at the end of the process, that is, its goal (telos). For Aristotle, telos designated an apparent internalized goal, not the purpose of an external agent.[11] Francisco J. Ayala, an evolutionary biologist, notes,

> A teleological explanation implies that the system under consideration is directively organized. For that reason, teleological explanations are appropriate in biology . . . Moreover, and most importantly, teleological explanations imply that the end result is the explanatory reason for the *existence* of the object or process which serves or leads to it . . . the use of teleological explanations in biology is not only acceptable but indeed indispensable.[12]

Ernst Mayr, similarly an evolutionary biologist, makes much the same point, arguing, "the occurrence of goal-directed processes is perhaps the most characteristic feature of the world of living systems."[13] Natural selection itself, the ultimate explanation within biology, should be considered a teleological process in that it has the net effect of increasing maximal repro-

---

8. Ibid., 201.
9. Ibid.
10. Ibid.
11. McGrath, *Darwinism and the Divine*, 189.
12. Ayala, "Teleological Explanations in Evolutionary Biology," 12.
13. Mayr, "Teleological and Teleonomic," 104.

A Modern Depiction of Natural Theology

ductive fitness. W.D. Ross interprets *telos* as end to be the "final cause" in nature, which is a structure common to a "whole *infima species*," to which "individual members of the species strive *without* conscious purpose."[14]

Considered in this context, therefore, it seems to be fully justified to designate the process of evolution by natural selection, as Ayala does, as teleological or end-directed.[15] This is the case because survival or reproductive success can be indeed viewed as the end toward which they naturally tend even if without conscious purpose. Teleological mechanisms in living organisms are biological adaptations that have arisen as a result of natural selection. Such teleological explanations are both appropriate and inevitable in biology, and remain fully compatible with standardized causal accounts. They should not be reduced to non-teleological explanations, for they would then lose their explanatory power.

I take issue, however, with Aquinas's attempt to *prove* the existence of God by his fifth way, that of teleology, as per his statement directly to that effect in *Summa theologica* I.2.3. I say this because one cannot demonstratively prove the existence of God through reference to teleology. Rather, the congruence of such a position with the existence of God can be read from the interpretation of nature. In contradistinction to Aquinas and in dialogue with McGrath, I posit that natural theology can be pictured as the process of "seeing" nature from the perspective of a Trinitarian ontology.[16] Christian theology provides an interpretative framework by which nature may be "seen" in a way that connects with the transcendent. The enterprise of natural theology would thus be one of discernment, of viewing it through a particular set of spectacles, as it were, which acknowledges nature as a legitimate, but limited, conduit to the divine reality.[17] This type of natural theology holds that nature reinforces an *existing* belief in God through the resonance between observation and theory.[18] When properly understood, a renewed, defensible, natural theology represents a distinctively Christian way of viewing, beholding, envisaging, and appreciating the natural order—in ways that are not necessarily mandated by nature itself.

The enterprise of natural theology has, if anything, been given a new lease of life through the rise of evolutionary thought. The traditional

14. Ross, *Aristotle*, 74.
15. Ayala, "Teleological Explanations in Evolutionary Biology," 11
16. McGrath, *Darwinism and the Divine*, 201.
17. McGrath, *The Open Secret*, 3.
18. Ibid., 5.

approach to natural theology, aptly demonstrated by Aquinas, is one option among many; the rise of evolutionary thought supplemented an existing and vigorous theological critique of this approach. Natural theology needs to emerge from the shadows of this traditional approach and rediscover, retrieve, and renew alternative approaches. Natural theology cannot be understood to concern *proving* God from nature. Christians must do natural theology, rather, beholding the same realities as the general populace, and recast it as a process of "seeing" the domain of nature as affirming the resonance of what they observe with tenets of the Christian faith, without claiming that this observed resonance *proves* the truth of Christianity. After all, "the world at which the theologian looks and the world at which the secularist looks are one in the same."[19] This interpretive lens does not prove its truth; it does however, demonstrate its utility, opening up in the process further areas of exploration and engagement.

Whitehead's Construction of Natural Theology

Whitehead repeats, supplements, and alters the position he stated in *Science and the Modern World* in his *Religion in the Making*. The repetition and supplementation is illustrated in the following passage: "The universe exhibits a creativity with infinite freedom, and a realm of forms with infinite possibilities; but ... this creativity and these forms are together impotent to achieve actuality apart from the completed ideal harmony, which is God."[20] Speaking of God, Whitehead writes:

> He is the binding element in the world. The consciousness which is individual in us, is universal in him: the love which is partial in us is all-embracing in him. Apart from him there could be no world, because there could be no adjustment of individuality. His purpose in the world is quality of attainment. His purpose is always embodied in the particular ideals relevant to the actual state of the world. Thus all attainment is immortal in that it fashions the actual ideals which are God in the world as it is now. Every act leaves the world with a deeper or a fainter impress of God. He then passes into his next relation to the world with enlarged, or diminished, presentation of ideal values.[21]

---

19. Smith, *The Free Man*, 45.
20. Whitehead, *Religion in the Making*, 119–20.
21. Ibid., 158–59.

A Modern Depiction of Natural Theology

Thus, God makes possible order and value in the world, the world then acts upon God, and God's new relation to the world is affected.[22]

God is, however, a very special type of actual entity. He is contrasted with all others by virtue of being "nontemporal."[23] "The definite determination which imposes ordered balance on the world requires an actual entity imposing its own unchanged consistency of character on every phase."[24] Indeed,

> He must include in himself a synthesis of the total universe. There is, therefore, in God's nature the aspect of the realm of forms as qualified by the world, and the aspect of the world as qualified by the forms. His completion, so that He is exempt from transition into something else, must mean that his nature remains self-consistent in relation to all change.[25]

In *Science and the Modern World*, Whitehead presents four metaphysical principles: the underlying substantial activity and its three attributes—eternal objects, actual entities, and the principle of limitation.[26] In *Religion in the Making*, subtle changes occur in the understanding of these four elements in the philosophic system. First, the underlying substantial activity is now called *creativity*.[27] Whereas substantial activity was that of which all the other three were attributes in *Science and the Modern World*, creativity is accorded no such favored place. Rather, complete interdependence of the four principles is stressed rather than the primacy of any one.[28] God is an actual entity who envisages and orders the realm of eternal possibilities, thereby ensuring a measure of order and value in a situation that could otherwise be only chaotic and indeed could achieve no actuality at all. What finally is the relation of God to creativity? Whitehead's *Process and Reality: An Essay in Cosmology* directly addresses this question.[29] Indeed, in 1927 and 1928, Whitehead gave the Gifford Lectures, which focused on natural theology, and later was expanded into his *Process and Reality* of 1929. In this title, Whitehead calls pure possibilities *eternal objects*, and Whitehead

22. Cobb, Jr., *A Christian Natural Theology*, 91.
23. Whitehead, *Religion in the Making*, 90.
24. Ibid., 94.
25. Ibid., 98–99.
26. Whitehead, *Science and the Modern World*.
27. Whitehead, *Religion in the Making*, 90.
28. Ibid., 90–93, 156–57.
29. Whitehead, *Process and Reality*.

calls *creativity* the ongoingness of activity in nature, and I claim that creativity is the Spirit of God.

For Whitehead, the initial aim determines just what an occasion shall aim to become.[30] Whitehead writes of the initial aim both that it is always at the best possible actualization, given that situation,[31] and that it includes indeterminations awaiting determination by the occasion itself in subsequent phases of its inner development.[32] These statements appear to be in some tension with each other. If the initial aim is at the best possibility, must it not be quite specific and must not its development in subsequent phases be a deviation away from this specific ideal? On the other hand, if the initial aim is indeterminate, how can it be directed toward the ideal? The solution is found in Whitehead's idea of graded relevance.[33] Some particular possibility must be ideal, given the situation. But closely related to this possibility are others, appropriate to the situation although deviating from the ideal. The initial aim thus involves the envisagement of a set of related and relevant possibilities from among which the final satisfaction of the occasion will in fact be chosen. These are all bounded by the definite limits required for the maintenance of minimal order. Yet they allow for so large a measure of self-determination that higher levels of order are subject to destruction by occasions that reject the ideal possibilities they confront in favor of others of lesser value. Whitehead shows here the sensitive balance between the freedom and the determinism of the cosmos, and how order is sustained and enhanced while constantly threatened by the possibility of decay.[34]

The initial aim of each occasion is derived from God.[35] God's aim is expressed in the ordering, by the laws of nature, of potentiality or pure possibilities, which Whitehead calls eternal objects.[36] Whitehead believes God's aim is the increase of value, which I reinterpret as the increase of complexity. God's aim operates in the world by participation through the Spirit in the actualization of actual occasions. For the majority of entities, God's aim is simply to absorb and transmit energy, yet this process even-

---

30. Cobb, *A Christian Natural Theology*, 93.
31. Whitehead, *Process and Reality*, 134–35, 195, 373.
32. Ibid., 74, 342–43, 375.
33. Ibid., 248. See also Ibid., 315, 425, 522.
34. Cobb, *A Christian Natural Theology*, 91.
35. Whitehead, *Process and Reality*, 104, 343, 373, 527.
36. Cobb, *A Christian Natural Theology*, 95.

tually led to an increase in complexity. The Divine aim is both restricted and empowered by the Spirit's primordial ordering of potentiality. Thus, according to Whitehead, God is not only the principle of limitation but the principle of potentiality as well.[37] According to Cobb, Whitehead refers to God as the organ of novelty.[38] What Whitehead attributes to God generically, I attribute to the Spirit of God specifically.

Whitehead's final summary of the interactions between God and the world are nicely summed up in the following passage:

> There are thus four creative phases in which the universe accomplishes its actuality. There is first the phase of conceptual origination, deficient in actuality, but infinite in its adjustment of valuation. Secondly, there is the temporal phase of physical origination, with its multiplicity of actualities. In this phase, full actuality is attained; but there is deficiency in the solidarity of individuals with each other. This phase derives its determinate conditions from the first phase. Thirdly, there is the phase of perfected actuality, in which the many are one everlastingly, without the qualification of any loss either of individual identity or of completeness of unity. In everlastingness, immediacy is reconciled with objective immortality. This phase derives the conditions of its being from the two antecedent phases. In the fourth phase, the creative action completes itself. For the perfected actuality passes back into the temporal world, and qualifies this world so that each temporal actuality includes it as an immediate fact of relevant experience.[39]

The attack upon traditional Western theism is especially clear in Whitehead's famous antitheses:

> It is as true to say that God is permanent and the World fluent, as that the World is permanent and God is fluent.

> It is as true to say that God is one and the World many, as that the World is one and God many.

> It is as true to say that, in comparison with the World, God is actual eminently, as that, in comparison with God, the World is actual eminently.

---

37. Whitehead, *Process and Reality*, 257.
38. Cobb, *A Christian Natural Theology*, 99.
39. Whitehead, *Process and Reality*, 532.

> It is as true to say that the World is immanent in God, as that God is immanent in the World.
>
> It is as true to say that God transcends the World, as that the World transcends God.
>
> It is as true to say that God creates the World, as that the World creates God.[40]

Whitehead's argument for the existence of God is primarily the traditional one from the order of the universe to a ground of order.[41] Order is indisputably in the world, whether or not there may also be disorder, and the order may be understood either as entirely imposed or as arising out of the nature of things themselves. Whitehead believes that elements of both are essential to an adequate analysis. There must be, then, some source of order that transcends the objects of scientific investigation, whether it is beyond or within the ordered world. If the world is viewed in organic terms, then the principle of life, order, and growth must be immanent to the organisms, which I herein attribute to the Spirit of God. Whitehead is careful to assert that, "God is not to be treated as an exception to all metaphysical principles, invoked to save their collapse. He is their chief exemplification."[42]

A Constructive Natural Theology

Whereas deist natural theologies portrayed God as the grand designer, and Aquinas's natural theology pictured his existence as provable by nature, the defensible natural theology that I argue for declares that God is attested to by the order of nature; he is signified by, or indicated *within*, the natural order. It is my position that the process of discerning God in nature is grounded in the philosophy of panentheism. Whereas claims to natural theology and panentheism abound, the uniting principle amongst these concepts is lacking. In all these cases, what is lacking appears to be the metaphysical basis of natural theology, which is a lacuna that a kenosis-based perspective could perhaps adequately fill. Indeed, perhaps the development of a kenotically-relational metaphysical basis for natural theology in the natural world will succeed in linking panentheism, the possibility of natural theology, and God. Using an expanded view of kenosis that

---

40. Whitehead, *Process and Reality*, 528.
41. Cobb, *A Christian Natural Theology*, 107.
42. Whitehead, *Process and Reality*, 521.

includes the pouring of the Spirit into creation offers a "pneumatological assist" to Darwin's, Whitehead's, and Cobb's writings and assists us also in constructing a modern relation of theology and science. Fittingly, the Spirit necessarily in-fills all of matter from its very origin, and as such, there is no distinction between matter and Spirited-entities.

Preliminary Conclusions: A New Turn to Natural Theology

Provided my understanding of kenosis as developed in previous chapters and recapitulated here, both creation and the incarnation are kenotic acts of *self-offering* since God makes space for creation and pours Himself into it. Moreover, a defensible natural theology for the twenty-first century holds that the true meaning of nature is capable of being unlocked, but doing so requires the employment of a hermeneutical key that nature itself cannot provide. In such a view, nature attests, declares, and makes manifest the God that is *already* known by and through faith. Seen as such, faith precedes the demonstration of teleology in nature, and does not result from it—that is, it is not based on proof. It cannot be maintained that Darwin's theory caused the "abandonment of natural theology."[43] The enterprise may have been refined and redirected by Darwin's theory, but it was certainly not abandoned. Rather, Darwin's theory of evolution by natural selection demands the reform and restatement of teleology—the "wider teleology" of which Huxley spoke—not its abolition.

In fact, it could be argued that Darwin's theory opened up new possibilities for natural theology, if we take the angle that it is through evolution that God makes his creation more complex. Indeed, as Charles Kingsley, a nineteenth century Anglican divine noted, "We knew of old that God was so wise that He could make all things: but behold, He is so much wiser than even that, that He can make all things make themselves."[44] This is because he is radically interior to everything within creation due to the interpenetrating Spirit that permeates it. In sum, the perspective of this chapter regarding natural theology is that it is about maximizing the intellectual "traction" between the Christian vision of reality and the observations of scientists.

---

43. Russett, *Darwin in America*, 43.
44. Kingsley, "The Natural Theology of the Future," xxvii.

11

A Critical Analysis and Response to Hume from a Pneumatological Perspective[1]

IN THE COURSE OF the history of Christianity, one of the most advocated and denigrated concepts is the verity of the miraculous. One finds that the opponents of Christianity have perpetually attempted to belie the status of the miraculous in order to overturn the entire worldview of the Christian. On the other hand, one also finds that at various times Christians have overemphasized the importance of the miraculous to their worldview in general. The situation in which Scottish philosopher David Hume lived (1711–1776) was the most ripe for the apparent refutation of the miraculous (and thereby, it was thought, of Christianity) of any time in the history of the movement. As Brown states, "no work on miracles penned in the seventeenth, eighteenth, or nineteenth centuries receives greater attention today than Hume's slim essay."[2] Antony Flew avers that, "the section 'Of Miracles' has probably provoked more polemic than anything else Hume ever wrote."[3] After a lengthy critical analysis of Hume, it will be argued in this chapter that he did not successfully negate either the possibility of the miraculous or the plausibility of the miraculous. Instead, it will be herein asserted that the modern Renewal movement (generated largely from the Pentecostal-charismatic imagination)—with its *renewed* emphasis on pneumatology—has given new weight to the affirmation of miracles. Both the

---

1. A previous version of this essay appeared in *Journal of Pentecostal Theology* 26 2 (2017) 233–51.

2. Brown, *Miracles and the Critical Mind*, 79.

3. Flew, *Hume's Philosophy of Belief*, 171.

possibility and the plausibility of the miraculous are crucial to the Renewal movement's emphasis upon the present-day activity of the Holy Spirit, and therefore a proper response to Hume is in order, as his causal analyses are still the predominant paradigm within the Western world.

In keeping with classical theists, who generally ground the *possibility* of a miracle in God's omnipotence, whereas they ground the *probability* of the miraculous in God's omnibenevolence, the Renewal movement also grounds both the possibility and plausibility of the miraculous on the nature of God. The Renewal movement, moreover, in keeping with classical theism, depicts God as opposite that of the prevalent form of deism (i.e., Christianity's Godhead is not impersonal or disinterested). Building upon this Classical Christian understanding, the panentheistically informed pneumatological understanding of the God/world relationship herein developed will lay the groundwork for future extension in that it posits God the Spirit as one who offers action that is at once personal, direct and specific. The import of this position for those within the Pentecostally-related Renewal movement is enormous, not only for practical reasons, but also for theological reasons.

In part two of this chapter, I will attempt to place Hume within a historical context, which will give important insights into the development of Hume's own notions regarding the verity of the miraculous. In part three of this chapter, I will seek to flesh out what a Humean miracle is in truth. After all, as Thomas Huxley (commonly referred to as Darwin's "bulldog") states: "The first step in this, as in all discussions, is to come to a clear understanding as to the meaning of the term employed. Argumentation about whether miracles are possible and, if possible, credible, is mere beating the air until the arguers have agreed what they mean by the word."[4] In part four of this chapter, I will focus upon the rejection and unraveling of Hume's arguments. And in part V of this chapter, I will proffer an embryonic response to Hume from a panentheistically informed pneumatological position.

Hume in Context

In this section, I will cover disparate background information regarding David Hume, which were formative to his worldview in the eighteenth century. I will cursorily provide a rough schematic of the various influences upon Hume's thinking. Many movements and developments of thought

---

4. Huxley, *The Works of T. H. Huxley*, 153.

regarding the miraculous, ranging from medieval scholastics, to pre-modern scientists, to pre-modern manifestations of Deistic understandings of the God/world relationship, will be identified as important to the development of Hume's position on the miraculous. Also, the establishment of a truly free press, it will be argued, added the avenue of expression that Hume needed to advance his positions regarding the miraculous. Moreover, it will be asserted in this section that Christianity itself, by internal bickering between various subsections within the movement, gave Hume intellectual ammunition with which to attack the verity of the miraculous.

The background behind Hume's argument against miracles goes back to at least Aquinas, who offered that a miracle is an occurrence whose cause "lies outside of nature."[5] After Aquinas, Spinoza extended this thought and defined a miracle as something that is "contrary to the order of nature."[6] Moreover, the Newtonian worldview, which viewed creation as a machine that was governed by inexorable and eternal laws, gave rise to Hume's understanding of the term "law."[7] Newton's system of thought therefore leads, by logical extrapolation, to the view that miracles are "violations" of the laws of nature, and hence were incoherent.

Voltaire epitomized the attitude of the Deistic age which directly preceded Hume, an age in which it was perceived incredible that God would intervene in this world on behalf of people. Voltaire's God, indeed the God of all of the deists, was simply the cosmic architect who engineered the cosmic machine, and then left it to its own devices.[8] Deistic attacks on the credibility of the miraculous began to increase in the seventeenth century, which resulted in a contemporaneous response of extremism from those who supported the accounts of miracles within Christianity.[9] Moreover, the attack on belief of miraculous accounts was strengthened by the fact that during this period the most vociferous advocates of the miraculous were not conservative theologians, but their liberal counterparts instead. In addition, deism was the most widely accepted form of religious orientation amongst the cultural and educated elite strata of society within this period, which furthered its influence. Deism can be succinctly characterized by a denial of the necessity of revelation (note that the deists of this period

---

5. Aquinas, *Summa theologica*, Q. 110, Art 4, 1022.
6. Yaffe, *Spinoza's Theologico*, xxi.
7. Craig, "The Problem of Miracles," 16.
8. Ibid.
9. Burns, *The Great Debate on Miracles*, 96.

often deemed revelation as self-contradictory). Moreover, deists in the period directly preceding Hume argued against the verity of the miraculous accounts in Scripture from *a posteriori* objections, as well as from objections based upon the existence of similar miracles in other religions. This situation gave Hume precedence to likewise use the same arguments in his polemic against miracles.[10]

Another condition influencing the argument about miracles in the first half of eighteenth century Europe arose from the principle of toleration, which was ensured in 1694 by the establishment of a truly "free press."[11] Prior to this date, no publication was allowed without a government-granted license (heavily influenced by the church). This establishment of a 'free press' allowed dissenting voices to actively publish material that was contrary to that which was formerly sanctioned by the church. As a result, dissenters to commonly propounded notions of Christianity gained a veritable voice with which to disseminate their objections.

Additionally, in arguing against transubstantiation, Tillotson gave Hume a pattern with which to construct his own argument against the miraculous. Tillotson wrote that if "Transubstantiation be part of the Christian Doctrine, it must have the same confirmation with the whole, and that is Miracles."[12] According to Tillotson, the founding miracles of Christianity are based upon the senses, for they are attested to by "eyewitnesses." Because Transubstantiation is counter a person's sense perception, it cannot be a part of Christian doctrine. Consequently, Transubstantiation is an errant doctrine, for it seeks to establish a notion contrary to what the person perceives by their senses (i.e., that the wafer becomes the body of Christ, and that the wine becomes the blood of Christ). Thus, Transubstantiation is not a miraculous occurrence. This argument by Tillotson gave Hume the proverbial ammunition that he needed to attempt to debunk the verity of any and all accounts of the miraculous.[13]

Already in 1667, Robert Boyle, an orthodox believer, taught and wrote that miracles validated Christianity, and as such, included them within his threefold structure of "grand arguments" for Christianity.[14] Hume, knowing that miracles were seen as validation of Christianity, had therefore

10. Ibid., 72.
11. Ibid., 11.
12. Tillotson, "A Discourse upon Transubstantiation," 297.
13. Reich, *Hume's Religious Naturalism*, 76.
14. Burns, *The Great Debate on Miracles*, 18.

an ardent desire to debunk the verity of the miraculous. Moreover, John Locke, as a moderate empirical-evidentialist, gave both background and substance to Hume's later arguments against the miraculous.[15] Indeed, Locke advocated that the miraculous had an essential role to play within Christianity as supplying the "credentials" that guaranteed the authenticity of divine revelation.[16] John Locke made another important (negative) contribution to Hume's thought by not classifying information obtained through others as knowledge in the strict sense. Moreover, in Locke we find stress placed upon the probability of reports of others, as well as "the intrinsic likelihood of the event related."[17] In Locke, then, people are able, in certain situations, to refuse the testimony of otherwise reliable witnesses because the event that they recount is not in line with "our own knowledge, observation, and experience."[18] In applying this logic of Locke to reported miracles, Hume was able to refute the testimony of others in substantiating the occurrence of a purported miracle. Hume, in following and building upon Benedict de Spinoza's argument regarding the impossibility of the *occurrence* of a miracle, argues for the impossibility of the *identification* of a miracle.[19] As I will show in the next section, Hume, contrary to the Deists, had no good intentions in reference *to the faith once delivered to the saints* by publishing his material about miracles. In contrast, not only did he lack faith in traditional Christianity, he also did not believe in the "heavenly city of the eighteenth-century philosophers."[20]

Hume and Miracles

In this section, I will begin by noting that Hume's conception of the miraculous was essentially equivalent to a Pyrrhonists' understanding of the miraculous. I will then note how Hume extends and applies the Pyrrhonist understanding of the miraculous by citing Hume's own work. I will then offer a summarization of what I deem to be Hume's four arguments against the miraculous, and this will be thereafter supported and extended by other commentators.

15. Ibid., 47.
16. Ibid., 66.
17. Ibid., 60.
18. Locke, *The Reasonableness of Christianity*, 143.
19. Craig, "The Problem of Miracles," 17.
20. Wollheim, *Hume on Religion*, 15.

A Critical Analysis and Response to Hume

As aforementioned, Pyrrhonist thought permeates Hume. Pyrrhonists taught that all human claims to knowledge are untenable because it can never be rationally possible to know for certain that one really knows what one is inclined to believe one knows at any given moment. As a logical extension to this thought of the Pyrrhonists, Hume accepts the sentiment that humans can never gain absolute certainty regarding perceived truths, especially in the cases in which the perceived truths are based upon testimony of other humans. Furthermore, Hume extends Pyrrhonist thought insomuch as to claim that objective knowledge cannot ever be in fact attained.

Hume thereafter postulates that a miracle, by its very definition, is an extremely unlikely event, "a transgression of a law of nature . . . by the interposition of some invisible agent."[21] Hume advocates the notion that miracles run contrary to our constant and unhindered experience, "for nothing is esteemed a miracle if it ever happens in the common course of nature."[22] Moreover, to Hume, a miracle is an event that transgresses a "law of nature," with these laws being defined as "conclusions . . . founded on . . . infallible experience."[23] In other words, a miracle is an event, caused by some entity outside of nature, which is contrary to expected results—an event that appears to be impossible under the established norms of nature, and therefore is an event that requires an act of faith to believe. Thus, Hume thinks that because miracles are law-violating events, their probability is tantamount to zero, that is, that they are maximally improbable. From this understanding, Hume concludes that no amount of testimony, regardless of its *quantity* or *quality*, can raise that probability any significant degree.

According to Hume's analysis of the miraculous, it may be inferred that even if it is metaphysically possible that a deity could produce a miraculous event, it could never be demonstrated because in order to do so one would have to eliminate all possible naturalistic causes of the event in question (which would go on *ad infinitum*). Hume argues that, "No testimony is sufficient to establish a miracle unless that testimony be of such a kind that its falsehood would be more miraculous than the fact which it endeavors to establish."[24] Hume then goes on to assert that no miracle ever has, or ever will have, more evidence supporting it than it has opposing it.

---

21. Hume, *An Enquiry Concerning Human Understanding*, 115.
22. Ibid., 115.
23. Ibid., 114.
24. Ibid., 115–16.

Succinctly, Hume's four arguments against the miraculous found within part II of his *Enquiry* can be categorized as follows: 1). The number of witnesses is not sufficient; 2). Humans tend to exaggerate and be enthusiastic about the "marvelous"; 3). Stories of miracles abound among ignorant folk; and 4). Miracles of competing religions cancel each other out. Hume maintains in these four arguments that miracles are impossible, implausible, improbable, and indistinguishable. So then, one can accurately classify the case of Hume against the miraculous as consisting of four distinct (but linked by the overlapping aim) arguments in "Of Miracles." First, the beginning section argues against the possibility of miracles *apriori* (i.e., the *impossibility* argument). Second, the *implausibility* argument seeks to undermine the testimonial evidence given for supposed miracles. Third, Hume argues that the probability of the miraculous renders them unlikely (i.e., the *improbability* argument). Fourth, Hume proffers a case against humanity being able to distinguish what they claim as miracles from that which is mere anomalous (i.e. the *indistinguishability* argument).[25] Whatever else may be said of Hume's essay "Of Miracles," his "particular purpose" in it is to undermine belief in the founding miracle of Christianity, that is, the resurrection of Jesus.[26]

In a different, but somewhat compatible, understanding to the one offered in the previous paragraph, Craig contends that Hume argues against (in principle) the identification of any occurrence as a miracle, and then in the second part of his essay argues (in fact) what he thinks is the case.[27] Johnson asserts that Hume viewed the "*laws* of nature . . . as universal and nonprobabilistic generalizations which, furthermore, are *true*."[28] Therefore one may deduce that Hume pictured the laws of nature as unbreakable and inviolable. Thus, Hume posits that any evidence in favor of a miracle is not stronger than the evidence against a miracle.

Hume's Unraveling

In this section, I will note friendly receptions of Hume, but focus on the reception of Hume that has been negative. I will, in dialogue with various supporters of Hume's attack on the miraculous, pinpoint wherein their

---

25. Reich, *Hume's Religious Naturalism*, 73–75.
26. Ibid., 73.
27. Craig, "The Problem of Miracles," 18.
28. Johnson, *Hume, Holism and Miracles*, 9. Emphasis in original.

understanding(s) of Hume is deficient. I will intimate that their attempts to reinterpret Hume are lacking of substance and without merit.

Friendly writers such as Huxley, Mill, and Wollheim have all taken Hume's argument in "Of Miracles" to be explicitly condemning of testimony by others in reference to purported miracles, without even testing the testimony first. Hume asserts that the testimony of others is inherently less believable than personal experience. In arguing that there "is not to be found [any] miracle sufficiently attested by a sufficient number of men of such unquestioned good sense [and] undoubted integrity [that was] performed in such a public manner and in so celebrated a part of the world, as to render the detection unavoidable," Hume is mixing value judgments with "matter of fact statements."[29] Who is to determine the sufficient number of people who attest to a miracle in order for it to be credible? Who is to determine what "higher learning" exactly entails? What is "unquestioned integrity"? What is a "public manner"? What is a "celebrated part of the world"? Are we to take Hume to be the one who can establish such criteria?

If for Hume a miracle is truly a "violation" of a law of nature, then it seems that no matter where the purported miracle was derived from, there would be no need of further arguments against it; however, in part II, Hume offers a prolonged attack against the credibility of miracle stories. So then, Hume makes a question-begging argument in part one, only to then attempt to add credence to his *apriori* decision in part two. Stephen Naylor Thomas defines a question-begging argument in the following manner: "when reasoning, for one of its reasons or assumptions (whether explicit or suppressed), depends on a statement that is identical or equivalent to the drawn conclusion, then it is said to 'beg the question.' Such an argument, which assumes the very claim it is trying to prove, is also called 'circular' or is said to 'argue in a circle.'"[30] The popular theologian C.S. Lewis probably posits the best-known argument against Hume in this vein:

> Now we must agree with Hume that if there is absolute uniform experience against miracles, if in other words, they have never happened, why then they never have. Unfortunately, we know the experience against them to be uniform only if we know already that miracles never occurred. In fact, we are arguing in a circle."[31]

---

29. Mitchell, *David Hume's Anti-Theistic Views*, 47.
30. Thomas, *Practical Reasoning in Natural Language*, 370.
31. Lewis, *Miracles*, 134.

But Robert J. Fogelin claims that Lewis gets Hume's argument "backwards."[32] He also asserts that Hume stipulates that the more heavily attested testimony does not automatically falsify the singular testimony to the contrary, but merely makes "a decisively strong presumption... in favor of its (i.e., the second testimony's) falsehood."[33] Fogelin contends that there is no "circularity," therefore, in Hume's argumentation, and that Hume is not "question-begging."[34] He then asserts that Hume begins part II by claiming that no purported miracle has ever passed the 'direct' test (or Hume's first condition)—i.e., no miracle has had a sufficient number of well-educated people backing its claims. Fogelin claims that Hume offers a 'psychological' account (or Hume's second condition) of why some people believe in miracle attestations—i.e., they are metaphorically drunken with the desire for awe and wonder. Fogelin also contends that Hume's conditions placed upon testimony offer an "explanation of how beliefs in miraculous events gain their initial foothold."[35]

Thus, Fogelin posits that Hume does not argue against miracles *apriori* in part one of his essay "Of Miracles." Instead, he argues that Hume arrives at a conditional conclusion at the end of part one. Moreover, Fogelin argues, Hume does not argue *apriori* in part one because Hume acknowledges "that under certain circumstances it *could* be possible to establish the occurrence of a miracle on the basis of testimony."[36] I personally do not understand how Fogelin can posit such a position, for Hume explicitly dismisses what he acknowledges to be three heavily supported testimonies to the miraculous (i.e., Tacitus' reports of Vespasian, Cardinal de Retz, and those at the tomb of Abbé Paris), which seems to indicate that Hume disavows supported claims to the miraculous, reinforcing the traditionally perceived *apriori* conclusion of part one.

Houston recognizes that if we had no reason to suspect that a god could have any purpose in bringing about the event, then we would seek a natural explanation of the report.[37] In that case, Houston thinks that an inductive inference from our past experience of law-like events is entirely appropriate. What Houston objects to is Hume's automatic inference from

---

32. Fogelin, *A Defense of Hume on Miracles*, 19.
33. Ibid., 20.
34. Ibid.
35. Ibid., 21.
36. Ibid., 18. Emphasis in the original.
37. Houston, *Reported Miracles*, 161.

"the event reported would violate a law" to "the event reported has the highest degree of improbability."[38] In making this inference, Houston asserts, Hume has violated his self-imposed condition of initial *neutrality* and thus begged-the-question against theism.

David Johnson similarly states that Hume's argument depends upon a "tendentious and, one would rightly say question-begging assumption about what a miracle must be."[39] Johnson goes on to state in reference to Hume's argument in part one that in order "to stave off an illusory apriori proof that there are no miracles, we must tinker either with the definition of 'miracle' itself, or with the definition of 'violation', or with the definition of 'laws of nature.'"[40] If a miracle is truly a "violation" of a law of nature (as Hume stipulates), then it is illogical to likewise assert that laws of nature are universal truths, for as Spinoza writes, "whatsoever is contrary to nature is contrary to reason, and whatever is contrary to reason is absurd and, *ipso facto*, to be rejected".[41] But there is no good reason to classify a miracle as a violation or as "*an exception to an exceptionless regularity . . .* [and] there is no good reason to define it in effect as *a past event of a kind which has never been observed.*"[42] Differing with Hume, Johnson stipulates that miracles are merely "violations" of *apparent* laws of nature.[43]

Hume is inconsistent in his definition of a miracle, not in small part by the evidence that he uses both *against* them and *for* the uniform status of natural law (i.e., personal experience relayed by testimony of others). How can Hume claim that the uniform experience of the laws of nature is the case against the testimony of a purported miracle, when in fact "uniform experience" is composed of testimony by others? In spite of this inconsistency, Hume nonetheless avers in his *Enquiry* that uniform experience trumps human testimony to the miraculous.

---

38. Ibid.
39. Johnson, *Hume, Holism and Miracles*, 19.
40. Ibid., 7.
41. Yaffe, *Spinoza's Theologico*, 76.
42. Johnson, *Hume, Holism and Miracles*, 19. Emphasis in original.
43. Ibid., 23. Also note that Johnson proposes three possible interpretations of what Hume means by "the common course of nature" (20): 1. an absolutely uniform observed course of nature, "where the past has been entirely regular and uniform"; 2. an absolutely uniform observed course of nature when nature is not interfered with (a'la Mackie) by something outside of nature; and 3. the commonly or usually observed course of nature.

Antony Flew states that part one of "Of Miracles" allows for the theoretical possibility of miracles.[44] The strength of Flew's interpretation of part one of "Of Miracles" is that it gives clear purpose for Hume's argument in part two. Contrary to Flew, however, it seems that Hume was indeed arguing that even if testimonies of the miraculous are passed through rigorous testing, they are still false. So then, part two of "Of Miracles" builds upon part one. In support of this assertion, note Hume when he writes, "[t]he wise and learned are contented, in general, to deride its [i.e., the miracle's] absurdity, without informing themselves of the particular facts."[45] Therefore, Flew's reinterpretation of Hume is not palatable.

There are also other people (not positively inclined toward Hume), however, who argue against this *traditional* understanding of Hume's argument.[46] These newer interpreters posit that part two of Hume's essay "Of Miracles" gives the proper judgment (according to Hume) to the slight inference that can be drawn from part one (i.e., that some specific testimony may be able to establish the credibility of an account of a miracle). I find their position less than convincing, however. As a third option, some interpreters have taken a middle-ground position in reference to the relationship between part one and part two of Hume's essay, and posit that Hume's original essay, composed in embryonic form during the later part of the 1730's, was constituted by the proof of part one, and only later did Hume add the condition that high-quality testimony was needed to establish the verity of a purported miracle (apparently to soften its offense to advocates of the miraculous). Though this interpretation has some merit, it is essentially indemonstrable, and as such, one must work with the text as they find it (i.e., consisting of part one and part two together as a whole).

In weighing the probabilities of miracles, Hume is entirely consistent with his epistemological foundation; however, the problem is that Hume confuses evidence with probability. Indeed, it is certainly not correct to assert that people should always believe the most probable; it is reasonable instead to believe an improbable event if sufficient evidence establishes that it has happened. Even when Hume concedes that it is possible that an improbable event may occur, he qualifies such a concession by immediately stating that it likely has a natural explanation. But the only way that Hume can rightly argue that no evidence is sufficient to warrant belief that

---

44. Flew, *God and Philosophy*, 185–86.
45. Hume, *Enquiry*, 120.
46. cf. Earman, *Hume's Abject Failure*.

a violation of natural law has occurred is if "violations of natural law are maximally improbable. However, one can only know that violations are maximally improbable if one already knows that they [never] could or have never occurred."[47]

Blomberg, in re-applying Stein's criteria of authenticity for the sayings of Jesus, provides at least four crucial criteria for establishing the reliability of the historical witness(es) (i.e., testimony) for the miraculous. First, accounts of the miraculous pervade every putative source of the canonical tradition (i.e., they are attested by multiple sources). Second, incidental details contained within the narratives that include miraculous occurrences lend credence to said events, as they are perceived to be true-to-life. Third, both internal coherence as related by various authors, as well as external coherence as related by historians affirm that Jesus was a miracle-worker. Fourth, dissimilarity to other purported miracles in the ancient world offers credence to the stories of the miraculous as posited by the New Testament texts.[48]

Concerning the weight of human testimony, when there is a preponderance of evidence in favor of regularity, but the evidence for the miraculous is nonetheless strong, Houston notes that one might be the most wise to suspend judgment entirely.[49] Houston goes on to suggest that Hume's manner of evaluating claims of the miraculous is quite unsatisfactory because he fails to recognize how theistic assumptions would positively affect the credibility of a reported putative miracle.[50] In so doing, Hume merely assumes the outcome to be negatively disposed against the verity of the miraculous. In an apparent inconsistency within his argumentation against the miraculous, Hume notes that the Indian Prince could well change his mind in reference to believing that water turns into ice if he is made privy to further information (by means of testimony).[51] I am immediately struck by Hume's allowance of the Indian Prince to be convinced and converted to a new way of thinking by testimony, when he disallows the non-believer in the miraculous to be persuaded by the very same type of reasoning. Why testimony can convince the Indian Prince of the notion that water some-

---

47. Beckwith, *David Hume's Argument Against Miracles*, 35.

48. Blomberg, "Concluding Reflections," 446–49.

49. Houston writes, "Suspensions of belief may well be more appropriate [than taking either side, i.e.]" (Houston, *Reported Miracles*, 126).

50. Ibid., 127.

51. Hume, *Enquiry*, 122.

times turns into a solid, and equivalent testimony cannot convince a skeptic that someone has risen from the dead, is inexplicable without ceding the notion that Hume was ardently anti-miraculous. As Earman questions, "Why isn't the passing of water from a liquid state to a solid state just as contrary to the prince's experience as the springing to life of a dead man"?[52]

Moreover, if we take for granted that humans originated somewhere in Africa about six million years ago, then our corporate ancestor had no conception of what "frozen water" (i.e., ice) was or even looked like. If Hume were to apply his logic to the first instance of a report given by someone having seen ice, dismissal of said report from our corporate ancestor would be permitted (it is thus easy to reduce Hume's position to absurdity). In applying this same reasoning to Hume's argument against the miraculous, testimony should be capable of establishing the veracity of a purported miracle. It is apparent, then, that one must emphasize the communal character of all knowledge, that testimony is crucial to the establishment of that knowledge, and that testimony, contra Hume, can take precedence over personal experience. This line of reasoning was perhaps perceived by Hume himself, as Earman notes that Hume most likely added part II of his essay "Of Miracles" because the proof "from experience is not the final word since it may be opposed by a proof from testimony".[53]

As Houston writes, "[b]ecause human experience provides a direct and full proof of natural laws and therefore, in Hume's view, against miracles whose occurrence would violate these laws, the strongest possible evidence for a miracle, being also a direct and full proof, could only equal that against [it]."[54] Though Hume argues that the logical way to determine the truth between two contradictory situations is to ascertain which of the events has more supporting evidence, Hume is errant in assuming that the mere adding up of the events in order to determine truth is sufficient, because truth is regularly attained by minority vote. Hume intimates that as a miracle is essentially an argument against the established norms of nature, there is by definition always greater evidence against the occurrence of a miracle than for it.

Colin Brown has observed that the criteria Hume places on establishing an account of the miraculous are "such as would preclude the testimony of anyone without a Western university education, who lived outside

---

52. Earman, *Hume's Abject Failure*, 34.
53. Ibid., 43.
54. Houston, *Reported Miracles*, 134.

A CRITICAL ANALYSIS AND RESPONSE TO HUME

a major cultural center in Western Europe prior to the sixteenth century, and who was not a public figure."[55] While it is granted that some stories of antiquity regarding the miraculous are the product of ingenious minds craving for wonder, it is not appropriate to extend such a concept to all alleged miracles of antiquity. To do so would be to commit what is commonly called the *fallacy of false analogy*. Indeed, it is quite absurd to expect a witness in history to have the same level of education and possess the same worldview that we possess in this (post)modern age. We should base the validity of a witness not on such factors as culture, education, and worldview, but on their honesty, proximity to alleged events, and their motives.

In "Of Miracles," Hume confuses matters of *science* with matters of *history*. That dead men generally do not rise from the dead is a matter of *science*, and such a statement to the contrary is clearly naturally impossible. However, the testimony that a dead man (e.g., Jesus of Nazareth) did rise from the dead is *not* a matter of science, but a matter of *history*. Thus, Hume is guilty of arguing from a categorical mistake. Hume's argumentation against the verity of the miraculous diminishes historical reasoning and the ability to reconstruct historical occurrences, as the historian must be open to novel occurrences, and not exclude apriori their possibility, merely because they do not conform to present experience.[56]

Contra Hume, and in dialogue with modern probability theory, Earman notes that, "given some mild assumptions, which can be made plausible . . . results about the incremental confirmation of hypotheses about miracles and religious doctrines proper can be proved as theorems of probability."[57] Perhaps my critique of Hume in reference to his straight rule of induction is a little harsh. After all, Bayesian mathematics was in the process of being developed in this same general time frame, and as such, Hume was not privy to it. Although the forms of Bayesian mathematics are manifold, there are several characteristics of Bayesianism that apply universally. For example, Bayesians contend that epistemology should not be construed as an all-or-nothing belief, but in terms of degrees of belief instead.[58] Moreover, Bayesians likewise state that degrees of belief should

---

55. Brown, *Miracles and the Critical Mind*, 97.

56. cf. Neibuhr's argument against Troeltsch, as found in Niebuhr, *Resurrection and Historical Reason*, 168–170.

57. Earman, *Hume's Abject Failure*, 72.

58. For further information regarding Bayesian thought, reference Jaynes, *Probability Theory*; and Howson and Urbach, *Scientific Reasoning*.

be in accordance with probability calculus. Third, Bayesians posit that when a person encounters a learning experience, then the person's degree of belief is in direct relation to said person's prior beliefs.[59] So then, Hume's conception of inductive inferences is impoverished due to a lack of mathematical development; but this fact does not excuse his arrogance in promoting his essay as a "check" that will never be surmounted.[60]

When Hume applies his logic to particular miraculous claims, his logic is superficial and without substance. Indeed, Hume sets forth the appearance of a powerful argument against the miraculous claim, but in truth only presents ambiguities. Instead of unassailable logic, Hume inundates one with hyperbole, sarcasm and forceful prose. Earman claims that those who have been engendered by Hume's argument in his essay "Of Miracles" have been impressed "not by content, but by the nice ring of the language of Hume's formulation."[61]

George Mavrodes states that even if a Christian accepts Hume's interpretation of the miraculous event(s) they "need not be greatly disturbing to any religious person or any 'friend of miracles.'"[62] Mavrodes is confident in asserting such a bold claim because even if these "violations" have undermined "natural law", that does not mean that they did not occur. Mavrodes contends further,

> Nothing that the objector has said tends to show at all, or make it in any way probable, that Jesus did not turn water into wine, that he did not calm a storm with a word or raise Lazarus from the dead, and so on. Nor does it tend to show that these events did not have a profound religious significance. It does not even tend to show that these things, if they happened, were not miracles. At most (for better or worse) it tends to show that they are not *Humean* miracles.[63]

If one *shares* Hume assumption that the universe is an entirely closed, orderly whole, completely constituted by what Hume calls the "common course of nature," then Hume's argument against the *possibility* and the *plausibility* of the miraculous is coherent. Beckwith challenges Hume's notion of the miraculous, however, and instead posits that a "miracle is a

---

59. Earman, *Hume's Abject Failure*, 26.
60. Hume, *Enquiry*, 115.
61. Earman, *Hume's Abject Failure*, 42.
62. Mavrodes, "Miracles and the Laws of Nature," 337. Emphasis in original.
63. Ibid.

divine intervention which occurs contrary to the regular course of nature within a significant historical-religious context."[64] This definition offered by Beckwith, then, necessarily entails that a miracle is rationally inexplicable by scientific law, and that a miracle is an event for which God is responsible (though not necessarily the God of Christian theism). So then, one ought to not necessarily characterize the miraculous as a "violation" or "transgression'" of the natural law. Rather, it might be better to think of miracles as "*supra*-natural" and not "*contra*-natural." Moreover, a miracle could be "teleologically" thought of instead of merely "scientifically" thought of, for it is well possible that science could explain the immediate process, but be silent as to the unusual or purposeful nature of it.[65]

Hume unfortunately uses his "straight rule of induction" in such a manner that it is descriptively inadequate to actual scientific practice, and which would stultify scientific inquiry.[66] Indeed, unless testimony is allowed to over-ride prior improbabilities, there is no way in which humans can make inferences in everyday life or in science, which leads to a virtual paralysis of indecision and uncertainty. Testimony of an event cannot be refuted by experiences and observations to the contrary alone, it may be deduced.[67]

Contemporary scientists, in addition, consider "scientific laws" (i.e., natural laws) to be descriptive, and not prescriptive. So then, in contemporary idiom, when a scientist speaks of a scientific law, they are speaking not of what *must* occur *apriori*, but describing instead what *generally* happens. Moreover, "scientific laws" (i.e., natural laws) are now seen to be more like approximations than uniform expectations. As Swinburne notes, "[t]o say that a certain such formula is a law is to say that in general its predictions are true and that any exceptions to its operation cannot be accounted for by another formula which could be taken as a law."[68] The benefit of this newer understanding of scientific/natural law is that it does not rule-out the possibility of the miraculous outright.

---

64. Beckwith, *David Hume's Argument*, 7.
65. Geisler, *Miracles and Modern Thought*, 56.
66. Earman, *Hume's Abject Failure*, 31.
67. Craig, "The Problem of Miracles," 24.
68. Swinburne, *The Concept of Miracle*, 1.

PART FOUR: PNEUMATOLOGY, PHILOSOPHY, & SCIENCE

A Pneumatological Response to Hume

Any epistemology that does not allow for the possibility that evidence, whether from eyewitness testimony or from some other source, can establish the credibility of a UFO landing, a walking on water, or a resurrection is inadequate.[69] Thus, miracles should not be discounted apriori. It was Hume's underlying, proverbially atheistic (at least at this stage in his life) worldview that drastically affects his view of the evidence for the occurrence of a miracle. If there is no god, the possibility of a god's so acting that there is a departure from nature's regular course can be discounted.[70] However, given the existence of God, miracles are not incredible. Moreover, granted the existence of God the Spirit, if a miracle occurs, it would not be a violation of natural cause and effect, as per se, but an entirely new effect produced by the panentheistically present Spirit.

But there is truly no irreconcilable relation between human experience and Christian miracles, for miracles, though different from our ordinary experience (i.e., *contraria*), are not contradictory (i.e., *contradictoria*) to experience in general.[71]

Understanding a miracle as something that is naturally impossible (i.e., nature in and of itself acting exclusively), but not logically impossible, is an appropriate conceptioning of the embryonic panentheistically informed pneumatological position herein advocated. Thus, properly conceived, miracles neither render natural law uncertain, nor unable to predict with a degree of certainty what will happen with future events when given its antecedents.[72] Natural law is not abolished because of a few discreet exceptions, as the counter-instance must occur repeatedly in order to truly render the natural law falsified.

David Hume's essay represents the kind of writing that perennially gives philosophy a bad name. Throughout his essay "Of Miracles," Hume claims more than he delivers. Contrary to Hume, and given the reliability of witnesses, convergence to certainty can ensue as the number of witnesses also increases. Bilynski succinctly provides four criteria for identifying some event E as a miracle, which are instructive in reference to Hume:

---

69. Beckwith, *David Hume's Argument*, 4.
70. Houston, *Reported Miracles*, 143.
71. Campbell, *The Works of George Campbell*, 1:23.
72. Craig, "The Problem of Miracles," 33.

1. the evidence for the event E is at least as credible for other accepted but unusual events in similar distance from the inquiry with respect to time and space as event E;
2. explanations of natural causal powers for event E are impotent;
3. there is no evidence of natural causal powers for event E; and
4. there is reason to expect a supernatural explanation for event E, outside of its inexplicability by natural causal powers.[73]

Whereas all of Hume's criticisms have some force, his postulations cannot be used, however, to in/validate any particular argument for the miraculous. Rather, in the era post-Hume, those who accept the possibility of the miraculous must be cautious in their pronouncements concerning purported miracles. I agree with Davis who avers that Hume is both right and wrong.[74] Hume is right in claiming that rational expectation of what will occur should be based on what has occurred, that people ought to always believe the lesser of two miracles, as well as that rational people should require strong evidence before ever conceding the verity of a miracle. Hume is also right in intimating that advocates of the miraculous often exaggerate greatly the strength of their arguments, while downplaying the difficulties within them. However, Hume is wrong in stating that our past experience—in and of itself—establishes that a miracle cannot happen, that the purported miracle is always a greater "miracle" than the testimony to it being false, and that it can never be rational to assert that a miracle has occurred.[75]

It is easy to see how natural law became viewed as immutable, for this view arose out of the Deist controversy. However, it is more in line with modern science to see natural law as being descriptive, and not prescriptive. Advances in modern physics have rendered it probable that the Newtonian world-machine is an inadequate framework to conduct scientific inquiry, and that natural law, as such, is not absolutely final. Understanding natural law to be descriptive rather than prescriptive reopens possibilities for anomalous events to occur in the natural environment, of which miracles may aptly be titled the exemplar.

---

73. Bilynskyj, "God, Nature, and the Concept of Miracle," 10–42.
74. Davis, "The Miracle At Cana," 430–31.
75. Burns, *The Great Debate on Miracles*, 223.

Part Four: Pneumatology, Philosophy, & Science

Preliminary Conclusions

The pneumatology herein advocated affirms that the Spirit of God "poured Himself out" into creation, thereby giving rise to a panentheistic orientation of God in reference to the world. More pointedly, the possibility of the miraculous is not a problem for someone who accepts this panentheistically informed pneumatological understanding of the God/world relationship. Since God created, maintains, sustains, and permeates the entirety of the created world, he certainly has the power and accessibility to intervene into the natural order of things as he desires. Purtill therefore proffers that miracles be thought of as "exceptions" to natural law, or more apropos, exceptions to the "natural order of things."[76] Given that the universe is orderly, understandable, and comprehensible, it is logical to propose that such a state exists (i.e., its rationality) because of its coinherence in and with God through his Spirit. In support of my embryonic, panentheistically informed pneumatological position regarding the God/world relationship, Purtill asserts that the view of nature that entails it to possess an "inherent principle of order" is not rational, and that therefore it is best to surmise a rational agent, a God if you will, to be the ordering principle within the universe.[77] And since it is rational to propose that this God is the basis of order for the universe, it is similarly rational to propose that said God could manipulate and/or alter events at various times.

It also must not be *apriori* assumed that God cannot violate the natural law, or that God can only violate said natural laws through what is commonly labeled as the miraculous. Rather, I postulate that God should be conceived as inhering within the intricacies of nature so that he could (panentheistically) control how nature effects its ends. This panentheistically informed pneumatological position would affirm both the uniformity of nature, as well as God's providential working within nature. So then, divine omnipotence, in this view, could be preserved and also allow for the relative integrity of natural processes. Moreover, this panentheistically informed pneumatological position rejects the metaphysical limitations imposed by both a strict determinism and a strictly defined theology of the God/world relationship. In working from a panentheistically informed pneumatological position, I am able to affirm the pervasiveness of God's special providence, as well as the simultaneous existence of evil, all the

---

76. Purtill, *Thinking About Religion*, 68.
77. Ibid., 69.

while positing that both God and His intentions for humanity are good. Indeed, a panentheistically informed pneumatological understanding of the God/world relationship offers credence to the notion that people can—and even should—expect the miraculous. This panentheistically informed pneumatological understanding of the God/world relationship should, then, be a welcome addition to the budding theology found within the Renewal movement, as it affirms the continuing personal, direct and specific action of God the Spirit in the world today.

12

Causation, Vitalism, and Hume[1]

CAUSATION HAS TROUBLED PHILOSOPHERS at least since the time of Aristotle, and philosophers have consequently sought to clarify the concept of causation. The main reason for the quest to clarify causation concerns its implications for other philosophical issues, as clarity regarding causation is intrinsically vital for clarity in the areas of metaphysics, epistemology, the philosophy of science, the philosophy of language, as well as the philosophy of logic.[2] To believe in causation is simply to believe that there is something fundamental about nature in virtue of which the world is regular in its behavior and that something is *what* causation is, or is at least is an essential *component* of what causation involves.[3] It may be added that the concept of causation involves the notion of one thing deriving from another.

In the seventeenth century, there was much debate regarding the notion of vitalism,[4] and this debate heavily influenced the discussion regarding causation. Additionally, the topic of causation was prominent in seventeenth century philosophy in large part because of the need to reconcile mechanistic physics with traditional beliefs regarding the relation between God and creation. Prior to the seventeenth century, Western philosophy largely considered the concept of causation as unproblematic, and

---

1. A previous version of this chapter appeared in *Philosophy and Theology* 29 2 (2017) 341–51.

2. Brand, ed., *The Nature of Causation*, 1.

3. Strawson, *The Secret Connexion*, 85.

4. Note that the term vitalism, as used within this chapter, could be roughly equated with the concept of teleology, as understood in today's terminology.

its intelligibility was not an issue. However, during this early modern period many philosophers questioned the intelligibility of causal interactions and the notion of causation itself.[5] As a consequence of this debate, causes were no longer seen as the active initiators of a change, but as inactive nodes in a law-like implication chain. An important characteristic of the early modern conception of cause was that causation and determinism became virtually equivalent, thus denying any sort of vitalistic impulse within matter. The crux of the debate between the broad categorization of those who were rationalists and those who were empiricists during this early modern period pertained to the nature of cause.

The structure of the modern scientific revolution, onset by advances within the early modern period, became a mechanistic one, and vitalism eventually became a term of contempt in the mind of the mechanists. The primary distinction between mechanism and vitalism is in terms of vitalism's self-organization. In mechanism, causation is external: the configuration of beings is determined. In vitalism, causation is largely self-caused. Vitalism is opposed to mechanistic materialism and its thesis that life emerges from a spontaneous complex combination of organic, carbon-based matter.

In this chapter, I will focus on how early modern philosophers reacted to the notion of vitalism, which was formerly seen to be the primary agent of causation within philosophy. I will trace the development of vitalism cursorily through history, noting how the discussion regarding vitalism culminates with the reduction of all causation to mere efficient causation, as apparent in Hume. The early modern philosophers, almost wholesale and culminating with Hume, discard talking about the Aristotelian four causes, and reduce what we can epistemically know regarding causation to efficient causation only, which implicitly denied the *recognition* of any sort of vitalistic impulse. Hume, for all intents and purposes, is still the paradigm of both Western philosophy and Western science, especially in regards to the notion of causation.

Vitalism in History Prior to the Early Modern Period

In this section I will give a general definition of vitalism, and thereafter expand on its origins as well as its reception prior to the early modern period. Moreover, I will explain what it is, principally, that distinguishes vitalism

---

5. Loeb, *From Descartes to Hume*, 17.

PART FOUR: PNEUMATOLOGY, PHILOSOPHY, & SCIENCE

from other competing theories of causation. And then I shall conclude with how early modern philosophers responded to the notion of vitalism, which will segue into the next section.

Definition and Derivation of Vitalism

Vitalism is the doctrine that the causation of a living organism is due to a vital principle distinct from physicochemical forces.[6] According to vitalism, living organisms are *fundamentally* different from non-living entities because they contain some non-physical element or are governed by different principles than are inanimate things.[7] Aristotle's explanations of biological phenomena are thought of as vitalistic; therefore, Aristotle is regarded as the father of all vitalistic theories.[8] It is from Aristotle that vitalism gains a conception of an active and immaterial factor inherent within the matter that constitutes life.[9] Moreover, Aristotle believed that the soul, as a modality of life-energy, kept the organism alive. Another source of influence for vitalism comes from the Greek anatomist Galen who, in the third century CE, held that vital spirits were necessary for life.[10]

Implications of Vitalism

In its simplest form, vitalism posits that living entities contain some distinctive immaterial impulse within it that causes its emergence. In more sophisticated forms, the vitalistic impulse is a substance *infusing* bodies and giving life to them. So then, vitalists believe that the laws of physics and chemistry alone cannot explain life functions and processes. Vitalism, as used within this chapter, is primarily concerned with what one might call dynamic teleology. Dynamic teleology posits that there is internal purposiveness to the processes in matter, as opposed to descriptive (or static) teleology, which is only teleological in the sense of having order.[11] Vitalism was addressed in varying manners by the emergence of modern science

---

6. Schubert-Soldern, *Mechanism and Vitalism*, 8.
7. Ibid., 10.
8. Driesch, *The History and Theory of Vitalism*, 11.
9. Schubert-Soldern, *Mechanism and Vitalism*, 14.
10. Galen, *On Anatomical Procedures*, 34.
11. Ibid., 6.

during the late seventeenth and early eighteenth centuries, as well as by the philosophers of that age who reacted against it.

A Survey of Hume's Thinking Regarding Causation

David Hume (1711–1776) represents the culmination of the debate on causation in the eighteenth century. In this section, I will analyze Hume's simplification, secularization, and epistemological treatment of causation, which thereby delimits the role in which any sort of vitalism could be epistemically knowable in causation. I will address Hume's response to, and critique of, earlier causation theories. As Hume is still the paradigm for causation within the Western world, I will analyze Hume's view of causation within *A Treatise of Human Nature* in the second section.[12] Then, in the third section, I will present Hume's view of causation within *An Enquiry concerning Human Understanding*.[13] The second and third sections, respectively, set up the transition to the New Hume Debate, which is found in the fourth section. The New Hume Debate, I argue, is critical to attain an adequate view of causation today. Although Hume, in this *new* understanding, allows for causation outside of efficient causation, he nonetheless stipulates that speculation on the nature of such causation is fruitless, for one knows not the "causal joint."[14]

Hume's Response to Earlier Causation Theories

By far the most important relation for Hume is causation, for that, "relation alone can lead us beyond the immediate impressions of our memory and senses."[15] Hume writes, "There is no question, which on account of its importance, as well as difficulty, has caus'd more disputes both among antient and modern philosophers, than this concerning the efficacy of causes, or that quality which makes them be follow'd by their effects."[16]

---

12. References to the *Treatise* abbreviated "SBN" give the corresponding page numbers to: Hume, *A Treatise of Human Nature*.
13. References to the *Enquiry* abbreviated "SBN" give the corresponding page numbers to David Hume, *An Enquiry concerning Human Understanding*.
14. Note that this is modern idiom, not attributable to Hume himself.
15. Hume, *Treatise*, 1.3.6.7, SBN 26.
16. Ibid., 1.3.14.2, SBN 156.

Hume had at least four traditions that he targeted with his writings: the vitalists, the scholastics, the rationalists, and the occasionalists. Hume directly challenged the traditional vitalistic account of causation, as well as the occasionalist's understanding of causation because he perceived God's agency within both models. In attempting to belie the notion that God is the total efficient cause of all things, Hume deemed it true that created things have authentic causal capacities, whereas they could not if God—and *only* God—is causally efficacious. Hume therefore reacts negatively toward earlier causation theories.

In fact, Hume, "for the first time in the history of philosophy examines the notion of power and declares it to be spurious."[17] It is not until Hume that we have the empiricist principle formulated with great rigor, as well as a more rigorous critique of metaphysical knowledge.[18] Hume strikes "at the root of our common sense notion" of causation, and analyzes the situation more *thoroughly* than anyone else before him.[19] Hume's greatest contribution to the philosophy of causation is not that he solved the problems of causation, however, but that he raised the questions and made the philosophical problems of causation readily apparent instead.[20] Chakraboti asserts, "whoever understands Hume's arguments on causality understands Hume's purport in his *Treatise* and *Enquiry*."[21] In his implicit attack upon vitalism, Hume writes: "the terms of *efficacy, agency, power, force, energy, necessity, connexion,* and *productive quality,* are all nearly synonymous; and therefore "tis an absurdity to employ any of them in defining the rest."[22] Whereas the Aristotelian/scholastic model of causation centered God as the active cause of everything within his creation, Hume jettisons that model in favor of explanations without God, substantial forms, or even substances.[23]

Hume's View of Causation Within the Treatise

Hume gives at least two different definitions of the term "cause" within his *Treatise*. In his first definition, Hume writes, "We may define a CAUSE to be

17. Chakraboti, *Hume's Theory of Causality*, 52.
18. Messinese, *Problem of God in Modern Philosophy*, 12.
19. Chakraboti, *Hume's Theory of Causality*, 26.
20. Ducasse, "Critique of Hume's Analysis," 68.
21. Chakraboti, *Hume's Theory of Causality*, vii.
22. Hume, *Treatise*, 1.3.14.4, SBN 157; emphasis in original.
23. Clatterbaugh, *The Causation Debate*, 7.

'An object precedent and contiguous to another, and where all the objects resembling the former are plac'd in like relations of precedency and contiguity to those objects that resemble the latter.'[24] In his second definition of cause within the *Treatise*, Hume notes:

> If this definition be esteem'd defective, because drawn from objects foreign to the cause, we may substitute this other definition in its place, viz. "A CAUSE is an object precedent and contiguous to another, and so united with it, that the idea of the one determines the mind to form the idea of the other, and the impression of the one to form a more lively idea of the other."[25]

The first of these two definitions defines causation in terms of a *realist* perspective, whereas the second definition cause within the *Treatise*, building upon the first, seems to refer to dispositions of the mind (a *regularity* perspective). Hume, I postulate, was a regularity theorist in the *Treatise*. Indeed, he writes,

> The only conclusion we can draw from the existence of one thing to that of another, is by means of the relation of cause and effect, which shews, that there is a connexion betwixt them, and that the existence of one is dependent on that of the other. The idea of this relation is deriv'd from past experience, by which we find, that two beings are constantly conjoin'd together, and are always present at once to the mind.[26]

Moreover, Hume also writes in the *Treatise* that, "the constant conjunction of objects constitutes the very essence of cause and effect."[27] Contra Strawson, who claims that, "Hume does not hold anything like the strong Regularity theory of causation in the *Treatise*,"[28] I deem it true that Hume indeed was a regularity theorist in the *Treatise*, though he had changed his position on causation prior to the writing of the *Enquiry*, to which I now turn.

---

24. Hume, *Treatise*, 1.3.14.31, SBN 170.
25. Ibid., 170.
26. Ibid., 212.
27. Ibid., 173.
28. Strawson, *The Secret Connexion*, 169.

Hume's View of Causation Within the Enquiry

There are not only two definitions of the term "cause" in the *Treatise*, but there are also two definitions of the term "cause" within the *Enquiry*. And although the analysis of causation by Hume is different in the *Treatise* versus the *Enquiry*, the conclusion is essentially the same. Notably, the *Treatise* highlights the necessary connection in the mind, whereas the *Enquiry* does not. Strawson stipulates that the *Enquiry* was more representative of Hume's mature views than the *Treatise*, for in the *Treatise*, Hume was inclined toward "dramatic overstatement in his polemic."[29] In Hume studies, it is generally recognized that whenever statements find their place within both writings, the more mature view is to be given precedence. Thus, I shall now identify Hume's two definitions of cause within the *Enquiry*, as they do differ in expression, if not in essence, from those found within the *Treatise*. In his first definition of cause within the *Enquiry*, Hume writes:

> [W]e may define a cause to be *an object, followed by another, and where all the objects, similar to the first, are followed by objects similar to the second*. Or in other words, *where, if the first object had not been, the second never had existed*.[30]

In his second definition herein, Hume says that we can "form another definition of cause; and call it, *an object followed by another . . . whose appearance always conveys the thought to that other*."[31]

The New Hume Debate

One of the major disputes in Hume scholarship in the past thirty years has been the "new Hume" (or skeptical realist interpretation) position, which holds that Hume does *not* deny that there are real causal connections among external objects. Annas and Barnes note, "scepticism consists precisely in the fact that there is something there to be known which... [we are] not in a position to know."[32] The skeptical realist interpretation of Hume is called such because Hume is a realist, as he thinks that there is a reality that the human can perceive. However, Hume is a skeptic in that what is real to us, at its most fundamental level, is ungraspable by the human mind. So then,

---

29. Ibid., 8.
30. Hume, *Enquiry*, SBN 76; emphasis in original.
31. Ibid., 77; emphasis in original.
32. Annas and Barnes, *The Modes of Scepticism*, 97–98.

whereas one cannot penetrate into the essence of matter or real power, one is nonetheless compelled to believe that they exist. In this view, Hume combines reliance on experiment with the conviction that the ultimate secrets of nature cannot be discovered by our enquiries.[33] Hume, then, is making the negative skeptical epistemological claim that we cannot know anything regarding the nature of causation, but he is not making the non-skeptical, dogmatic, ontological-metaphysical claim that there is no such thing as causation. Part of the inspiration for this skeptical realist interpretation is that Hume does write a lot about the "hidden powers", and one way to take these statements is to interpret them as *affirmations* that there are indeed hidden powers (or even vitalistic impulses).[34]

Galen Strawson is a prominent scholar who defends the skeptical realist interpretation of Hume's theory of causation. He argues that Hume believes in real causal power, and does so not only in common life, but also as a philosopher.[35] Strawson suggests that it never really occurred to Hume to question real causal power, that is, that there must be—and is—something about nature and reality that enables it to be ordered and regular in the way that it is—even in his most skeptical mode. Rather than denying causal power, Hume insists that we have no real grasp of its nature, despite our conviction to the contrary. Hume writes, "experience only teaches us, how one event constantly follows another; without instructing us in the secret connexion, which binds them together, and renders them inseparable."[36] Hume notes that the causal powers are "secret" in that we cannot discover their true nature, because that nature is not revealed through sensory experience. However, Hume concedes that they exist nonetheless, although we can only speculate about them.[37] Additionally, although Hume notes "we are ignorant of those powers and forces, on which this regular course and succession of objects totally depends,"[38] it is nonetheless significant that he admits that the objects "totally depend" upon said powers and forces (or vitalistic impulse). As a true and thorough skeptic, "Hume continually stresses the fact that there may exist aspects of reality which are not only

33. Smith, *The Philosophy of David Hume*, 62.

34. Strawson writes that there are "objective, 'fundamental forces' governing the behavior of the world . . . [and] [t]hese forces are features of—they are essentially constitutive of—the nature of matter" (Strawson, *The Secret Connexion*, 90–91).

35. Ibid., 1.

36. Hume, *Enquiry*, 66.

37. Ibid., 73–74.

38. Ibid., 55.

unknown by us, but are also unknowable by us, beyond our powers of comprehension, and in that sense utterly unintelligible to us."[39]

Preliminary Conclusions

After Hume, I contend, science and philosophy are once more in accord regarding the notion of causation. Indeed, with Hume, both science and philosophy are rescued from the foolish notion that what we perceive to be the cause of change(s) is not the true cause.[40] Laden with irony, however, Alfred North Whitehead writes, "causation has emerged from its treatment by Hume like the parrot after its contest with the monkey."[41] Contemporary discussions of causation are invariably influenced by Hume's views on the subject, as the relationship between causes and effects is seen as a purely *external* affair. Another aspect of this influence is that all we can definitively know of causation is regular succession.

However, the Aristotelian notion of causation is closer to the truth than the early modern or contemporary manifestation of the same, as it contains the closely related concepts of power (or efficacy) and necessity (or compulsion), as well as allowing for different causation methodologies (i.e., efficient, formal, material, and final). Unfortunately, most contemporary philosophers have eschewed the notion of other types of causation, reducing instead causation to mere efficient terms (or regular, temporal succession). The cause of an event, after Hume, is now almost universally supposed to be some condition or set of conditions that temporally precedes some other in time.

This chapter has shown that Hume is a realist in terms of *known* causes, but allows for secret "powers." Whereas Hume admits that there may exist secret powers or "unknown qualities" in nature, we are unable to *know* anything of their natures, and as such our causal explanations cannot employ them. Hume's description of causal power(s) allows one "to *refer* to it while having absolutely no sort of positive conception of its nature."[42] In effect, then, philosophy post-Hume has reduced all knowable instances of causation to mere efficient causal language, denying the reality and import of material, formal, and final causality.

---

39. Strawson, *The Secret Connexion*, 53.
40. Clatterbaugh, *The Causation Debate*, 206.
41. Whitehead, *The Interpretation of Science*, 57.
42. Strawson, *The Secret Connexion*, 52. Emphasis in original.

13

Triangulating Peirce, Gould, and Conway Morris into a Thematic Understanding of the Theology and Science Relationship

Themes of Evolutionary Thought

Two themes regarding the nature of evolutionary thought, that of it being pictured as descent with modification and as it being marked by an over-reliance on genetics and a high emphasis upon contingency, mark the historical development of Darwinism broadly construed. I would like to hope that we, in the twenty-first century, can move beyond these two models, and enter into a Darwinism as potentially marked by an evolutionary developmental philosophy assisted by Charles Sanders Peirce and a proposed period of stability between the competing extremes of an over-emphasis on contingency on one side, and strict predictability on the other. Each of the two aforementioned themes may be thought to correspond to a phase in the evolution of Darwinism. The first such phase was the period from the publication of *The Origin of Species* (1859) to the early twentieth-century. Although there were positions put forth regarding various evolutionary theories and the competing debates about those evolutionary theories before *The Origin of Species*, it was Darwin's work that succeeded in convincing both the scientific community and the wider public of the fact that all species are related to one another.[1] Darwin's phrase "descent with modification," which he preferred to the term "evolution," sums up clearly

---

1. Brooke, *Science and Religion*, 226–74.

the concept of evolutionary continuity that the original form of Darwinism supposed.

Again, each of these themes may be thought of as corresponding to a phase in the evolution of Darwinism. The first such phase was the period from the publication of *The Origin of Species* (1859) to the early-twentieth century. This first phase of Darwinism came to fruition in the *Modern Evolutionary Synthesis*, during the 1930s through the 1940s, when the importance of natural selection as an explanation of evolutionary change was confirmed, following also from the synthesis of natural selection with the rediscovery of Gregor Mendel's theory of particulate inheritance. This coupling led it to be termed the "Neo-Darwinian" synthesis.

The second phase in the history of Darwinism may be thought of as originating in the 1970s with various pressures on the Neo-Darwinian synthesis.[2] A feature common to the consequent expansions of the Neo-Darwinian synthesis is the theme of contingency. As David J. Depew and Bruce H. Weber say of current evolutionary biology,

> Just as Darwin's work exploded the Victorians cozy sense of space and time, so contemporary evolutionary speculation is forcing twentieth century Darwinians to adjust to the even more expansive, chancy, contingent worldview that is already present in modern cosmology but that has so far been contained in evolutionary biology by the comforting rationalism of our talk about adaptations, according to which, even if we do not invoke God, we still seem to be able to give good reasons for what we see around us.[3]

Into this modern retrieval of the import of chance in evolutionary explanations, I would like to propose that Peirce's evolutionary developmental philosophy is a mediating third way between total chance on one side and total determination on the other. For Peirce, the element of chance in the universe is the essential agency by which the whole process of (macro-) evolution is brought about.[4] Indeed, the consensus view among biologists at the early part of the twenty-first century is that all genetic mutations occur by "chance" or at "random" with respect to adaptation. However, the discovery of some molecular mechanisms enhancing mutation rate in response to environmentmental conditions has given rise to discussions among biologists, historians, and philosophers of biology about the

2. Depew and Weber, eds. *Evolution at a Crossroads*, 14.
3. Ibid., 15.
4. Peirce, "Design and Chance," 219.

"chance" vs. "directed" character of mutations (1980s–2000s). Nevertheless, I would like to proceed with the aforementioned delineations.

Theme 1: Darwinism as Relayed by Darwin Himself

After returning home from his sea voyage on the Beagle, Darwin's earlier belief in the special creation of each distinct species transmutated into a strong suspicion that the origin of different living species had occurred gradually, in a purely natural way. Among the many questions that Darwin and other naturalists who thereafter studied the specimens he collected on the voyage began to ask was, Why do small but distinct variations appear among geographically distributed species of birds and other animals? Specific differences in species, Darwin began to suppose, could be accounted for without divine special creation if there had been minute, cumulative changes in living organisms over an immensely long time. In fact, following his return from the voyage of the Beagle, Darwin writes of his own views, "The old argument from design in nature, as given by Paley, which formerly seemed to me so conclusive, fails, now that the law of natural selection has been discovered. There seems to be no more design in the variability of organic beings and in the action of natural selection, than in the course which the wind blows."[5]

In offering the mechanism of natural selection, Darwin gave a new kind of answer to what had previously been viewed as a strictly theological question. After he published his theory in 1859, Darwin effectively made natural science the new kind of ultimate explanation by making science itself able to provide a new answer to a very old theological question. After all, if natural science can account for something as complex as living organisms, including things as simple as the fish's eye and eventually as complex as even the human brain, had not science then taken over theology's place in the task of making life's designs fully intelligible? If natural selection is the ultimate cause of apparent design, do classic theological explanations matter at all? What good is theology if science can provide a satisfying answer to one of humanity's most burning questions?[6] These questions are still quite alive today—over one hundred and fifty years later.

---

5. Charles Darwin, *Autobiography,* http://darwin-online.org.uk/content/frameset?itemID=F1497&viewtype=text&pageseq=1.

6. Haught, *Making Sense of Evolution,* 13.

PART FOUR: PNEUMATOLOGY, PHILOSOPHY, & SCIENCE

Theme 2: A Darwinism as Identified by Neo-Darwinists

The second phase of Darwinism came to fruition in the 1930s and 40s, during which the importance of natural selection as an explanation of evolutionary change was confirmed, following from the synthesis of natural selection with Gregor Mendel's rediscovered theory of particulate inheritance. This coupling led it to be termed the "Neo-Darwinian" synthesis. A feature common to the consequent expansions of the Neo-Darwinian synthesis are the over reliance on genetics and the theme of contingency.

Theme 3: A Darwinism Potentially Marked by an Evolutionary Developmental Philosophy of Peirce:

Into this distinctly modern retrieval of the import of chance in evolutionary explanations, I would like to propose that Charles Sander Peirce's evolutionary philosophy is a mediating third way between total chance on one side and total determination on the other. For Peirce, the element of chance in the universe is the essential agency by which the whole process of (macro-)evolution is brought about.[7] The operation of chance in evolution, however, shows an uncanny tendency to bring about unlikely events by various means under varying circumstances, a point which this chapter will later argue has implications for a modern view of the relation between theology and science.

The God of Chance

In the present section of this chapter, I will argue that ontological randomness is genuine. God does not determine the outcome of every scientifically random event, but instead controls randomness by setting broad boundaries, such as the range of possible outcomes of a random event and the probability of each outcome. God then allows particles, systems, and organisms to interact according to natural laws within these boundaries, producing a wide range of beautifully complex results. So then, we live in a world of chance and randomness. But how much is truly random? This chapter looks at how, through paleontological examination, randomness and chance, which are inextricably linked,[8] shape the world from the bottom

---

7. Peirce, "Design and Chance," 219.
8. Sweetman, *Evolution, Chance, and God*, 110.

up.[9] While I appreciate Brendan Sweetman's distinction between the two terms—an event came about by *chance* means it could have been otherwise, whereas *randomness* refers to there being no goal toward which an event strives—I do intentionally highlight that even he admits the two terms are tightly linked with one another. However, this is not the end of the story. Indeed, the phenomena known as convergence, which this chapter also explicates with reference to dagger-like canines in animals and several examples of the multiple convergences in camera-like and compound eyes in animals, indicates that though evolution through natural selection may proceed along various paths, the destinations are few. So then, there is a dichotomy: randomness is constrained within pattern.

In order to understand the events and generalities of life's pathway, we must go beyond principles of evolutionary theory to a paleontological examination of the contingent pattern of life's history on our planet—the single actualized version among millions of plausible alternatives that did not occur. Such a view of the history of life is highly contrary to both the conventional deterministic models of Western science and to the deepest social traditions of Western culture wanting for a history culminating in humanity as life's most magnificent expression.

In his magnum opus, *The Structure of Evolutionary Theory*, Stephen Jay Gould emphasizes the importance of recognizing both the reality of structural constraint and that structures have historical origins, and in so doing, he helps unite insights from both sides of the age-old debate between functionalist and formalist biologists. The functionalists—such as Darwin and Jean-Baptiste Lamarck—typically stressed that features of organisms existed for utilitarian reasons (they were adaptations to their environmentments), and formalists—such as Étienne Geoffroy Saint-Hilaire and Johann Wolfgang von Goethe—stressed the structural unity of type common across similar organisms. A formalist often denied the possibility of evolution because they believed that only superficial change, not fundamental change, was possible. This division was permanently undermined when Darwin showed that structures had evolved through natural selection, although after their emergence, these structures may constrain the evolutionary pathways available to organisms. In this, Darwin fundamentally reoriented the functionalist-formalist debate by adding a new dimension

9. Ibid.

to the functional (active adaptation) and formal (constraints of structure) dichotomy: historical contingencies.[10]

Life's pathway certainly includes many features predictable from the laws of nature, but these aspects are too broad and general to explain evolution's particular results—cats, dogs, mushrooms, people, and so forth. Organisms adapt to, and are constrained by, physical principles. Three features of the paleontological record stand out in opposition to the conventional view of the history of life as a broadly predictable process of gradually advancing complexity through time: the constancy of modal complexity; the concentration of major events in short bursts interspersed with long periods of stability; and the role of external impositions—primarily mass extinctions—in disrupting patterns of "normal" times.[11] These three features, combined with the more general themes of chaos and contingency, require a rethinking of the oft-accepted framework for conceptualizing the history of life.

According to Gould, the history of life is not progressive, necessarily, and it is certainly not predictable. The earth's biota has evolved through a series of fortuitous events. Homo *sapiens sapiens*, for example, did not appear on the earth in one glorious moment of time; humans arose, rather, as a contingent outcome of thousands of linked events, any one of which could have occurred differently and thereby led evolutionary history on a pathway that possibly could not have led to the derivation of consciousness. To mention just four examples among many:

1. If a member of our chordate phylum, *Pikaia*—which shows its relation to humans by its possession of a notochord—had not been among the survivors of the initial radiation of multicellular animal life in the Cambrian explosion ca. 520 million years ago, then it is unlikely that vertebrates would have inhabited the earth at all.

2. If a small group of lobe-finned fishes had not evolved with a radically different limb skeleton, with a strong central axis perpendicular to the body, capable of bearing weight on land, then vertebrates possibly would never have become terrestrial.

3. If a meteorite had not struck the earth ca. 65 million years ago, then dinosaurs would probably still be dominant today and mammals would still be small creatures living within the dinosaurs' world; and

10. Gould, *The Structure of Evolutionary Theory*, 251–60.
11. Gould, *The Richness of Life*, 212.

4. If a small lineage of primates had not evolved upright posture on the African savannas just two million years ago, then our ancestry might have wound up as a line of ecologically marginal apes.[12]

We are an item of evolutionary history and not an embodiment of general evolutionary principles.

In 1989, Gould published *Wonderful Life: The Burgess Shale and the Nature of History*, perhaps the most successful book on a paleontological subject since Darwin's *Origin*. Although seemingly a historical account of the discovery of the Burgess Shale invertebrate fossils, found high in the Canadian Rockies, Gould uses the book to advance a number of claims about the very nature of evolution. According to Gould, Charles Doolittle Walcott misinterpreted the fossils that he first found in the Burgess Shale in 1909, due in large part because of his conventional view of life that insisted upon evolution being marked by a steady, progressional rise of complexity. *Wonderful Life* shatters this conception, instead promoting the notion that Walcott committed a cardinal error by "shoehorning" the Burgess Shale fauna into existing phyla and classes.[13]

Walcott's interpretations of the Burgess fossils remained uncontested for more than fifty years until a group, spearheaded by Harry Whittington at Cambridge University in 1971, published a monograph that not only reexamined Walcott's conclusions, but also radically reinterpreted the Burgess Shale fauna, and with it the view of life—even our own evolution. *Wonderful Life* recounts this reinterpretation of the Burgess Shale fossils, and the ideas that emerged from this work by Whittington's group. Three paleontologists dominate the center stage in *Wonderful Life*, as they did the bulk of the technical work in anatomical description and taxonomic placement: the aforementioned Whittington, who at the time was the world's leading expert on trilobites, and two men who began their careers as his understudies and then built their careers on the Burgess fauna—Derek Briggs and Simon Conway Morris, the latter of which we will again meet in the next section of this chapter.

Gould employs the fossils of the Burgess Shale to further his arguments for the importance of historical contingency relative to natural selection and adaptation in the history of life. Indeed, Gould makes three primary arguments. First, rather than "the cone of increasing diversity"—which he

---

12. Gould, *Full House*, 3.
13. Gould, *Wonderful Life*, 108.

indicates is the primary iconography of evolution—the fauna of the Burgess Shale supports a model of rapid increase in morphologic disparity, a Christmas tree pattern, followed by the elimination of many lineages and diversification of the successful lineages, which indicates that the morphologic disparity (note, not "diversity") was a *primary* feature of the Cambrian explosion, and not a consequence of the subsequent evolutionary history.[14] He avers that the familiar accounts of evolution are meant to reinforce a comfortable view of human inevitability and superiority, arrived at after a ladder of progress. However, he contends, "Life is a copiously branching bush, continually pruned by the grim reaper of extinction, not a ladder of predictable progress."[15] So then, in Gould's view, evolutionary innovation was primarily focused in the events of the Cambrian, with later history largely "generating endless variants upon a few surviving models."[16]

Gould refers to this pattern as "decimation" because he can combine the literal and vernacular senses of the term to suggest the two cardinal aspects stressed throughout the book: the largely random sources of survival or death, and the high probability of extinction. Gould suspects that in the great majority of cases, the traits that enhance survival during an extinction event do so incidentally, and are not related to the causes of their evolution in the first place. While animals evolve their sizes, shapes, and morphologies under natural selection during normal times and for specific reasons, when a mass extinction comes along, what may have been advantageous before could turn out to be deleterious, whereas a trait without particular significance before the mass extinction event might attain one afterward. He asserts that there can be no causal correlation in principle between the derivation of a trait in that circumstance and its new usage. After all, a species "cannot evolve structures with a view to their potential usefulness millions of years down the road—unless our general ideas about causality are markedly awry, and the future can control the present."[17] With regard to randomness, he notes that, "decimate" comes from the Latin *decimare*: "to

---

14. Ibid., 38. For the general pattern of the Christmas tree, see 525–542; Raup and Gould, "Stochastic Simulation and Evolution of Morphology," 305–22; Gould et al., "The Shape of Evolution," 23–40; Gould, Gilinsky, and German, "Asymmetry of Lineages and the Direction of Evolutionary Time," 1437–441. We may interpret this bottom-heavy pattern in many ways; Gould sees it as "early experimentation and later standardization" (Gould, *Wonderful Life*, 304).

15. Gould, *Wonderful Life*, 35.

16. Ibid., 47.

17. Ibid., 307.

take one in ten," which referred originally to the standard punishment for members of the Roman army who were found to be guilty of mutiny—one soldier out of every ten was selected by lot and put to death. With regard to the probability of extinction, he points out that decimate connotes how most—say, 90 percent—of the individual entities in the Burgess fauna were extinguished without leaving any significant lineage. Stereotypy—the cramming of most species into a few anatomical plans—is the mark of modern life forms.[18]

The model of maximal increase in morphologic disparity early in the history of Metazoa as a whole leads to the second major argument of *Wonderful Life*, which is Gould's thought experiment of replaying the tape of life over. The Burgess pattern of decimation shows that groups may prevail or die for reasons that are not related to Darwinian selection processes. This leads him to stipulate that if it were possible to "replay the tape" of evolution, the outcome would almost certainly be very different, both in detail and in general. Gould's argument represents the culmination of his fight against overly adaptive storytelling and inferred evolutionary progress:

> Any replay of the tape would lead evolution down a pathway radically different from the road actually taken. But the consequent differences in outcome do not imply that evolution is senseless, and without meaningful pattern; the divergent route of the replay would be just as interpretable, just as explainable *after* the fact, as the actual road. But the diversity of possible itineraries does demonstrate that eventual results cannot be predicted at the outset. Each step proceeds for cause, but no finale can be specified at the start and none would even occur a second time in the same way, because any pathway proceeds through thousands of improbable stages. Alter any early event, ever so slightly and without apparent importance at the time, and evolution cascades into a radically different channel.[19]

For Gould, this is the essence of contingency. Gould's third argument in *Wonderful Life* builds on the pattern of disparity and the import of contingency to conclude that natural selection and adaptation play a less significant role in evolution than acknowledged by most evolutionary biologists.

We do not know why most of the early experiments were failures, with only a few surviving to become modern phyla. It is tempting to say that the

---

18. Ibid., 49.
19. Ibid., 51.

victors won by virtue of greater complexity, better fitness, or some other predictable feature of the conventional Darwinian struggle.[20] But nothing in particular unites the victors, and a radical alternative must be considered: that each early experiment received little more than a proverbial ticket in the largest "lottery" ever played on our planet—and that the surviving lineages, including our own phylum of vertebrates, survived more by the luck of the draw than by any intrinsic merit.[21]

The transforming power of the Burgess message can be seen in its affirmation of historical contingency as the chief determinant of life's direction, and it shows that the fantastic explosion of early disparity is followed by decimation, largely based in terms of what can be pictured as a lottery. Gould concedes that the origin of life on earth was virtually inevitable, given the early chemical composition of oceans and the atmosphere, along with the nature of self-organizing systems. In fact, Gould states, "I suspect that given the composition of early atmospheres and oceans, life's origin was a chemical necessity. Contingency arises later, when historical origin enters the picture of evolution."[22] While the laws of nature impact the general forms and functions of organisms, the channels are so broad that the details are left to chance. The physical channels do not specify "arthropods, annelids, mollusks, and vertebrates, but, at most, bilaterally symmetrical organisms based on repeated parts."[23] Much less do they specify the essential answers related to our own origin, such as why mammals evolved, why primates moved from land to the trees, and why the fragile lineage of Homo *sapiens sapiens* emerged and survived in Africa. This evidence suggests that God does not determine the outcome of every scientifically random event, but instead controls randomness by setting broad boundaries. God thereafter allows organisms to interact according to natural laws within these boundaries, producing a wide range of beautifully complex results. Sweetman, who argues explicitly for determinism, even admits that this definition of randomness works well within the discipline of biology.[24] I disagree with Sweetman, one may surmise, when he further stipulates that it is the "simple fact that it is not true that the cause (or more accurately causes) of any event in the universe could have been different than

---

20. Gould, *The Richness of Life*, 217.
21. Gould, *Wonderful Life*, 239.
22. Ibid., 309.
23. Ibid., 290.
24. Sweetman, *Evolution, Chance, and God*, 109.

they in fact were . . . In short, we are looking at a completely deterministic universe."[25]

The God of Purpose

Perhaps the most sustained critique of Gould's contingency argument has come from Simon Conway Morris. Conway Morris is Professor of Evolutionary Palaeobiology at the University of Cambridge. He notes that in the phenomena known as convergence, similar patterns appear in widely divergent groups, and he has compiled manifold amounts of examples of convergence and employed them to argue that despite apparent contingency, evolution is far more predictable than admitted by Gould (Conway Morris 1998,[26] 2004,[27] 2009[28]). He writes, however, that, "the likelihood of 'exactly the same cognitive creatures—with five fingers on each hand, a vermiform appendix, thirty-two teeth, and so on'[29] evolving again if, somehow, the Cambrian explosion could be rerun is remote in the extreme."[30] But what about the emergence of more general features in the evolutionary epic?

A few overarching themes emerge from the literature on convergence. The most obvious is that convergent features arise in response to similar processing demands. Convergence operates at all levels of biological organization. Conway Morris writes,

> To paraphrase much of this book, life may be a universal principle, but we can still be alone. In other words, once you are on the path it is pretty straightforward, but finding a suitable planet and maybe getting the right recipe for life's origination could be exceedingly difficult: inevitable humans in a lonely Universe. Now, if this happens to be the case, that in turn might be telling us something very interesting indeed. Either we are a cosmic accident, without either meaning or purpose, or alternatively . . .[31]

The central theme of *Life's Solution* depends on the realities of evolutionary convergence: the recurrent tendency of biological organization to

25. Sweetman, *Evolution, Chance, and God*, 113.
26. Conway Morris, *The Crucible of Creation*.
27. Conway Morris, *Life's Solution*.
28. Conway Morris, "The Predictability of Evolution," 1313–337.
29. Conway Morris, *Life's Solution*, 6–7.
30. Ibid., xii.
31. Conway Morris, *Life's Solution*, xiii.

arrive at the same "solution" to a particular "need." Within it, there are four conclusions: First, what we regard as complex is usually inherent in simpler systems: the real unanswered question in evolution is not novelty *per se*, but how things are put together. Second, the number of evolutionary endpoints is limited, meaning that in no way is everything possible. Third, what is possible has usually been arrived at multiple times. Finally, all this takes billions of years to become increasingly inevitable.[32] Convergence tells us at least two things: that evolutionary trends are real, and that adaptation is not some occasional component in the organic machine, but is central to the explanation of derivation of life.

It is surprising in light of the high probability for novelty in (macro-) evolution, to find—in similar niches—high morphological similarity in distinctly different genetic lines. Evolution is indeed constrained, if not bound. Despite the immensity of biological hyperspace, Conway Morris argues that nearly all of it must remain forever empty, not because our chance drunken walk failed to wander into it, but because the possibilities were from the beginning unavailable. This implies that it matters little what our starting point may have been, as the different routes will not prevent a convergence to similar ends, and that we may be on the verge of glimpsing a deeper structure to life.

Conway Morris gives an example from the world of predator-prey relationships. The dagger-like canines, in both placental cats (the sabre-tooth cats)[33] and a group of South American marsupials known as the thylacosmilids, independently evolved.[34] In fact, the evidence suggests that even within the placental cats the sabre-tooth habit evolved several times.[35] Although as a group the marsupials are best known as kangaroo and wombat species, they tend to be regarded in some generalized sense as inferior to the placentals.[36] So, too, the rich, but now largely extinct, diversity of South American marsupials is widely regarded as having been competitively inferior to the placental mammals that surged south when the Panamanian

---

32. Ibid., xii–xiii.

33. See, for example, Churcher, "Dental functional morphology," 201–20.

34. See, for example, Turnbull, "Another look at dental specialization," 399–414.

35. Antón and Turner point out that sabres have evolved at least three times in the placentals (Antón and Turner, *The Big Cats*, 30–31).

36. Kirsch, "The Six-Percent Solution," 276–88. Interestingly, Kirsch suggests that the marsupium—that is, the pouch in which the young develop—actually arose several times independently within the marsupials, an argument that presupposes that primitively this group of mammals lacked the pouch.

isthmus was formed several million years ago. In contradistinction to the prevailing notion, the sabre showed a number of design advantages when compared with the placental equivalents in the marsupial thylacosmilids, including the possession of a protective flange, a self-sharpening mechanism, and a deeper insertion into the skull that presumably afforded a more secure housing for the canine. Despite this manifest convergence, neither group escapes its hallmark of phylogenetic history, which is marked in the specific structure of the teeth.[37]

Not only are the dagger-like canines convergent, but also are other features in nature. For example, cats of all varieties see through the dilated pupils of its camera eyes, whereas the mosquito sees through its compound eyes. Not only have both these types of eye—camera and compound—evolved several times, but even the neural architecture underlying the sight mechanism has shown multiple convergences. The existence of camera and compound eyes reminds us that solutions to biological evolution need not be unique, but are simply very strongly constrained. When considering convergences between camera-eyes, it is almost inevitable that comparisons will be drawn between the camera-eyes of vertebrates and those of the advanced cephalopods,[38] notably the squid and octopus. Of course, there are well-known differences; most notable is those between the relative position of the light-sensitive layer, the retina, which arise as a result of the different embryologies in vertebrates and mollusks. In mollusks, the retina is derived from the ectoderm (the outer layer); as it *in*volutes to make the eyecup, the associated nerve cells extend into the body to make their connection with the brain. The vertebrate retina, in contrast, is effectively an *out*growth of the central nervous system. The net result of this process is that in the vertebrates the nerve cells overlie the retina. The exit point of these nerves to the optic tract, which then leads to the brain, results in a "blind spot" in the retina. The arrangement of nerve cells and retina in mollusks and vertebrates is reversed, however, with the cephalopods arguably having the better design of the nervous layer being beneath the sensory retina (which definitively runs counter to progressional thinking regarding Homo *sapiens sapiens*).

These differences are important, but it is still the case that the similarities between the human eye and those of a cephalopod are very striking.

---

37. See Koenigswald and Goin's remarks on enamel structure in, "Enamel Differentiation in South American Marsupials," 129–68.

38. Budelmann, "Cephalopod Sense Organs," 13–33.

PART FOUR: PNEUMATOLOGY, PHILOSOPHY, & SCIENCE

What is less well known is that a similar camera-eye has evolved independently in several other groups; for instance, the most notable is in a group of marine annelids (alciopids), which are close relatives of the more familiar earthworms.[39] These eyes are strikingly similar to those of the vertebrates and cephalopods, and because the annelids are also relatively closely related to the mollusks, the retina has the same arrangement as in the latter group. There is, moreover, another convergence in the alciopid eye—the so-called accessory retinas, which are light sensitive patches located nearer to the front of the eye; these are convergent on similar structures found in some deep-sea fish and cephalopods.[40] Returning to the mollusks, considering this time the gastropods (snails), we find that in this group a camera-like eye seems to have evolved independently at least three times.[41]

Nor does the list of convergently evolved camera-eyes quite end there; there are two more examples that Conway Morris recounts, each in their own way surprising.[42] The first example comes from the primitive cubozoans, which are a type of jellyfish renowned both for their highly toxic stings and for their remarkable eyes. The eyes are similar in construction to other camera-eyes, with a large lens located in front of the retina.[43] Cubozoan jellyfish belong to a primitive group of animals, the cnidarians, which also includes the sea anemones and corals. While primitive eyespots are known in other cnidarians, at first sight the sophistication of the cubozoan eyes, which typically total eight arranged around the margin of the swimming bell, is quite surprising. What is particularly interesting is the relative simplicity of their nervous system, which consists of a nerve net linked to a series of four pacemakers, a neural architecture that is effectively imposed by the jellyfish body plan. There is no brain.[44] Yet there are complex eyes

---

39. Conway Morris, *Life's Solution*, 152.

40. Wald and Raypart, "Vision in annelid worms." They remark, "The presence of accessory retinas in alciopid eyes offers a prime instance of the phenomenon of evolutionary convergence" (1437). They suggest that they may function to detect light of long wavelength, which penetrates more deeply into the sea, and could thus be used to judge depth.

41. A general overview of the camera-like eyes in both the heteropods (such as Pterotrachea) and also Littorina and Strombus, is given by Charles, "Sense Organs (less cephalopods)," 455–521.

42. Conway Morris, *Life's Solution*, 154.

43. See Pearse and Pearse, "Vision of Cubomedusan Jellyfishes," 458.

44. Evidence for the visual abilities of cubozoans is given by Hamner, Jones, and Hamner, "Swimming, Feeding, Circulation and Vision," 985–90.

and sophisticated behavior. So then, even considering rudimentary forms of life, the pattern of convergence dominates, suggesting that there may be a God of purpose behind it all, wooing, if you will, creation forward in complexity.

The God of Chance & Purpose

In the concluding section of this chapter, I suggest that we must suppose an element of absolute chance, sporting, spontaneity, originality, and freedom in nature. I explicate three models of evolution as presented by Peirce—comprised of tychism, anancasm and agapism. Together, this threefold description provides a plausible account of evolution that is in some sense explainable by reference to teleology. Moreover, I explain how Peirce, by virtue of his developmental teleology, brought a unique understanding of reality to philosophy. In fleshing out my constructive proposal in this section of the chapter, I further dialogue with Peirce, drawing from him a developmental teleological view, which is then applied to a modern rendition of teleology that perhaps could be made palatable for the modern evolutionary sciences. An "evolutionary developmental teleology" will be proposed, whereby the telos of evolution is seen to be, broadly, increased complexity, a telos of which is ever growing and not exact in what it calls for to actualize its completion. This means, then, that there are no definite end games according to which the creation of complexity corresponds. The ever-intensifying growth of complexity, which is apparent in the incipient complexification of matter, is the *general* telos according to which creation leads. At present, humans are the pinnacle, but what this might mean for the future is, at the present moment, unknown, for we have no definite looking glass into what the future might hold for the evolution of species.

Also in the final section, I note how Charles Sanders Peirce contends that bodies indeed obey the laws of mechanics, but it may be true that if our means of measurement were better, or if we were able to wait inconceivable ages for an exception, exceptions to any law would perhaps be found. In fact, it may be that chance, in the Aristotelian sense of there being the absence of a general, necessitating cause, has to be admitted as being relevant in our universe. Aristotle, in his *Physics*, writes,

> It is clear then that chance is an incidental cause in the sphere of those actions for the sake of something which involve purpose. Intelligent reflection, then, and chance are in the same sphere, for

purpose implies intelligent reflection ... It is necessary, no doubt, that the causes of what comes to pass by chance be indefinite; and that is why chance is supposed to belong to the class of the indefinite and to be inscrutable to man, and why it might be thought that, in a way, nothing occurs by chance. For all these statements are correct, because they are well grounded. Things do, in a way, occur by chance, for they occur incidentally and chance is an incidental cause. But strictly it is not the cause—without qualification—of anything; for instance, a housebuilder is the cause of a house; incidentally, a fluteplayer may be so.[45]

Preliminary Conclusions: A Proper Balance

In this section of the chapter, I argue for a balance between the competing extremes of an overemphasis on contingency— à la Gould—and the strong predictability thesis of Conway Morris. I also attempt to dismiss the French physicist Pierre-Simon de Laplace's claim that a sufficiently informed intelligence could forecast everything that is going to happen in the whole universe—and, working backwards—tell you everything that did happen, not by direct citation and rebuke, but rather by implicit argumentation and demonstration of the God of *chance* and *purpose*. History also includes too much contingency, or the shaping of present results by long chains of unpredictable antecedent states, rather than immediate determination, for a position—such as Laplace's—to be palatable.

It should be noted that the thirteenth century Christian philosopher Thomas Aquinas insisted that a perfect universe must contain randomness to allow humans their autonomy.[46] I argue that while ontological randomness is indeed genuine, as God does not directly determine the outcome of every scientifically random event, he nevertheless instead generally controls randomness by setting broad boundaries. God then allows particles, organisms and even systems to interact according to natural laws within these boundaries, producing a wide range of beautifully complex results. So then, we live in a world of both chance and purpose, and both chance and purpose are critical to account for in a modern relation of theology and science. One may even go so far as to state that this world is designed for both chance and purpose, though one needs to be wary of allowing overly

---

45. Aristotle, *Physics* II, 29.
46. Aquinas, *Summa Contra Gentiles*, III.80.3.

anthropomorphic notions to creep into the analysis. Rational beings, in this scenario, are not ipso facto required for God to control randomness, as the degree of influence the deity has is dependent upon the level of sentience that the entity in relation possesses.

In this chapter, I have argued for a balance between the competing extremes of an overemphasis on contingency—à la Gould—and the strong predictability thesis of Conway Morris. The preceding analysis of Gould's and Conway Morris's postulates suggests two things that are relevant for the purposes of this book. First, there is ontological randomness in nature. Theologically interpreted, God uses this randomness in order to achieve the population of creation by maintaining dynamic equilibria in complex systems. But this ontological randomness does not preclude the derivation of propensities toward the expression of similar form, even among widely divergent evolutionary lines. These findings strengthen the case that mechanical optimization can drive evolution, contributing to the long-standing debate over the evolutionary roles of randomness versus physical constraints that limit the solutions that are feasible in living creatures.

14

Conclusion

A Modern Relation of Theology & Science

THIS PROJECT GROWS OUT of my overall desire to have a functional and potent relationship between science and theology in my personal and academic life. I am a biologist by initial training, a former atheist due to my personal Traumatic Brain Injury and the entailments thereof, I also worked for numerous years at Emergent Genetics making things that God did not, and then—only after a long process—I converted to Christianity.

In this book, the ever-present call for dialogue between theology and science has been taken seriously. While I do not wish to repeat myself in this conclusion, I will recapitulate some salient points. A modern relation of theology and science is fundamentally based on a monistic, process-based view of the world. This modern relation consists of, principally, an overlapping of the two domains of theology and science. It has panentheism as a main or even key tenet. Kenosis, understood as a divine pouring of the Spirit into creation, provides the basis for this panentheistic postulation. Charles Sanders Peirce, and his evolutionary developmental teleology is critical to this modern construction of the theology and science relationship. I build principally off the insights of Stephen Jay Gould as well, garnering from him the import of chance, or the tychism of the evolutionary process to use Peircean terminology. I will note that I have strong sympathies with the position of Gould, highlighting as he does the import of historical contingency in evolution; using Peirce enables me to maintain the most significant elements of Gould's views. The telos that I propose

Conclusion

herein is *not* specific, unlike other popular forms of teleology but is of a *general* type instead: that is, increased complexity. With Peirce, I posit that final causation without efficient causation is blind, and efficient causation without final causation is worse than blind—it is mere chaos.

My argument in this book builds upon itself, and works outward in a logical manner over thirteen distinct chapters: The first chapter is introductory in its nature, and set the scene for the remainder of the title. Indeed, in chapter 1, I outline several historical depictions of the science & theology relationship, with the intent of showing them to be lacking.

Chapters 2–5 are the fulcrum upon which the thesis of this book depends. These four chapters are constructive in their nature, and cover emergence, kenosis, and theology. In them, I develop a kenotic-relational theology that is based principally on the uncontrolling love of God, and I make inroads to linking my kenotic view of nature with the philosophical construct of emergence theory as aptly presented by Philip Clayton. These chapters are so important, in fact, that I feel as if I must refocus your attention to them rather than attempting to summarize them. Nevertheless, chapter 2 defends Amos Yong's pneumatological emergence theory against criticisms by a couple of modern scholars. The third chapter develops and advocates a Wesleyan-based view of kenosis and emergence; in this third chapter, we find kenosis being the metaphysical basis of emergence theory. Chapter 4 develops a kenosis of the Spirit into creation, which serves as the foundation of my proposed panentheistic viewpoint. Chapter 5 draws upon John Paul II's Thomistic Personalism and relates this theorizing with my kenotic theory of divine action.

Chapters 6–9 focus upon teleology and theology. In fact, chapter 6 introduces a teleological viewpoint on divine action due the illustrated difficulties with other models of divine action. Chapter 7 brings to the fore some Catholic contributions to my modern relation of theology and science. It does this primarily by coalescing an Aquinas-inspired teleological theory that is consistent with the modern evolutionary synthesis. Chapter 8 dialogues with Peirce—especially his posits of tychistic, anancastic, and agapastic evolution—that is, evolution based on chance, determination, and love (which incorporates the others), respectively. I argue that Peirce's three-fold agapastic form of evolution is employed by him as a mediating third way between total chance on one side (i.e. tychism), and total determination on the other (i.e. anancasm). Further, in chapter 9, I extend these

Part Four: Pneumatology, Philosophy, & Science

thoughts upon kenosis and emergence in linking them with final causality, which has not been done heretofore by anyone else.

Chapters 10–13, respectively, dialogue with Thomism, Hume, Darwin and Whitehead, along with Charles Sanders Peirce, Stephen Jay Gould, and Simon Conway Morris. Indeed, chapter 11 garners a modern depiction of natural theology in dialogue with Aquinas, Darwin, and Whitehead. Chapter 12 is the first of two chapters that dialogue with Hume, and which show forth a pneumatological theory of divine action. The twelfth chapter develops a response to vitalism from the perspective of a modern relation of theology and science. In chapter 13, I make a *key* presentation to philosophy based upon the *God of Chance and Purpose*, which is based upon the philosophy of Peirce, with me aligning myself, if I had to choose, with Gould's "chancy" contingency argument of ontological randomness; in this chapter, I argue that God sets broad parameters for evolution, within which it proceeds, and the *details* are left to chance or randomness.

My summation of the relation of theology and science as a whole may be delineated in three movements, historically speaking, and a fourth movement that I propose. The historical movements correspond to the three general phases in the evolution of Darwinism: Phase one is marked by an attendant emphasis upon continuity, which is correlated to the time before Darwin's "On the Origin of Species" in 1859 to the first quarter of the twentieth century. At this time, the Catholic monk Gregor Mendel's experimental genetics work with pea plants was rediscovered and wedded with Darwinism to form what would become known as the Neo-Darwinian Synthesis (this refers to the period of time between 1859 to the late 1920s/early 1930s).

This led to the second Phase, which was characterized by an emphasis on particulate inheritance. This was the phase of Darwinism in which Mendel's genetics work was applied to Darwinism at large, expanded by various thinkers to all facets of what was then known as the Neo-Darwinian Synthesis, and was, for all intents and purposes, the paradigm of Darwinism. This period corresponds to the time between the 1930s and the 1970s. Phase three is marked by an emphasis upon contingency, and it corresponds to the paradigm shift following the publication of Stephen Jay Gould and Niles Eldredge's 1972 seminal paper entitled, "Punctuated Equilibria: The Tempo and Mode of Evolution Reconsidered," wherein they argue that evolution is marked by long periods of stasis, after which rapid (geologically speaking) advancements of complexity occur, which is in contradistinction to

Conclusion

the gradualism of historic Darwinism. Neo-Darwinism got shell-shocked. Moreover, this theory avers that contingency is the primal aspect of evolution, not natural selection; that is, if the tape of life were to be re-run, the specific outcomes—and even the broad outlines—of evolution would be drastically different: you would not get anything like the same thing(s) or entities twice.

Into this situation, I would like to propose, in the coming years, a *fourth* general phase of Darwinian evolution: *correlationism,* wherein Peirce's evolutionary developmental teleology, as I have roughly outlined it in this book, is a mediating third way between total chance on side and total determination on the other. In this conceptioning, I am aided by Haught's theorizing regarding "layered explanations," wherein all explanations are multiply explicable: that is, science operates upon one level of understanding, and theology operates on a deeper level of understanding in its explanations of all things.

This book, in sum, has sought to salvage a form of teleology for the postmodern era and allow for the Godhead to have at least secondary influence in all things. Moreover, it seeks to build from the insights of Peirce, Gould, and Conway Morris to develop a modern relation of theology and science that is *monistic, Process*-based, and marked by an *overlapping* of the two domains (or magisteria) of theology and science. It has been assisted by a series of insights from emergence and kenosis.

Bibliography

Allen, Colin. "Teleological Notions in Biology." *The Stanford Encyclopedia of Philosophy* (Winter 2009 Edition), edited by Edward N. Zalta. http://plato.stanford.edu/archives/win2009/entries/teleology-biology.

Alexander, Samuel. *Space, Time, and Deity*. The Gifford Lectures for 1916–18, 2 vols. London: Macmillan, 1920.

Alston, William P. "Divine Action: Shadow or Substance." In *The God Who Acts: Philosophical and Theological Explorations*, edited by Thomas F. Tracy, 41–62. University Park, Pennsylvania: Pennsylvania State University Press, 1994.

Ambrose. *Hexaemeron*. In *Fathers of the Church: A New Translation*, edited by Joseph N. Magee. Washington, DC: Catholic University of America Press, 1947.

Annas, Julia, and Jonathon Barnes. *The Modes of Scepticism*. Cambridge: Cambridge University Press, 1985.

Antón, Mauricio, and Alan Turner. *The Big Cats and Their Fossil Relatives: An Illustrated Guide to Their Evolution and Natural History*. New York: Columbia University Press, 1997.

Aquinas, Thomas et al. *Aquinas on Creation: Writings on the "Sentences" of Peter Lombard, Book 2, Distinction 1, Question 1*. Toronto: Pontifical Institute of Mediaeval Studies, 1997.

Aquinas, Thomas. "On Natural Science, Mathematics, and Metaphysics." In *Expositio super Librum Boethii de Trinitate*, 2. Questions 5–6. *Thomas Aquinas: Selected Philosophical Writings*. Translated by Timothy McDermott. Oxford: Oxford University Press, 1993.

———. *Quaestiones Disputatae de Anima*. Translated by John Patrick Rowan. London: B. Herder, 1949.

———. *Quaestiones Disputatae De Potentia Dei*. Translated by the English Dominican Fathers. Westminster, Maryland: The Newman Press, 1952.

———. *Quaestiones Quodlibetales*. Translated by Sandra Edwards. Mediaeval Sources in Translation, 27. Toronto: Pontifical Institute of Mediaeval Studies, 1983.

———. *Summa Contra Gentiles*. Translated by Anton C. Pegis et al. New York: Hanover House, 1955–57.

———. *Summa Theologiae of St. Thomas Aquinas*. Translated by the Fathers of the English Dominican Province. London: Burns, Oates, & Washbourne, 1920.

Aristotle. *De Anima*. Translated by J. A. Smith. Internet Classics Archive.

———. *Physics* II. In *The Complete Works of Aristotle: The Revised Oxford Translation*, vol. 1. Translated by R.P. Hardie and R.K. Gaye, edited by Jonathon Barnes. Princeton, New Jersey: Princeton University Press, 1984.

Bibliography

Augustine. *Confessions, Fathers of the Church* 21. Edited by Joseph N. Magee, 1–421. Washington, DC: Catholic University of America Press, 1947.

———. *The Trinity.* In *The Works of Saint Augustine: A Translation for the 21st Century*, 2nd ed, edited by John E. Rotelle, 7–247. Translated by Edmund Hill. New York: New City Press, 2011.

Ayala, Francisco J. "Teleological Explanations in Evolutionary Biology." *Philosophy of Science* 37 1 (1970) 1–15.

Barbour, Ian. "God's Power: A Process View." In *The Work of Love: Creation as Kenosis*, edited by John Polkinghorne, 1–20. Grand Rapids, Michigan: Eerdmans, 2001.

Barbour, Ian. *Religion in an Age of Science.* New York: HarperCollins, 1990.

———. *When Science Meets Religion: Enemies, Strangers, or Partners?* New York: HarperOne, 2000.

Bartholomew, David J. *God of Chance.* London: SCM, 1984.

Bauer, Walter, and Frederick William Danker. *A Greek-English Lexicon of the New Testament and Other Early Christian Literature*, 3rd ed. Chicago, Illinois: University of Illinois Press, 2001.

Beckwith, Francis J. *David Hume's Argument Against Miracles: A Critical Analysis.* Lanham, Maryland: University Press of America, 1989.

Bedua, Mark. "Weak Emergence." In *Philosophical Perspectives: Mind, Causation, and World*, vol. 11, edited by James E. Tomberlin, 375–99. Malden, Massachusetts: Blackwell, 1997.

Bergmann, Sigurd. *Creation Set Free: The Spirit as Liberator of Nature.* Translated by Douglass W. Stott. Grand Rapids, Michigan: Eerdmans, 2005.

Bilynskyj, Stephen S. "God, Nature, and the Concept of Miracle." PhD Dissertation: Notre Dame, 1982.

Blanchette, Olivia. *The Perfection of the Universe According to Aquinas: A Teleological Cosmology.* University Park, PA: The Pennsylvania State University Press, 1992.

Blomberg, Craig L. "Concluding Reflections on Miracles and Gospel Perspectives." In *Gospel Perspectives: The Miracles of Jesus*, vol. 6, edited by David Wenham and Craig Blomberg, 443–469. Sheffield: JSOT, 1986.

Blumer, Michael J.F., et al. "Ocelli in a Cnidaria Polyp: The Ultrastructure of the Pigment Spots in Stylocoronella riedli (Scyphozoa, Stauromedusae)." *Zoomorphology* 115 (1995) 221–227.

Bonting, Sjoerd. "Spirit and Creation." *Zygon: Journal of Religion & Science* 41 3 (2006) 713–26.

Bradnick, David. *Evil, Spirits, and Possession: An Emergentist Theology of the Demonic.* Leiden: Brill, 2017.

Brand, Myles, ed. *The Nature of Causation.* Chicago, Illinois: University of Illinois Press, 1976.

Broad, C. D. *The Mind and Its Place in Nature.* London: Routledge and Keegan Paul, 1925.

Brooke, John Hedley, and Geoffrey Cantor. *Reconstructing Nature: The Engagement of Science and Religion* (Glasgow Gifford Lectures). Oxford: Oxford University Press, 2000.

Brooke, John Hedley. *Science and Religion: Some Historical Perspectives.* Cambridge: Cambridge University Press.

Brower, Jeffrey, and Susan Brower-Toland. "Aquinas on Mental Representation." In *Philosophical Review* 117 (2008) 193–243.

Brown, Colin. *Miracles and the Critical Mind.* Grand Rapids, Michigan: Eerdmans, 1984.

BIBLIOGRAPHY

Browning, Douglass. *Philosophers of Process*. Manhattan: Random House, 1965.
Brunner, Emil "Natur und Gnade: Zum Gespräch mit Karl Barth." In *Ein offenes Wort. Voträge un Aufsätze 1917-1934*, ed. Rudolf Wehrli (Zürich: Theologischer Verlag, 1981), 354-378.
Budelmann, B. U. "Cephalopod Sense Organs, Nerves and the Brain: Adaptations for High Performance and Life Style." In *Marine and Freshwater Behaviour and Physiology* 25 (1994) 13-33.
Bulgakov, Sergius. *The Comforter*. Translated by Boris Jakim. Grand Rapids, Michigan: Eerdmans, 2004.
Burns, R. M. *The Great Debate on Miracles: From Joseph Glanvill to David Hume*. East Brunswick: Associated University, 1981.
Chrysostom, John. "Homilies on the Gospel of Saint John and Epistle to the Hebrews." In *The Nicene and Post-Nicene Fathers*, vol. 14, edited by Philip Schaff. Electronic edition. Oak Harbor: Logos Research Systems, 1997.
Callen, Barry L. *God as Loving Grace: The Biblically Revealed Nature and Work of God*. Nappanee, Indiana: Evangel, 1996.
Campbell, George. *The Works of George Campbell*. 6 vols. London: Thomas Tegg, 1840.
Campbell, Neil A. *Biology*. 3rd ed. Menlo Park: Benjamin Cummings, 1991.
Carroll, William E. "Creation, Evolution, and Thomas Aquinas." *Revue des Questions Scientifique* 171 4 (2000) 319-47.
Chakraboti, Tapan Kumar. *Hume's Theory of Causality*. Calcutta: Raghunauh, 1972.
Charles, G.H. "Sense Organs (less cephalopods)." In vol. II of *Physiology of Mollusca*, 455-521, edited by K. M. Wilbur and C. M. Yonge. London: Academic, 1966.
Churcher, C.S. "Dental Functional Morphology in the Marsupial Sabre-tooth *Thylacosmilus atrox* (Thylacosmilidae) Compared to that of Felid Sabre-tooths." In *Australian Mammalogy* 8 (1985) 201-20.
Clarke, Adam. *Clarke's Commentary: Genesis*. Electronic edition. Logos Library System. Albany, Oregon: Ages Software, 1999.
Clarke, W. Norris. *Person and Being*. Milwaukee: Marquette University Press, 2006.
Clatterbaugh, Kenneth C. *The Causation Debate in Modern Philosophy 1671-1739*. New York: Routledge, 1999.
Clayton, Philip, and Paul Davies, eds. *The Re-Emergence of Emergence: The Emergentist Hypothesis from Science to Religion*. Oxford: Oxford University Press, 2008.
Clayton, Philip, and Zachary Simpson, eds. *Adventures in the Spirit: God, World, Divine Action*. Minneapolis, Minnesota: Fortress, 2008.
Clayton, Philip. "Conceptual Foundations of Emergence Theory." In *The Reemergence of Emergence: The Emergentist Hypothesis From Science to Religion*, edited by Philip Clayton and Paul Davies, 1-34. Oxford: Oxford University Press, 2006.
―――. "Divine Causes in the World of Nature." In *God, Life, and the Cosmos: Christian and Islamic Perspectives*, 271-92, edited by Ted Peters, et al. Aldershot: Ashgate, 2002.
―――. "Emergence from Physics to Theology: Toward a Panoramic View." *Zygon: Journal of Religion and Science* 41 3 (2006) 675-87.
―――. "Emergence of Spirit: From Complexity to Anthropology to Theology." *Theology and Science* 4, no. 3(2006) 291-307.
―――. "Emergence of Spirit and Four Responses." *CTNS Bulletin* 20 4 (2000) 3-20.
―――. *God and Contemporary Science*. Edinburgh: Edinburgh University Press, 1997.
―――. "Kenotic Trinitarian Panentheism." *Dialog: A Journal of Theology* 44 3 (2005) 250-55.

Bibliography

———. *Mind & Emergence: From Quantum to Consciousness*. Oxford: Oxford University Press, 2004.

———. "On the Value of the Panentheistic Analogy: A Response to Willem Drees." *Zygon: Journal of Religion and Science* 35 (2000) 699–704.

———. "Panentheism in Metaphysical and Scientific Perspective." In *In Whom We Live and Move and Have Our Being: Panentheistic Reflections on God's Presence in a Scientific World*, edited by Philip Clayton and Arthur Peacocke, 73–94. Grand Rapids, Michigan: Eerdmans, 2004.

———. "The Panentheistic Turn in Theology." *Dialog: A Journal of Theology* 38 (1999) 289–93.

Cobb, Jr. John B. *A Christian Natural Theology*. 2nd ed. Louisville: Westminster John Knox, 2007.

———. *Grace and Responsibility: A Wesleyan Theology for Today*. Nashville, Tennessee: Abingdon, 1995.

———. "Human Responsibility and the Primacy of Grace." In *Thy Nature and Thy Name is Love: Wesleyan and Process Theologies in Dialogue*, edited by Brian P. Stone and Thomas Jay Oord, 95–110. Nashville, Tennessee: Kingswood, 2001.

Cohen, S. Marc. "Aristotle's Metaphysics." In *The Stanford Encyclopedia of Philosophy* (2012 Edition), edited by Edward N. Zalta. http://plato.stanford.edu/archives/sum2012/entries/aristotle-metaphyics. Accessed 10/7/16.

Conway Morris, Simon. *Life's Solution: Inevitable Humans in a Lonely Universe*. Cambridge: Cambridge University Press, 2004.

———. *The Crucible of Creation*. Oxford: Oxford University Press, 1998.

———. "The Predictability of Evolution: Glimpses into a Post-Darwinian World." *Naturwissenschaften* 96 (2009) 1313–37.

———. *The Runes of Evolution: How the Universe became Self-Aware*. West Conshocken, Pennsylvania: Templeton, 2015.

Cooper, John W. *Panentheism: The Other God of the Philosophers: From Plato to the Present*. Grand Rapids, Michigan: Baker Academic, 2006.

Copleston, Frederick. *A History of Philosophy Vol. IV: Descartes to Leibniz*. London: Burns Oates and Washbourne, 1959.

Corrington, Robert S. *An Introduction to C. S. Peirce: Philosopher, Semiotician and Ecstatic Naturalist*. Lanham, Maryland: Rowman and Littlefield, 1993.

Craig, William L. "The Problem of Miracles: A Historical and Philosophical Perspective." In *Gospel Perspectives* vol. 6: *The Miracles of Jesus*, edited by David Wenham and Craig Blomberg, 9–48. Sheffield: JSOT, 1986.

Crain, Steven. "God Embodied In, Bodying Forth the World: Emergence and Christian Theology." *Zygon: Journal of Religion and Science* 41 3 (2006) 665–74.

Creegan, Nicola H. "A Christian Theology of Evolution and Participation." *Zygon: Journal of Religion and Science* 42 2 (2007) 499–518.

Cross, Richard. "Dun Scotus and Divine Necessity." In *Oxford Studies in Medieval Philosophy*, vol. 3, edited by Robert Pasnau, 128–144. Oxford: Oxford University Press, 2015.

Dabney, Lyle D. "Naming the Spirit: Towards a Pneumatology of the Cross." In *Starting with the Spirit*, edited by Gordon Preece and Stephen Pickard, 51–62. Adeliade: Open Book, 2001.

Bibliography

Dabney, D. Lyle. "The Nature of the Spirit: Creation as a Premonition of God." In *The Work of the Spirit*, ed. Michael Welker, 71-86. Grand Rapids, Michigan: Eerdmans, 2006.

Darwin, Charles. *Autobiography*, http://darwin-online.org.uk/content/frameset?itemID=F1497&viewtype=text&pageseq=1.

Darwin, Francis, ed. *The Life and Letters of Charles Darwin*, 3 vols. London: John Murray, 1887.

Davis, Ellen F. and Richard B. Hays, eds. *The Art of Reading Scripture*. Grand Rapids, Michigan: Eerdmans, 2003.

Davis, Stephen T. "The Miracle At Cana: A Philosopher's Perspective." In *Gospel Perspectives* vol. 6: *The Miracles of Jesus*, edited by David Wenham and Craig Blomberg, 419-42. Sheffield: JSOT, 1986.

Dawkins, Richard. *The Selfish Gene*, 2nd ed. Oxford: Oxford University Press, 1989.

Deacon, Terrence W. "Emergence: The Hole at the Wheel's Hub." In *The Re-Emergence of Emergence: The Emergentist Hypothesis from Science to Religion*, edited by Phillip Clayton and Paul C. Davies, 111-150. Oxford: Oxford University Press.

———. "The Hierarchic Logic of Emergence." In *Evolution and Learning*, edited by Bruce H. Weber and David J. Depew, 273-308. Cambridge, Massachusetts: MIT, 2003.

Dennett, Daniel C. *The Intentional Stance*. Cambridge, Massachusetts: MIT, 1987.

Denton, Michael. *Evolution: A Theory in Crisis*. Chevy Chase, MD: Adler & Adler, 1986.

Depew, David J. and Bruce H. Weber, eds. *Evolution at a Crossroads: The New Biology and the New Philosophy of Science*. Cambridge, Massachusetts: MIT Press, 1989.

Dodds, Michael J. *Unlocking Divine Action: Contemporary Science and Thomas Aquinas*. Washington, DC: Catholic University of America Press, 2012.

Doncel, Manuel G. "The Kenosis of the Creator and of the Created Co-creator." *Zygon: Journal of Religion and Science* 39 (2004) 791-800.

Dostal, Robert J. "Gadamer: The Man and His Work." In *The Cambridge Companion to Gadamer*, 13-35, edited by Robert J. Dostal. Cambridge: Cambridge University Press, 2002.

Draper, John William. *History of the Conflict between Religion and Science*. New York: Appleton, 1874.

Drees, Willem B., Hubert Meisinger, and T. A. Smedes, eds. *Creation's Diversity: Voices from Theology and Science*. London: T. & T. Clark, 2008.

Drees, Willem B. "Gaps for God?" In *Scientific Perspectives on Divine Action*, vol. 2: *Chaos and Complexity*, 223-38, edited by Robert John Russell et al. Vatican City: Vatican Observatory, 1995.

———. *Religion, Science, and Naturalism*. Cambridge: Cambridge University Press, 1996.

Driesch, Hans. *The History and Theory of Vitalism*. Translated by C.K. Ogden. New York: Macmillan, 1914.

Ducasse, C. J. "Critique of Hume's Analysis." In Myles Brand, ed. *The Nature of Causation*, 67-76. Chicago, Illinois: University of Illinois Press, 1976.

Dun Scotus, *Lect.* II, d. 12, q. un., n. 30 (Vatican, XIX, 80). Translated by Richard Cross, "Duns Scotus on Essence and Existence." In *Oxford Studies in Medieval Philosophy*, Vol. 1, 171-92, edited by Robert Pasnau. Oxford: Oxford University Press, 2013.

Dunn, James D. G. "Towards the Spirit of Christ: The Emergence of the Distinctive Features of Christian Pneumatology." In *The Work of the Spirit*, edited by Michael Welker, 3-26. Grand Rapids, Michigan: Eerdmans, 2006.

Earman, John. *Hume's Abject Failure*. Oxford: Oxford University, 2000.

Bibliography

Edwards, Denis. *Breath of Life: A Theology of the Creator Spirit*. Maryknoll, New York, New York: Orbis, 2004.

———. *How God Acts: Creation, Redemption, and Special Divine Action* (Theology and the Sciences). Minneapolis, Minnesota: Fortress, 2010.

———. *The God of Evolution: A Trinitarian Theology*. New York: Paulist, 1999.

el-Hani, Charbel Nino, and Antonio Marcos Pereira. "Higher-Level Descriptions: Why Should We Preserve Them?" In *Downward Causation: Minds, Bodies and Matter*, 118–42, edited by Peter Bøgh Anderson et al. Aarhus: Aarhus University Press, 2000.

Eldredge, Niles, and Stephen Jay Gould. "Punctuated Equilibria: An Alternative to Phyletic Gradualism." In *Models in Paleobiology*, 82–115, edited by T. J. M. Schopf. San Francisco: Freeman Cooper, 1972.

Eldredge, Niles. *The Myths of Human Evolution*. New York: Columbia University Press, 1984.

Ephraem. *Sancti Patris Nostri Ephraem Syri Opera Omnia*, edited by J. A. Assemani. Rome, 1737.

Farrer, Austin. *A Science of God?* London: Geoffrey Bles, 1966.

Feser, Edward. *Aquinas*. Oxford: One World, 2009.

Flew, Antony. *God and Philosophy*. New York: Harcourt, Brace and World, 1966.

———. *Hume's Philosophy of Belief*. London: Routledge & Kegan Paul, 1961.

Fogelin, Robert J. *A Defense of Hume on Miracles*. Princeton, New Jersey: Princeton University Press, 2003.

Fowler, Thomas B., and Daniel Kuebler. *The Evolution Controversy*. Grand Rapids, Michigan: Baker Academic, 2006.

Freeman, Walter J. "Consciousness, Intentionality and Causality." *Journal of Consciousness Studies* 6 11–12 (1999) 143–172.

———. "Nonlinear Brain Dynamics and Intention according to Aquinas." In *Mind and Matter* 6 2 (2008) 207–234.

———. *Societies of Brains: A Study in the Neuroscience of Love and Hate*. Hillsdale, New Jersey: Lawrence Erlbaum Associates, 1995.

Fretheim, Terence E. *God and World in the Old Testament: A Relational Theology of Creation*. Nashville, Tennessee: Abingdon, 2005.

Futuyma, Douglas J. *Science on Trial: The Case for Evolution*. New York: Pantheon, 1983.

Galen. *On Anatomical Procedures*. Translated by W.L.H. Duckworth, edited by M. C. Lyons and B. Bowers. Cambridge: Cambridge University Press, 1962.

Geisler, Norman L. *Miracles and Modern Thought*. Dallas, Texas: Zondervan, 1982.

Giberson, Karl W. and Donald A. Yerxa. "Providence and the Christian Scholar." *Journal of Interdisciplinary Studies* 1 1 (1999) 123–40.

Gilson, Etienne. *From Aristotle to Darwin and Back Again: A Journey in Final Causality, Species, and Evolution*. Translated by John Lyon. South Bend, Indiana: University of Notre Dame Press, 1984.

———. *The Philosopher and Theology*. Translated by Cecile Gilson. New York: Random House, 1986.

Goergen, Donald J. *Fire of Love: Encountering the Holy Spirit*. Mahwah, New Jersey: Paulist, 2006.

Goodenough, Ursula, and Terrence W. Deacon. "From Biology to Consciousness to Morality." *Zygon: Journal of Religion & Science* 38 4 (2003) 801–19.

BIBLIOGRAPHY

Goris, Harm J. M. J. *Free Creatures of an Eternal God: Thomas Aquinas on God's Infallible Foreknowledge and Irresistible Will.* Peeters Leuven: Thomas Instituut Te Utrecht, 1996.

Görman, Ulf, Willem B. Drees, and Hubert Meisinger, eds. *Creative Creatures: Values And Ethical Issues in Theology, Science And Technology* (Issues in Science and Theology 3). London: T. & T. Clark, 2005.

Gould, Stephen Jay, et al. "The Shape of Evolution: A Comparison of Real and Random Clades." In *Paleobiology* 3 (1977) 23–40.

Gould, Stephen Jay, and Niles Eldredge. "Punctuated Equilibria: The Tempo and Mode of Evolution Reconsidered." In *Models in Paleobiology*, edited by T. J. M. Schopf, 82–115. San Francisco, California: Freeman, Cooper and Company, 1972.

Gould, Stephen Jay, et al. "Asymmetry of Lineages and the Direction of Evolutionary Time." "Asymmetry of lineages and the direction of evolutionary time." In *Science* 236 4807 (1987) 1437–41.

Gould, Stephen Jay. "Evolution and the Triumph of Homology, or why History Matters." *American Scientist* 74 (1986) 60–69.

———. *Rock of Ages: Science and Religion in the Fullness of Life.* New York: Ballantine, 2002.

———. "The Evolution of Life." In *Evolution!: Facts and Fallacies*, edited by J. William Schopf, 1–14. Amsterdam, UK: Academic, 1998.

———. *The Richness of Life: The Essential Stephen Jay Gould.* New York: W.W. Norton & Company, 2007.

———. "The Shape of Evolution: A Comparison of Real and Random Clades." In *Paleobiology* 3 (1977) 23–40.

———. *The Structure of Evolutionary Theory.* Cambridge, Massachusetts: Belknap, 2002.

———. *Wonderful Life: The Burgess Shale and the Nature of History.* London: Penguin, 1989.

Graham, Loren R. *Between Science and Values.* New York: Columbia University Press, 1981.

Green, Joel B. "Scripture and Theology: Uniting the Two So Long Divided." In *Between Two Horizons: Spanning New Testament Studies & Systematic Theology*, edited by Joel B. Green and Max Turner, 23–43. Grand Rapids, Michigan: Eerdmans, 2000.

Gregersen, Neils Henrik. "Emergence: What is at Stake for Religious Reflection?" In *The Reemergence of Emergence: The Emergentist Hypothesis From Science to Religion*, edited by Philip Clayton and Paul Davies, 279–302. Oxford: Oxford University Press, 2006.

Gregersen, Niels Henrik. "Emergence in Theological Perspective: A Corollary to Professor Clayton's Boyle Lecture." *Theology and Science* 4 3 (2006) 309–20.

Gregory of Nyssa. "On the Making of Man." In *The Nicene and Post-Nicene Fathers Second Series Vol. 5*, edited by Philip Schaff. Electronic edition. Oak Harbor: Logos Research Systems, 1997.

Griffin, David Ray. *Unsnarling the World-Knot: Consciousness, Freedom, and the Mind-Body Problem.* Oakland: University of California Press, 1998.

Grondin, Jean. "Gadamer's Basic Understanding of Understanding." In *The Cambridge Companion to Gadamer*, edited by Robert J. Dostal, 36–51. Cambridge: Cambridge University Press, 2002.

Gruenwald, Oskar. "Philosophy as Creative Discovery: Science, Ethics and Faith." *Journal of Interdisciplinary Studies* XI (1999) 157–74.

Bibliography

Gunton, Colin. *The Triune Creator*. Grand Rapids, Michigan: Eerdmans, 1998.

Haag, James W. *Emergent Freedom: Process Dynamics in Theological, Philosophical, and Scientific Perspective*. PhD dissertation, Graduate Theological Union, 2007.

Hamner, W. M. et al., "Swimming, Feeding, Circulation and Vision in the Australian box jellyfish, *Chironex fleckeri* [Cnidaria: Cubozoa]." *Marine and Freshwater Research* 46 (1995) 985–90.

Hartshorne, Charles. *Creativity in American Philosophy*. Albany: State University of New York Press, 1984.

———. *Man's Vision of God and the Logic of Theism*. Chicago, Illinois: Willett, Clark & Company, 1941.

———. *The Logic of Perfection and other Essays in Neoclassical Metaphysics*. La Salle: Open Court, 1962.

Hausman, Carl R. *Charles S. Peirce's Evolutionary Philosophy*. Cambridge: Cambridge University Press, 1993.

Haught, John F. *Deeper than Darwin: The Prospect for Religion in the Age of Evolution*. Cambridge: Westview, 2003.

———. *Making Sense of Evolution: Darwin, God, and the Drama of Life*. Louisville, Kentucky: Westminster John Knox, 2010.

Houser, Nathan, and Christian J. W. Kloesel, eds. *The Essential Peirce: Selected Philosophical Writings, (1867–1893)*. Vol. 1. Bloomington, Indiana: Indiana University Press, 1992.

Houston, Joseph. *Reported Miracles: A Critique of Hume*. Cambridge: Cambridge University Press, 1994.

Howson, Colin, and Peter Urbach. *Scientific Reasoning: The Bayesian Approach*. Chicago, Illinois: Open Court, 2005.

Huchingson, James E. "Chaos, Communications Theory, and God's Abundance." *Zygon: Journal of Religion and Science* 37 (2002) 395–414.

Huchingson, James E. "Engaging James E. Huchingson's *Pandemonium Tremendum*: Chaos and Mystery in the Life of God." *Zygon: Journal of Religion and Science* 37 2 (2002) 395–414.

Hulswit, Menno. *From Cause to Causation: A Peircean Perspective*. New York: Springer, 2002.

———. "Peirce's Teleological Approach to Natural Classes." *Transactions of the Charles S. Peirce Society* 33 3 (1997) 722–72.

———. "Teleology: A Peircean Critique of Ernst Mayr's Theory." *Transactions of the Charles S Peirce Society* 32 2 (1996) 182–214.

Hume, David. *A Treatise of Human Nature*. Edited by L.A. Selby-Bigge, 2nd ed. Revised by P.H. Nidditch. Oxford: Clarendon, 1978.

———. *An Enquiry concerning Human Understanding*, edited by L.A. Selby-Bigge, 3rd ed. Revised by P.H. Nidditch. Oxford: Clarendon, 1975.

Huxley, Thomas H. *Lay Sermons, Addresses, and Reviews*. London: Macmillan, 1870.

———. *The Works of T.H. Huxley*. New York: Appleton, 1896.

Inbody, Tyron L. "Reconceptions of Divine Power in John Wesley, Panentheism, and Trinitarian Theology." In *Thy Nature and Thy Name is Love: Wesleyan and Process Theologies in Dialogue*, edited by Brian P. Stone and Thomas Jay Oord, 169–92. Nashville, Tennessee: Kingswood, 2001.

Jackelén, Antje. "Emergence Everywhere?! Reflections on Philip Clayton's Mind and Emergence." *Zygon: Journal of Science and Religion* 41 3 (2006) 623–32.

Bibliography

Jansen, Henry. *Relationality and the Concept of God*. Amsterdam: Rodopi B.V. Editions, 1995.
Jaynes, E. T. *Probability Theory: The Logic of Science*. Cambridge: Cambridge University Press, 2003.
Johnson, David. *Hume, Holism and Miracles*. Ithaca, New York: Cornell University Press, 1999.
Johnson, Monte Ransome. *Aristotle on Teleology*. Oxford: Clarendon, 2005.
Johnson, William S. "Reading the Scriptures Faithfully in a Postmodern Age." In *The Art of Reading Scripture*, edited by Ellen F. Davis and Richard B. Hays, 109–24. Grand Rapids, Michigan: Eerdmans, 2003.
Kaufman, Gordon D. "A Religious Interpretation of Emergence." *Zygon: Journal of Religion and Science* 42 4 (2007) 915–28.
———. *God the Problem*. Cambridge, Massachusetts: Harvard University Press, 1972.
———. *In the Beginning... Creativity*. Minneapolis, Minnesota: Fortress, 2004.
Kauffman, Stuart A. "Beyond Reductionism: Reinventing the Sacred." *Zygon: Journal of Religion and Science* (2007) 903–914.
———. *Investigations*. Oxford: Oxford University, 2000.
Keller, Catherine. *The Face of the Deep: A Theology of Becoming*. London: Routledge, 2003.
Kemp Smith, Norman. *The Philosophy of David Hume: A Critical Study of its Origins and Central Doctrines*. New York: Palgrave Macmillan, 2005.
Kim, Jaegwon. "Being Realistic about Emergence." In *The Reemergence of Emergence: The Emergentist Hypothesis From Science to Religion*, edited by Philip Clayton and Paul Davies, 189–202. Oxford: Oxford University Press, 2006.
Kim, Jaewong. "Making Sense of Emergence." *Philosophical Studies* 95 (1999) 3–36.
Kingsley, Charles. "The Natural Theology of the Future." In *Westminster Sermons*, vi–xxvii. London: Macmillan, 1874.
Kirsch, John A.W. "The Six-Percent Solution: Second Thoughts on the Adaptedness of the Marsupialia." In *American Scientist* 65 (1977) 276–288.
Kitcher, Philip. *The Advancement of Science*. New York: Oxford University Press, 1993.
Knight, Christopher C. *The God of Nature*. Minneapolis, Minnesota: Fortress, 2007.
———. "Theistic Naturalism and 'Special' Divine Providence." *Zygon: Journal of Religion and Science* 44 3 (2009) 533–42.
Koenigswald, Wighart V., and Francisco J. Goin. "Enamel Differentiation in South American Marsupials and a Comparison of Placental and Marsupial Enamel." *Palaeontographica, Abteilung A* 255 (2000) 129–68.
Kuhn, Thomas. *The Structure of Scientific Revolutions*. Chicago, Illinois: University of Chicago, Illinois Press, 1970.
Küng, Hans. *The Beginning of All Things: Science and Religion*. Translated by John Bowden. Grand Rapids, Michigan: Eerdmans, 2008.
Lang, Helen S. "Aristotelian Physics: Teleological Procedure in Aristotle, Thomas, and Buridan." *The Review of Metaphysics* 42 3 (1989) 569–591.
———. *Aristotle's Physics and Its Medieval Varieties*. SUNY Series in Ancient Greek Philosophy. New York: SUNY, 1992.
Langford, Michael J. *Providence*. London: SCM, 1981.
Leidenhag, Joanna. "A Critique of Emergent Theologies." *Zygon: Journal of Religion and Science* 51 4 (2016) 867–82.
Leidenhag, Mikael. "The Relevance of Emergence Theory in the Science-Religion Dialogue." *Zygon: Journal of Religion and Science* 48 4 (2013) 966–83.

Bibliography

Leidenhag, Mikael, and Joanna Leidenhag. "Science and Spirit: A Critical Examination of Amos Yong's Pneumatological Theology of Emergence." *Open Theology* 1 (2015) 425–35.

Lessa, Enrique P., and Richard A. Farina. "Reassessment of Extinction Patterns Among the Late Pleistocene Mammals of South America." *Palaeontology* 39 (1996) 651–62.

Lewis, C.S. *Miracles*. New York: Simon and Schuster, 1996.

Lewontin, Richard, et al. *Not in Our Genes: Biology, Ideology, and Human Nature*. Westminster, London: Penguin, 1990.

Locke, John. *The Reasonableness of Christianity*. Edited by I. T. Ramsey. London: A. & C. Black, 1958.

Lodahl, Michael E. "Creation Out of Nothing? Or Is Next to Nothing Enough?" In *Thy Nature and Thy Name is Love: Wesleyan and Process Theologies in Dialogue*, edited by Brian P. Stone and Thomas Jay Oord, 217–38. Nashville, Tennessee: Kingswood, 2001.

———. *From God to Creation: Pursuing the Trinitarian Reflections of Gregory of Nyssa as a Critique of Creation ex Nihilo*. Paper presented to the American Academy of Religion, 2004 Annual Meeting.

———. *God of Nature and of Grace: Reading the World in a Wesleyan Way*. Nashville, Tennessee: Kingswood, 2003.

———. *Shekhinah/Spirit: Divine Presence in Jewish and Christian Religion*. Mahwah, New Jersey: Paulist, 1992.

Linahan, Jane E. "Experiencing God in Brokenness: the Self-emptying of Holy Spirit in Moltmann's Pneumatology." In *Encountering Transcendence: Contributions to a Theology of Religious Experience*, edited by Lieven Boeve et al., 165–184. Belgium: Peeters, 2005.

Loder, James, and W. Jim Neidhard. *The Knight's Move: The Relational Logic of Spirit in Theology and Science*. Colorado Springs, Colorado: Helmers and Howard, 1992.

Loeb, Louis. *From Descartes to Hume*. Ithaca, New York: Cornell University Press, 1981.

Lucien, Richard. *Kenosis and Creation*. Mahwah, New Jersey: Paulist, 1997.

Maddox, Randy L. *Responsible Grace: John Wesley's Practical Theology*. Nashville, Tennessee: Abingdon, 1994.

Martyr, Justin. *The Ante-Nicene Fathers Vol. I: Translations of the Writings of the Fathers Down to A.D. 325*. Edited by Alexander Roberts et al. Electronic edition. Oak Harbor: Logos Research Systems, 1997.

Mavrodes, George "Miracles and the Laws of Nature." *Faith and Philosophy* 2 4 (1985) 333–46.

Mayr, Ernst. "Teleological and Teleonomic: A New Analysis." *Boston Studies in the Philosophy of Science* 14 (1974) 89–111.

———. *The Evolutionary Synthesis: Perspectives on the Unification of Biology*. Cambridge, Massachusetts: Harvard University Press, 1998.

———. *What Evolution Is*. New York: Basic, 2002.

McCall, Bradford. "Emergence and Kenosis: A Theological Synthesis." *Zygon: Journal of Science and Religion* 45 1 (2010) 149–64.

———. "Emergence and Kenosis: A Wesleyan Perspective." In *The Future of Wesleyan Theology: Essays in Honor of Laurence Wood*, ed. Nathan Crawford, 155–70. Eugene, Oregon: Pickwick, 2011.

———. "Emergence Theory and Theology: A Wesleyan-Perspective." *Wesleyan Theological Journal* 44 2 (2009) 189–207.

———. "The Kenosis of the Spirit into Creation." *Crucible* 1 1. http://www.crucibleonline.net/wpcontent/uploads/2016/09/McCall-Kenosis-of-the-Spirit-into-Creation-Crucible-1-1-May-2008.pdf.

———. "Thomistic Personalism in Dialogue with Kenosis." *Studia Elckie* 19 1 (2017) 21–32.

McFague, Sallie. *The Body of God: An Ecological Theology*. London: SCM, 1993.

McGrath, Alister E. *Darwinism and the Divine: Evolutionary Thought and Natural Theology*. West Sussex, UK: Wiley-Blackwell, 2011. Kindle Edition.

———. *The Open Secret: A New Vision for Natural Theology*. West Sussex, UK: Wiley-Blackwell, 2008. Kindle Edition.

McInerny, Ralph, and John O'Callaghan. "Saint Thomas Aquinas." *The Stanford Encyclopedia of Philosophy* (Winter 2010 Edition), edited by Edward N. Zalta. http://plato.stanford.edu/archives/win2010/entries/aquinas.

McKeon, Richard. *The Basic Works of Aristotle*. New York: Random House, 1947.

Meisinger, Hubert, et al., eds. *Wisdom or Knowledge? Science, Theology and Cultural Dynamics*. New York: T. & T. Clark, 2006.

Messinese, Leonardo. *Problem of God in Modern Philosophy*. Aurora: Davies Group, 2005.

Michaels, Lisa et al., eds. *Uncontrolling Love: Essays Exploring the Love of God, with Introductions by Thomas Jay Oord*. Sand Diego: SacraSage, 2017.

Mitchell, Timothy A. *David Hume's Anti-Theistic Views*. Lanham, Maryland: University Press of America, 1986.

Moltmann, Jürgen. *God in Creation: A New Theology of Creation and the Spirit of God*. Minneapolis, Minnesota: Augsburg Fortress, 1993.

———. "God's Kenosis in the Creation and Consummation of the World." In *The Work of Love: Creation as Kenosis*, 137–51, edited by John Polkinghorne. Grand Rapids, Michigan: Eerdmans, 2001.

———. *Science and Wisdom*. Translated by Margaret Kohl. Minneapolis, Minnesota: Fortress, 2003.

———. *The Spirit of Life: A Universal Affirmation*. Minneapolis, Minnesota: Augsburg Fortress, 1992.

———. *The Crucified God: The Cross of Christ as the Foundation and Criticism of Christian Theology*. Minneapolis, Minnesota: Fortress, 1993.

———. *The Trinity and the Kingdom of God*. Translated by Margaret Kohl. London: SCM, 1981.

Monod, Jacques. *Chance and Necessity: An Essay on the Natural Philosophy of Modern Biology*. New York: Vintage, 1972.

Montague, G. T. *The Holy Spirit: Growth of a Biblical Tradition*. New York: Paulist, 1976.

Montefiore, H. *The Probability of God*. London: SCM, 1985.

Morowitz, Harold J. *The Emergence of Everything: How the World Became Complex*. Oxford: Oxford University Press, 2002.

Murphy, Nancey, and George F.R. Ellis. *On the Moral Nature of the Universe: Theology, Cosmology, and Ethics*. Minneapolis, Minnesota: Fortress, 1996.

Murphy, Nancey. "Introduction." In Scientific Perspectives on Divine Action, vol. 4, *Neuroscience and the Person*, v–xv, edited by Robert John Russell et al. Vatican City: Vatican Observatory, 1999.

Nagel, Thomas. *Mind and Cosmos*. Oxford: Oxford University Press, 2012.

Neville, Robert C. *Creativity and God: A Challenge to Process Theology*. Albany, New York: State University of New York, New York Press, 1995.

Bibliography

Niebuhr, Richard R. *Resurrection and Historical Reason: A Study of Theological Method.* New York: Scribner's, 1957.

O'Connor, Timothy. "Emergent Properties." *American Philosophical Quarterly* 31 (1994) 91–104.

O'Rourke, Fran. "Aristotle and the Metaphysics of Evolution." In *Review of Metaphysics* 58 1 (2004) 3–59.

Ogden, Schubert M. "Process Theology and the Wesleyan Witness." In *Thy Nature & Thy Name Is Love: Wesleyan and Process Theologies in Dialogue*, edited by Bryan P. Stone and and Thomas Jay Oord, 21–46. Nashville, Tennessee: Kingswood, 2001.

Oord, Thomas Jay, and Michael Lodahl. *Relational Holiness.* Kansas City, Missouri: Beacon Hill, 2005.

Oord, Thomas Jay. *Defining Love: A Philosophical, Scientific, and Theological Engagement.* Grand Rapids, Michigan: Brazos, 2010.

———. "Essential Kenosis: An Open and Relational Theory of Divine Power: Between Voluntary Divine Self-Limitation and Divine Limitation by Those External to God." In American Academy of Religion, Open and Relational Theologies unit, San Diego, CA: November, 2007.

———. *The Nature of Love: A Theology.* St. Louis, Missouri: Chalice, 2010.

———. *The Uncontrolling Love of God: An Open and Relational Account of Providence.* Downers Grove, Illinois: IVP Academic, 2015.

Owens, Joseph. "The Teleology of Nature in Aristotle." *The Monist* 52 (1968) 159–73.

Paley, William. *A View of the Evidences of Christianity.* 2 vols. Westmead: Gregg International, 1970.

Palmer, Richard E. *Hermeneutics: Interpretation Theory in Schleiermacher, Dilthey, Heidegger, and Gadamer.* (Studies in Phenomenology and Existential Philosophy). Evanston, Illinois: Northwestern University Press, 1969

Pannenberg, Wolfhart. *Systematic Theology.* Vol. 1. Translated by W. Geoffrey Bromiley. Grand Rapids, Michigan: Eerdmans, 1991.

Pannenberg, Wolfhart. *Systematic Theology, vol. 2.* Translated by G. W. Bromiley. Grand Rapids, Michigan: Eerdmans, 1994.

Pasnau, Robert, and Christopher Shields. *The Philosophy of Aquinas.* Boulder, Colorado: Westview, 2004.

Pasnau, Robert. *Theories of Cognition in the Later Middle Ages.* Cambridge: CambridgeUniversity Press, 1997.

———. *Thomas Aquinas and Human Nature.* Cambridge: Cambridge University Press, 2002.

Patitsas, Chrestos. "Kenosis According to Saint Paul." *The Greek Orthodox Theological Review* 27 (1982) 67–82.

John Paul II. "Address to Members of the Pontifical John Paul Institute for Studies on Marriage and the Family." May 31, 2001. http://www.vatican.va/holy_father/john_paul_ii/speeches/2001/documents/hf_jp- ii_spe_20010531_istituto-jp-ii_en.html, § 2.

———. *Crossing the Threshold of Hope.* New York: Alfred A. Knopf, 1994.

———. *Redemptor Hominis.* Boston, Massachusetts: Pauline Books & Media, 1979.

Peacocke, Arthur R. *All That Is: A Naturalistic Faith for the Twenty-First Century*, edited by Philip Clayton. Minneapolis, Minnesota: Fortress, 2007.

Bibliography

———. "Biological Evolution: A Positive Theological Appraisal." In *Scientific Perspectives on Divine Action*, vol. 3. *Evolutionary and Molecular Biology*, edited by Robert J. Russell et al., 357–76. Vatican City State: Vatican Observatory, 1998.

———. *Creation and the World of Science: The Re-Shaping of Belief*. Oxford: Oxford University Press, 2004.

———. "Emergence, Mind, and Divine Action." In *The Re-Emergence of Emergence: The Emergentist Hypothesis from Science to Religion*, edited by Philip Clayton and Paul Davies, 257–78. Oxford: Oxford University Press, 2008.

———. *God and the New Biology*. London: Dent, 1986.

———. "God's Interaction with the World: The Implications of Deterministic 'Chaos' and of Interconnected and Interdependent Complexity." In *Scientific Perspectives on Divine Action*, vol. 2: *Chaos and Complexity*, edited by Robert J. Russell et al., 263–87. Vatican City State: Vatican Observatory, 1995.

———. "Introduction: In Whom We Live and Move and Have Our Being?" In *In Whom We Live and Move and Have Our Being: Panentheistic Reflections on God's Presence in a Scientific World*, edited by Philip Clayton and Arthur Peacocke, xi–xxii. Grand Rapids, Michigan: Eerdmans, 2004.

———. *Paths from Science Towards God: The End of All Our Exploring*. Oxford: One World, 2001.

———. "The Cost of New Life." In *The Work of Love: Creation as Kenosis*, edited by John Polkinghorne, 21–42. Grand Rapids, Michigan: Eerdmans, 2001.

———. *Theology for a Scientific Age: Being and Becoming–Natural, Human, and Divine*. Minneapolis, Minnesota: Fortress, 1993.

———. *Theology in an Age of Science*. Oxford: Blackwell, 1990.

———. "The Sound of Sheer Silence: How Does God Communicate with Humanity?" In *Scientific Perspectives on Divine Action Series*, vol. 4: *Neuroscience and the Person*, edited by Robert John Russell, et al., 215–47. Vatican City: Vatican Observatory, 1999.

Pearse, John S., and Vicki B. Pearse. "Vision of Cubomedusan Jellyfishes." *Science* 199 (1978) 458.

Peirce, Charles Sanders. "One, Two, Three: Kantian Categories." In *The Essential Peirce: Selected Philosophical Writings, vol. 1: (1867–1893)*, edited by Peirce Edition Project. Bloomington, Indiana: Indiana University Press, 1992.

———. *The Essential Peirce: Selected Philosophical Writings, vol. 2: (1893–1913)*, edited by Peirce Edition Project. Bloomington, Indiana: Indiana University Press, 1998.

———. *The Collected Papers of Charles Sanders Peirce*, vols. 1-6, edited by Charles Hartshorne and Paul Weiss. Cambridge, Massachusetts: Harvard University Press, 1936.

———. *Reasoning and the Logic of Things: The Cambridge Conferences Lectures of 1898*, edited by Kenneth Lane Ketner. Cambridge, Massachusetts: Harvard University Press, 1993.

———. "Design and Chance." In *Selected Philosophical Writings, vol. 1: (1867–1893)*, edited by Nathan Houser and Christian J. W. Kloesel, 132–56. Bloomington, Indiana: Indiana University Press, 1992.

———. *Selected Philosophical Writings, vol. 1: (1867–1893)*, edited by Nathan Houser and Christian J.W. Kloesel. Bloomington, Indiana: Indiana University Press, 1992.

Perler, Dominik, ed. *Ancient and Medieval Theories of Intentionality*. Leiden: Brill, 2001.

Bibliography

Peterson, Gregory R. "Species of Emergence." *Zygon: Journal of Religion and Science* 41 3 (2006) 691–701.

Peters, Ted, and Martinez Hewlett. *Evolution from Creation to New Creation: Conflict, Conversation, and Convergence*. Nashville, Tennessee: Abingdon, 2003.

Peterson, Gregory R. "Species of Emergence." *Zygon: Journal of Religion and Science* 41 (2006) 689–712.

Pinnock, et. al., Clark H. *The Openness of God: A Biblical Challenge to the Traditional Understanding of God*. Downers Grove, Illinois: InterVarsity, 1994.

Plantinga, Alvin. "Why Darwinist Materialism is Wrong." *The New Republic*. November 16, 2012.

Plantinga, Alvin. "Science: Augustinian or Duhemian?" *Faith and Philosophy* 13 (1996) 368–94.

Polkinghorne, John C. *Belief in God in an Age of Science*. New Haven: Yale University, 1998.

———. "Chaos Theory and Divine Action." In *Religion and Science: History, Method, and Dialogue*, eds. W. Mark Richardson and Wesley J. Wildman, 243–52. London: Routledge, 1996.

Polkinghorne, John C. *Science and Christian Belief: Theological Reflections of a Bottom–Up Thinker*. London: SPCK, 1994.

———. "Kenotic Creation and Divine Action." In *The Work of Love: Creation As Kenosis*, edited by John C. Polkinghorne, 90–106. Grand Rapids, Michigan: Eerdmans, 2001.

———. *Science and Creation: The Search for Understanding*. London: SPCK, 1988.

———. *Science and Providence: God's Interaction with the World*. London: SPCK, 1989.

———. *Science and the Trinity: The Christian Encounter with Reality*. London: SPCK, 2004.

———. *Scientists as Theologians: A Comparison of the Writings of Ian Barbour, Arthur Peacocke and John Polkinghorne*. London: SPCK, 1996.

———. *Serious Talk*. Philadelphia, Pennsylvania: Trinity, 1995.

———. *The Faith of Physicist: Reflections of a Bottom-Up Thinker. The Gifford Lectures, 1993-94*. Minneapolis, Minnesota: Fortress, 1996.

———. "The Hidden Spirit and the Cosmos." In *The Work of the Spirit: Pneumatology and Pentecostalism*, edited by Michael Welker, 169–82. Grand Rapids, Michigan: Eerdmans, 2006.

———. "The Metaphysics of Divine Action." In *Scientific Perspectives on Divine Action, vol. 2: Chaos and Complexity*, edited by Robert J. Russell et al., 147–56. Vatican City State: Vatican Observatory, 1995.

———. ed. *The Work of Love: Creation as Kenosis*. Grand Rapids, Michigan: Eerdmans, 2001.

———. *Theology in the Context of Science*. New Haven, Connecticut: Yale University Press, 2009.

Popa, Radu. *Between Necessity and Probability: Searching for the Definition and Origin of Life*. New York: Springer-Verlag, 2004.

Popper, Karl. *A World of Propensities*. Bristol: Thoemmes, 1990.

Porter, Andrew P. *By the Waters of Naturalism: Theology Perplexed Among the Sciences*. Eugene, Oregon: Wipf & Stock, 2001.

Purtill, Richard L. *Thinking About Religion: A Philosophical Introduction to Religion*. Englewood Cliffs: Prentice-Hall, 1978.

Rahner, Karl. *The Trinity*. Translated by J. Donceel. New York: Crossroad Herder, 1999.

Bibliography

Raup, David M. et al. "Stochastic Models of Phylogeny and the Evolution of Diversity." In *Journal of Geology* 81 (1973) 525–42.

Raup, David M., and Stephen Jay Gould. "Stochastic Simulation and Evolution of Morphology–towards a Nomothetic Paleontology." *Systematic Zoology* 23 3 (1974) 305–22.

Reich, Lou. *Hume's Religious Naturalism*. Lanham, Maryland: University Press of America, 1998.

Reiss, John O. *Not By Design: Retiring Darwin's Watchmaker*. Berkeley, California: University of California Press, 2009.

Robert, Jason S. *Embryology, Epigenesis and Evolution: Taking Development Seriously*. Cambridge: Cambridge University Press, 2004.

Rolston III, Holmes. "Kenosis and Nature." In *The Work of Love: Creation As Kenosis*, edited by John C. Polkinghorne, 43–65. Grand Rapids, Michigan: Eerdmans, 2001.

Ross, W. D. *Aristotle*. London: Methuen & Co., 1949.

Russell, Robert John. *Cosmology: From Alpha to Omega*. Minneapolis, Minnesota: Augsburg Fortress, 2008.

Russett, Cynthia Eagle. *Darwin in America: The Intellectual Response*. San Francisco, California: W.H. Freeman, 1976.

Sailhamer, John. "Exegetical Notes: Gen. 1:1–2:4a." *Trinity Journal* 5 (1984) 77–89.

Sanders, John. *The God Who Risks: A Theology of Divine Providence*. Downers Grove: IVP Academic, 2007.

Sansbury, Timothy. "The False Promise of Quantum Mechanics." *Zygon: Journal of Religion and Science* 42 1 (2007) 111–21.

Saunders, Nicholas. *Divine Action and Modern Science*. Cambridge: Cambridge University Press, 2002.

Schubert-Soldern, R. *Mechanism and Vitalism*. Translated by C. E. Robin. Edited by P. G. Fothergill. South Bend, Indiana: University of Notre Dame, 1962.

Shanahan, Timothy. *The Evolution of Darwinism: Selection, Adaptation and Progress in Evolutionary Biology*. Cambridge: Cambridge University Press, 2004.

Shields, Christopher. *Aristotle*. New York: Routledge, 2007.

Short, T. L. "Peirce's Concept of Final Causation." *Transactions of the Charles S. Peirce Society* 17 3 (1981) 369–82.

Simmons, Ernest. "Towards Kenotic Pneumatology: Quantum Field Theory and the Theology of the Cross." *CTNS Bulletin* 19 2 (1999) 11–16.

Simpson, G. G. *The Meaning of Evolution*. New Haven: Yale University Press, 1971.

Smedes, T. A. *Chaos, Complexity, and God*. Leuven, Belgium: Peeters, 2004.

Smith, James K. A. and Amos Yong, eds. *Science and the Spirit: A Pentecostal Engagement with the Sciences*. Bloomington, Indiana: Indiana University Press, 2010.

Schubert-Soldern, Rainer. *Mechanism and Vitalism*. Translated by C. E. Robin. Edited by P. G. Fothergill. South Bend, Indiana: University of Notre Dame Press, 1962.

Shields, Christopher. *Aristotle*. New York: Routledge, 2007.

Shults, F. LeRon. *Reforming Theological Anthropology: After the Philosophical Turn to Relationality*. Grand Rapids, Michigan: Eerdmans, 2003.

Sibbes, Richard. *Works*, 7 vols. Edited by A. B. Grosart. Edinburgh: James Nichol, 1860–1864.

Simpson, George G. *The Meaning of Evolution*. New Haven: Yale University Press, 1971.

Simmons, Ernest. "Towards Kenotic Pneumatology: Quantum Field Theory and the Theology of the Cross." *CTNS Bulletin* 19 2 (1999) 11–16.

Bibliography

Smith, Ronald Gregor. *The Free Man: Studies in Christian Anthropology*. London: Collins, 1969.

Southgate, Christopher. *God, Humanity, and the Cosmos*. New York: T. & T. Clark, 2005.

Sponheim, Paul R. *Faith and the Other: A Relational Theology*. Minneapolis, Minnesota: Fortress, 1993.

Stein, Ross L. "An Inquiry into the Origins Of Life On Earth–A Synthesis of Process Thought In Science And Theology." *Zygon: Journal of Religion and Science* 41 4 (2006) 995–1016.

Stenmark, Mikael. *How to Relate Science and Religion: A Multidimensional Model*. Grand Rapids, Michigan: Eerdmans, 2004.

Stoeger, SJ, William R. "Describing God's Action in the World in Light of Scientific Knowledge of Reality." In *Scientific Perspectives on Divine Action, vol. 2: Chaos and Complexity*, edited by Robert John Russell et al., 239–61. Vatican City: Vatican Observatory, 1995.

———. "Contemporary Physics and the Ontological Status of the Laws of Nature." In *Scientific Perspectives on Divine Action, vol. 1: Quantum Cosmology and the Laws of Nature*, 209–34, edited by Robert John Russell et al. Vatican City State: Vatican Observatory, 1993.

———. "The Mind–Brain Problem, the Laws of Nature and Constitutive Relationships." In *Scientific Perspectives on Divine Action, vol. 4: Neuroscience and the Person*, edited by Robert John Russell et al., 129–46. Vatican City State: Vatican Observatory, 1999.

Stone, Brian P., and Thomas Jay Oord, eds. *Thy Nature and Thy Name is Love: Wesleyan and Process Theologies in Dialogue*. Nashville, Tennessee: Kingswood, 2001.

Strawson, Galen. *The Secret Connexion*. Oxford: Oxford University Press, 1989.

Swanson, James. *Dictionary of Biblical Languages with Semantic Domains: Hebrew (Old Testament)*. Oak Harbor: Logos Research Systems, Inc., 1997.

Sweetman, Brendan. *Evolution, Chance, and God: Understanding the Relationship between Evolution and Religion*. New York: Bloomsbury, 2015.

Swinburne, Richard. *The Concept of Miracle*. New York: Macmillan, 1970.

Tanner, Kathryn. *God and Creation in Christian Theology: Tyranny or Empowerment?* Oxford: Blackwell, 1988.

Tanner, Kathryn. "Workings of the Spirit: Simplicity or Complexity?" In *The Work of the Spirit: Pneumatology and Pentecostalism*, edited by Michael Welker, 87–108. Grand Rapids, Michigan: Eerdmans, 2006.

Taylor, John V. and David Wood. *The Go-Between God: The Holy Spirit and the Christian Mission*. Eugene, Oregon: Wipf & Stock, 2015.

Thomas, Stephen N. *Practical Reasoning in Natural Language*. 3rd ed. Englewood Cliffs: Prentice-Hall, 1986.

Tillotson, John. "A Discourse upon Transubstantiation." In *The Works of John Tillotson*, edited by Thomas Birch, 274–97. London: Richard Priestly, 1820.

Tkacz, Michael W. "Aquinas vs. Intelligent Design." *Catholic Answers Magazine* 19 9 http://www.catholic.com/magazine/articles/aquinas-vs-intelligent-design.

Tracy, Thomas F. "Divine Action and Quantum Theory." *Zygon: Journal of Religion and Science* 35 4 (2000) 891–900.

———. "Evolutionary Theologies and Divine Action." *Theology and Science* 6 1 (2008) 107–16.

———. "Particular Providence and the God of the Gaps." In *Scientific Perspectives on Divine Action, vol. 2: Chaos and Complexity*, edited by Robert John Russell et al., 289–307. Vatican City: Vatican Observatory, 1995.

———. "Scientific Perspectives on Divine Action?: Mapping the Options." *Theology and Science* 2 2 (2004) 196–201.

———. "Theologies of Divine Action." In *Oxford Handbook of Religion and Science*, edited by Philip Clayton, 596–611. Oxford: Oxford University Press, 2007.

Turnbull, Werner D. "Another Look at Dental Specialization in the Extinct Sabre-toothed Marsupial Thylacosmilus, Compared to its Placental Counterparts." In *Development, Function and Evolution of Teeth*, edited by Kenneth Alan Joysey and Percy Milton Butler, 399–414. London: Academic, 1978.

Turner, Alan, and Mauricio Antón. *The Big Cats and their Fossil Relatives: An Illustrated Guide to their Evolution and Natural History*. New York: Columbia University Press, 1977.

van Huyssteen, J. Wentzel. *Duet or Duel? Theology and Science in a Postmodern World*. Harrisburg, PA: Trinity, 1998.

Vanstone, William H. *Love's Endeavor, Love's Expense*. London: Darton, Longman and Todd, 1977.

Wald, G. and S. Raypart. "Vision in Annelid Worms." *Science* 196 (1977) 1434–39.

Wallace, William A. *Elements of Philosophy: A Compendium for Philosophers and Theologians*. New York: Alba House, 1977.

Wang, Henry. "Rethinking the Validity and Significance of Final Causation." *Transactions of the Charles S. Peirce Society* 41 3 (2005) 603–25.

Ward, Keith. *God, Chance, and Necessity*. New York: Oneworld, 1996.

———. *Divine Action: Examining God's Role in an Open and Emergent Universe*. London: Collins Religious, 1990.

Welker, Michael. *Creation and Reality*. Minneapolis, Minnesota: Augsburg Fortress, 1999.

———. "Spirit in Philosophical, Theological, and Interdisciplinary Perspectives." In *The Work of the Spirit*, edited by Michael Welker, 221–32. Grand Rapids, Michigan: Eerdmans, 2006.

Wesley, John. "On the Omnipresence of God." In *The Works of John Wesley*, edited by Albert C. Outler, 4:27–4:42. Nashville, Tennessee: Abingdon, 1987.

———. "On Divine Providence." In *The Works of John Wesley*, edited by Albert C. Outler, 2:517–2:538. Nashville, Tennessee: Abingdon, 1987.

———. "Predestination Calmly Considered." In *The Works of John Wesley*, edited by Thomas Jackson, 10:221–10:236. Grand Rapids, Michigan: Zondervan, 1958.

———. "The Signs of the Times." In *The Works of John Wesley*, edited by Albert C. Outler, 4:43–4:62. Nashville, Tennessee: Abingdon, 1987.

———. "Thoughts upon God's Sovereignty." In *The Works of John Wesley*, edited by Thomas Jackson, 10:361–374. Grand Rapids, Michigan: Zondervan, 1958.

———. "Upon our Lord's Sermon on the Mount, III." In *The Works of John Wesley*, edited by Albert C. Outler, 1:511–532. Nashville, Tennessee: Abingdon, 1987.

Whitehead, Alfred North. *Adventures of Ideas*. New York: Macmillan, 1933.

———. *Process and Reality. An Essay in Cosmology. Gifford Lectures Delivered in the University of Edinburgh During the Session 1927–1928*. New York: Macmillan, 1929.

———. *Religion in the Making*. Cambridge: Cambridge University Press, 2011.

———. *The Interpretation of Science: Selected Essays*. Indianapolis, Indiana: Bobbs-Merrill, 1961.

Bibliography

Wildman, Wesley J. "The Divine Action Project, 1988–2003." *Theology and Science* 2 1 (2004) 31–75.
Wiles, Maurice. *God's Action in the World*. London: SCM, 1986.
Wojtyla, Karol. *Love and Responsibility*. San Francisco, California: Ignatius, 1993.
Wollheim, Richard. *Hume on Religion*. London: Collins, 1963.
Wood, D. R. W. *New Bible Dictionary*. Downers Grove, Illinois: InterVarsity, 1996.
Wynkoop, Mildred Bangs. *A Theology of Love*. Kansas City, Missouri: Beacon Hill, 1972.
Yaffe, Martin. *Spinoza's Theologico: Political Treatise*. Newbury Port: Focus, 2004.
Yong, Amos. "A Review Symposium on: Amos Yong The Spirit of Creation: Modern Science and Divine Action in the Pentecostal-Charismatic Imagination." *Australian Pentecostal Studies* 15 1 (2013). http://aps-journal.com/aps/index.php/APS/article/view/122/119.
———. *Beyond the Impasse: Toward a Pneumatological Theology of Religions*. Grand Rapids, Michigan: Baker Academic, 2003.
———. "Discerning the Spirit(s) in the Natural World: Toward a Typology of 'Spirit' in the Theology and Science Dialogue." *Theology and Science* 3 3 (2006) 315–29.
———. "From Quantum Mechanics to the Eucharistic Meal: John Polkinghorne's Vision of Science and Theology." *The Global Spiral: A Publication of Metanexus Institute* 5:5 (2005). http://www.metanexus.net/Magazine/ArticleDetail/tabid/68/id/9285/Default.aspx.
———. *In the Days of Caesar: Pentecostalism and Political Theology, The Cadbury Lectures*. Grand Rapids, Michigan: Eerdmans, 2010.
———. "Ruach, the Primordial Chaos, and the Breath of Life: Emergence Theory and the Creation Narratives in Pneumatological Perspective." In *The Work of the Spirit: Pneumatology and Pentecostalism*, edited by Michael Welker, 183–204. Grand Rapids, Michigan: Eerdmans, 2006.
———. *The Cosmic Breath: Spirit and Nature in the Christianity-Buddhism-Science Trialogue*. Philosophical Studies in Science and Religion. Leiden: Brill, 2012.
———. "The Spirit at Work in the World: A Pentecostal-Charismatic Perspective on the Divine Action Project." *Theology and Science* 7 2 (2009) 123–40.
———. *The Spirit of Creation: Modern Science and Divine Action in the Pentecostal-Charismatic Imagination*. Pentecostal Manifestos. Grand Rapids, Michigan: Eerdmans, 2011.
———. *The Spirit Poured Out on All Flesh: Pentecostalism and the Possibility of Global Theology*. Grand Rapids, Michigan: Baker Academic, 2005.

www.ingramcontent.com/pod-product-compliance
Lightning Source LLC
Chambersburg PA
CBHW062017220426
43662CB00010B/1371